This Littler Light

This Littler Light

Some Thoughts on NOT Changing the World

A Memoir

Jesse James DeConto

CASCADE *Books* • Eugene, Oregon

THIS LITTLER LIGHT
Some Thoughts on NOT Changing the World: A Memoir

Copyright © 2013 Jesse James DeConto. All rights reserved. Except for brief quotations in critical publications or reviews, no part of this book may be reproduced in any manner without prior written permission from the publisher. Write: Permissions, Wipf and Stock Publishers, 199 W. 8th Ave., Suite 3, Eugene, OR 97401.

Cascade Books
An Imprint of Wipf and Stock Publishers
199 W. 8th Ave., Suite 3
Eugene, OR 97401

www.wipfandstock.com

ISBN 13: 978-1-62032-819-4

Cataloguing-in-Publication data:

DeConto, Jesse James.

This littler light : some thoughts on NOT changing the world: a memoir / Jesse James DeConto.

xvi + 228 pp. ; 23 cm.

ISBN 13: 978-1-62032-819-4

1. DeConto, Jesse James. 2. Evangelicalism—Biography. I. Title.

BX 5995 D2 2013

Manufactured in the U.S.A.

To Julie and the girls:
You are my world that God has made, and it is good.

Contents

Acknowledgments ix

Permissions xii

Introduction xv

1. Please, Jesus 1
2. Love Not the World 23
3. God's Work and the Good News 40
4. Girls and God 56
5. Making Love 80
6. Cub Reporter 102
7. I Will Sing for the Meek 129
8. No One Said It Was Easy 144
9. Dirty Sheets and Purple Horses 153
10. The Image of the Trinity 167
11. Intentional Community 189

    Epilogue: The Silence of the Lamb 217

Acknowledgements

A memoirist owes thanks to every person who has crossed his path, for better or worse, because every encounter shapes his life and his story. I won't acknowledge every teacher, mentor, editor, friend, and colleague who has made this book possible, for I would have to list everyone who has made my life possible. They would be mere names to you, reader, and they are so much more than that. I trust some of them will receive the thanks implicit in telling the stories of how they have made my life what it is. At times, some of them might not recognize themselves, as making this story readable required combining a few different people into one character where it would not diminish the deeper truth of the narrative. The central characters all play themselves, as well as I understand them.

There are characters in my story whose names I have changed, the facts of our relationships I've obscured for their protection, because this is *my* story, and no one else should have to own it. For them I give thanks, for whether we've built one another up, torn one another down, or simply lived life together, they have taught me about myself, about this mysterious existence on planet earth, and about the God who created us. Let me say a special thanks to the woman I've called "Joy," who encouraged me to write this story years before I started, though I've brought no great joy to her life. I have purposed in this book to do no harm, to her nor anyone else. I mean for this story to serve as a tiny gift to the world, not some vain self-justification. You, reader, will have to decide whether I've succeeded.

With that said, let me express my particular gratitude to those who have made this writing process possible. Thank you to Jason Byassee, Lucila Vargas, and John Utz, who helped me to plumb the connections between my faith and my writing. Tim Conder, Melissa and Kevin Mehm, Mackenzie and Philip Henry: Thanks for encouraging me to take the leap from a stable job to find the time to write this book, among other things. Thank you to Mark Schultz, who remains a supportive editor, even after I quit the job you hired me for! Thanks to Isaac Villegas and Lauren Winner, who oversaw Duke Divinity School's "Spiritual Autobiography" course at the old Durham Correctional Center in the summer of 2011. Isaac and the

Acknowledgements

inmate-classmates there read and heard early drafts of some of the stories that make up this book, and their encouragement pushed me to think bigger. That fall at Duke, another course on women's spiritual memoir with Rick Lischer required me to write one of these chapters, and I just kept going. When I got to chapter 7, I went back and poached from an old essay I wrote for Kevin Heath back at Cedarville College and another, "Midwestern Radicals," that Jim Sparrell had acquired and edited for the old and much-missed *Mars Hill Review*.

Margot Starbuck, Phil Christman, Enuma Okoro, Vince Rocchio, Philip Henry, Damon McGraw, Angela Miller, Kevin Meadows, Brett McKey, Chris Breslin, Cleve May, Abi Riak, Rebecca Kuhns, Susan McSwain, Tommy Grimm, Sarah Kate Fishback: Thank you for the constructive criticism that buffed my rough manuscript into something I hope is worth reading. Rodney Clapp, my editor: Thank you for believing in an unknown author; I can only hope that my writing might make a fraction of the difference for some reader that *A Peculiar People* made for me. Ben Barnhart: Thanks for guiding me through my first literary contract deliberations as the voice of grizzled experience! Greg Veltman and Benita Wolters-Fredland: Thank you for the opportunity to present part of this book at the Calvin Festival of Faith and Music. I had met Rodney at the Festival of Faith and Writing a year earlier, so this, my first book, is proof that Ken Hefner and the Calvin College Student Activities Office are making a difference in the lives of writers and musicians.

Mom and Dad: Thank you for a lifetime of encouraging me to spend my time doing the things I love, rather than always doing what's prudent or expected. And thanks for the free babysitting, real-estate brokering, and home repair advice and/or labor that help to free up my time to do what I love. And Marco, Katie, Suzanne, and Steven: Thank you for following me from New Hampshire and Florida and making our home here in North Carolina. I could not have lived through this story without you all.

Lily, thank you for our daughters, and for trying to love me inasmuch as you were capable. I have tried to care for you as best I can while telling my story as truthfully as I can.

A.D.G.P.D and C.R.E.G.P.D—thanks for putting up with a dad whose job seems to have no recognizable end each day. Living with a writer and musician is not the easiest thing for a kid, but I hope you can see me dreaming and you can dream yourself. You're not allowed to read this book until you're older, but when and if you do, I hope you'll see that your mom and I have always loved you and will always love you. Neither one of us is perfect, and there's not much use in blaming anybody for what happened between us. The important thing is that we all learn from one another's experiences.

Acknowledgements

That's what this book is for—to try and share what I've learned through some very painful times, in hopes that someone else might learn something, and maybe avoid the same mistakes. We have to tell the truth as best we can, even if it's painful, because knowing the truth can help us live "with the grain of the universe," instead of fighting against it.

Julie, I wrote this book because you wouldn't let me go to Mexico to research for another book. Your sixth sense for what's going to work in real life helps us dreamers to get things done. You are the reason this book exists, and not just because you gave me permission to blaze a new career trail when it didn't make much sense financially. Thank you for your work at home and at Reality Ministries, work that goes a long way toward sustaining our family, so I can take some risks in my own work. More importantly, thank you for building a redemptive life with me and the girls. You're the woman of my dreams, from "the days when I still dreamed, sowing peace together on the battlefield." You are a constant in a story of unresolved endings.

Permissions

All scripture quotations, unless otherwise indicated, are taken from the Holy Bible, New International Version®, NIV®. Copyright ©1973, 1978, 1984, 2011 by Biblica, Inc.™ Used by permission of Zondervan. All rights reserved worldwide. www.zondervan.com The "NIV" and "New International Version" are trademarks registered in the United States Patent and Trademark Office by Biblica, Inc.™

Scripture quotations marked NASB taken from the New American Standard Bible®, Copyright © 1960, 1962, 1963, 1968, 1971, 1972, 1973, 1975, 1977, 1995 by The Lockman Foundation Used by permission." (www.lockman.org)

Scripture quotations marked KJV taken from The Authorized (King James) Version. Rights in the Authorized Version in the United Kingdom are vested in the Crown. Reproduced by permission of the Crown's patentee, Cambridge University Press.

The author also acknowledges his use of quotations from the following works:

From *Bread for the Journey* © 1997 by Henri Nouwen. Reprinted by permission of HarperCollins. All rights reserved.

From *The Epistle to the Romans* © 1933 by Karl Barth. Reprinted by permission of Oxford University Press, USA. All rights reserved.

From *All We Are Saying* © 2000 by David Sheff. Reprinted by permission of St. Martin's Press. All rights reserved.

From *Slouching Toward Bethlehem* © 1968 by Joan Didion. Reprinted by permission of Farrar, Straus and Giroux. All rights reserved.

From "Flood" © 1995 by Jars of Clay. Reprinted by permission of Brentwood-Benson Music Publishing. All rights reserved. ASCAP.

Permissions

From "Bus Driver" © 1997 by Derek Webb. Reprinted by permission of Niphon, Inc. (admin. By Music Services) All rights reserved. ASCAP.

From "I Will Sing" © 1989 by Rich Mullins. Reprinted by permission of Universal Music — Brentwood Benson Publishing. All rights reserved. ASCAP.

From "Will You" ©1990 by Wade Baynham. Reprinted by permission of composer. All rights reserved.

From "Tourniquet" and "Pour Kid" © 2006 by Bill Mallonee. Reprinted by permission of composer. All rights reserved.

From "Days Go By" © 1996 by Duncan Sheik. Reprinted under fair use from Atlantic Records. All rights reserved.

From "I'm Happy With Myself" © 1994, "All I Need is Everything" © 1996, "Bothered" © 1997, "The World Can Wait" © 2001, and "Snow Angels" © 2007 by Over the Rhine. Reprinted by permission of composer. All rights reserved.

This little light of mine, I'm gonna let it shine!
This little light of mine, I'm gonna let it shine!
This little light of mine, I'm gonna let it shine!
Let it shine, let it shine, let it shine!

Hide it under a bushel, no! I'm gonna let it shine!
Hide it under a bushel, no! I'm gonna let it shine!
Hide it under a bushel, no! I'm gonna let it shine!
Let it shine, let it shine, let it shine!

Don't let Satan whoosh it out, I'm gonna let it shine!
Don't let Satan whoosh it out, I'm gonna let it shine!
Don't let Satan whoosh it out, I'm gonna let it shine!
Let it shine, let it shine, let it shine!

Let it shine till Jesus comes, I'm gonna let it shine!
Let it shine till Jesus comes, I'm gonna let it shine!
Let it shine till Jesus comes, I'm gonna let it shine!
Let it shine, let it shine, let it shine!

—"This Little Light of Mine," Harry Dixon Loes

Introduction

We used to sing this song in Sunday School, as far back as I can remember, way back when I was learning to use a big-boy potty and tie my shoes. The little light was our faith in Jesus, and letting it shine was sharing it with others, who didn't know him. Jesus loved the little children, all the children of the world, red and yellow, black and white, they were precious in his sight, Jesus loved the little children of the world. He would make us FISHERS! of men, FISHERS! of men, FISHERS! of men, if we followed him, if we followed him, if we FAW! LOWED! HIM! I should dare to be a Daniel, dare to stand alone, dare to have a purpose firm, dare to make it known. Even if they fed me to the lions.

It took almost thirty years for me to really see "This Little Light" in action. Before that, it was mostly an ideal standard that made me feel guilty for not living up to it, a measuring stick that set me in competition with all the other little lights around me; if I shined a little brighter, you'd try too. But two years before Occupy Wall Street demanded economic reform at the national level, the candles lit in Charlotte, North Carolina, as hundreds of protestors marched on Bank of America and Wachovia in the fall of 2009. In the midst of the subprime mortgage crisis, with people facing ballooning interest rates and foreclosures on their homes, organizers delivered a theological statement against what they called "usury"—the Old Testament sin of collecting interest from the poor.

"This little light of mine, I'm gonna let it shine!" sang seventy customers inside the cavernous lobby at BOA headquarters.

"Even in my bank, I'm gonna let it shine!" they sang, marching seven times along the gleaming glass and polished marble walls, like Jesus throwing the moneychangers from the temple, like the Israelites marching around the walls of Jericho, "and the walls came a'tumbl-in' down!"

"Till we get an answer, we're gonna let it shine!" they sang, as four Charlotte-Mecklenburg police officers arrived to confer with bank employees.

"Oh, I've got my card, y'all, I'm gonna let it shine!" they sang, assuring the bank officials sent as buffers from the upper floors that, yes, they were Bank of America customers and they just had some questions about the puzzling fees and rising interest rates that were showing up on their monthly statements, about why their friends and families were losing their homes.

I hadn't known "This Little Light of Mine" was an anthem of the Civil Rights movement. I hadn't known *this little light* might shine through simple acts of justice: sitting on a bus, ordering coffee at a lunch counter, or transferring your money to a credit union built for people, not profits. I didn't know all these little flames, brought together in a simple Sunday school song reverberating around an office building, could enflesh the presence of God, even if they weren't hot enough or bright enough to right the wrongs, or turn oppression into justice or usher in the kingdom of God. I didn't know it could be enough just to catch a glimpse of that kingdom, wherever two or three were gathered in Christ's name. I didn't know that when Jesus taught us to pray, "Forgive us our debts, as we forgive our debtors," he really meant debts—currency, paper, not just spiritual shortcomings. I didn't know *this little light* might actually free people, here on earth, not completely, but at least give them a bit more freedom from from things like debt, or hunger, or poverty, or violence, or loneliness. I didn't know "the light of the world," "the city on a hill," what Martin Luther King Jr. called "the Beloved Community" could *show* people what it meant to be a Christian, could "preach the gospel to every creature and use words only if necessary." I didn't know *this little light* really could be little, because there were lots of them, and even when they all shine together, they were never meant to replace the One Big Light.

I thought I had to use words. I thought lots of people had to hear those words. I thought I had to live up to those words. And I thought I had to do it alone. I thought the salvation of the world, at least some of it, depended on me.

1

Please, Jesus

For just the tiniest smidge of a fraction of a nanosecond, I opened my armor and let the pain show. I had to be strong, but Langley saw through me.

"Are you OK?" he asked when we met outside North Carolina Central Prison on St. Patrick's Day, 2006.

Hours earlier, I lay on an operating table and allowed a young urological resident to cut into my manhood, to sterilize me, to make sure I would never father a son, to protect my dear, sweet daughters from adding more stress to a home already full of it. I had scarred my body to save my marriage. Even as I lay there and let the doctor stick a knife in me, I was hoping for a miracle, hoping this fix wouldn't take.

Not long after our second daughter's birth, Lily had started pressuring me for a vasectomy. She'd been through two surprise pregnancies, one ending in a miscarriage that had sapped her will even to get out of bed. After we married—at twenty-two and twenty-three years old—she often said she'd never planned on a marriage or a family. When she said things like that, like when she wrote that short "story" imagining her life with that biker dude she'd rejected in favor of me back at our Baptist college, I took it to heart: She was unhappy, and it was my fault. Aurora had the little sister she'd asked for, and Lily was done. For a year and a half, my wife pestered me, relaying her Appalachian grandmother's concern: "When's he gonna get fixed?"

On the one hand, I thought it was the loving thing to do. Lily was constitutionally frail, with a minor heart condition, multiple allergies, and what you might call a low zest for life. She said birth control made her stomach hurt. We'd already had one condom fail. She'd given me two precious girls, she didn't want any more, and she certainly didn't want to endure another miscarriage, so how could I make her take that risk? And was I myself willing to take the risk, knowing the conflict in our home?

On a brief detour from my daily newspaper career, I was taking five graduate-school classes, working as a research assistant, freelance writing to make some extra cash, and trying to figure out my next career move so I could buy Lily a house. We were living in a brand new student family apartment at the University of North Carolina-Chapel Hill, and I worried about what the neighbors thought about my screaming: about her hot iron that burned a hole in the kitchen counter, about the uninsured bills we were paying to an alternative healer because Lily didn't trust mainstream pediatricians, about another meal left for me to cook or laundry to wash when I got home, about her hours of aimless web-surfing, about credit card bills that were eating into our savings because she had to have the best of everything. No one in my shoes would have wanted to deal with her selfish idiosyncrasies, and no one in her shoes would have wanted to deal with my hot temper.

I thought I understood her unhappiness, and why she tried to fix it with fancy clothes and fantasies of the good life. Not only had her parents abandoned her to her grandparents when she was a baby, but they had flitted into and out of her life, giving her glimpses of the wealth and freedom they seemed to have chosen over her. They flitted, that is, until her mother decided she didn't like me—or didn't like the idea of her daughter getting married—and refused to come to our wedding. That kind of rejection might make anyone turn inside herself and never come out. But my understanding it wouldn't mend the tear it caused in our marriage. In fact, it only played upon my weakness: my pride, my need not to fail, my intense probing to heal her wounds, which instead seemed to cut her deeper. The strife was the strife, regardless of how much I might have believed I would resolve it one day. How could I bring another child into this home?

Still, it didn't feel right, altering my body like this, permanently. I'd never even been able to pull the trigger on a tattoo, for goodness sake. It seemed to me there was something sturdy in the Vatican's ban on birth control, something worth reckoning with. I mean, I didn't think having six or seven kids would be the responsible thing to do, but was it right to say, *no, never, no more*, after just two? Didn't God make us male and female to procreate? Wasn't our creativity how we displayed the image of God on earth? And could you get any more creative than making a new human life? As much as Lily had insinuated, how could I feel guilty about

Please, Jesus

our first pregnancy, our precious, unexpected Aurora? Wasn't that God's plan for marriage? Weren't our little girls something to celebrate? Did I have a right to cut asunder what God had created? Was there any way to reconcile these two competing moral duties: Loving my own flesh and loving my wife?

I had thought about consulting the busy priest at our Episcopal church, or maybe Duke University's eminent theological ethicist Stanley Hauerwas, who worshiped with us and surely had thought about the ethics of birth control. But why bother them with something so personal? I had good, dear friends, but they were spread out all over the country, even the world, and I didn't think any of them could relate to my predicament. Whenever they asked, I would tell them that marriage was the hardest thing I'd ever had to do. Nothing they could say would ever change that. We were raised by churches that taught us divorce was wrong in all cases, but they never talked about what those cases might look like. It was like this: If there's adultery, the wounded party has to forgive. And if there's forgiveness for that, then there must be forgiveness for just about anything. If you were in a bad marriage, you just had to work harder. That sort of categorical imperative made sense to me: I thought I was as smart and capable as just about anybody, and where I was weak, I just had to outwork 'em. I thought I could keep my marriage intact by force of will. Just trust and obey.

Mom suggested maybe twenty-nine years old was a bit young for a vasectomy, but this was my cross to bear. As I saw it, this operation was my self-crucifixion, my obedient, joyless martyrdom, the climax of my tortured submission to my wife's will, the apogee of my stoic self-reliance, my sacrifice for our salvation. Six moves in six years of marriage because one day I'd be able to make her happy. Estrangement from my parents and siblings because she needed me all to herself. To prove my worth to Lily, I made myself worthless to another woman. I went all in. I was either going to knock the ball out of the catcher's mitt, or break my neck trying.

"Yeah, I'm fine," I told Langley. "I just had a minor surgery."

The doctor had told me to rest, but I couldn't miss this night. It might turn into a once-in-a-lifetime experience. See, this night Langley would get himself arrested with fourteen other activists protesting the execution of convicted murderer Patrick Moody. More importantly, some of Langley's friends would sit with Patrick's mother Rondelle on the night she knew her son would die. Lily always said activists like these were just looking for attention, and sometimes I thought maybe she was right. But no matter what I thought about civil disobedience or the death penalty, I had to acknowledge the suffering of a murderer's family: They had raised a child who became a killer, and now they had to watch him die. The only people who had it worse were the victims' families, but at least they had society on their side. If you think about it, a murderer's family had also been victimized in a way: They had lost the innocent child they once knew, and it was that innocent child—not just a cold-blooded killer—who would shake and sputter and finally stop breathing in that execution chamber. Not only that, but those families also had to suffer as guilty by association. Their son or husband or brother or father was a murderer. I shuddered to think of what that must feel like, and I had to admire people who offered their time to soothe some of that suffering.

"I kind of feel like Patrick's sick, and we know he's going to die, and that we're kind of together for a funeral, and it's kind of a natural thing, and not that, you know, he's going to be executed and he shouldn't be," Langley's wife Sheila had said the prior evening. She was two months pregnant, characteristically thin, in her late twenties with long, straight, brown hair, the daughter of a Catholic-hippie family from rural New York. Langley, also long-haired and skinny from a vegetarian diet and frequent fasting, had rearranged bedroom furniture around their home in Raleigh, North Carolina, to accommodate Patrick's extended family—his brother, aunt, uncle, stepfather, and mother.

"He's going to die and that's sad," Sheila went on, "but the fact that he's being executed isn't really being talked about, which is fine. It just feels like it's a regular funeral. You know?"

"Yeah, it's really interesting. You can see 'em get quiet, and they're thinking about it," said her housemate Roberta, in her forties, pensive, bookish, with pixie hair and dark-rimmed glasses, a mother of two boys, with her youngest, a teenager still at home. "And then they say, 'That is really sad.'"

Sheila: "Because how do you think about it?"

"I know," said Roberta, shaking her head, exhaling sharply, chuckling darkly.

Sheila: "I don't know how else you deal with it."

We were in the kitchen of Nazareth House, the Catholic Worker intentional community that Langley, Sheila, Roberta, and her husband Scott had recently opened to offer hospitality to the families of death-row inmates at North Carolina Central Prison. We lounged against the cabinets I had helped to scrape and paint, or sat on the old gray-on-white speckled countertop, just inside the back door with a little placard that said "Peace to All Who Enter Here." I'd been writing for newspapers and magazines for six years, and I, too, was trying to make peace—not only for people suffering through no fault of their own, but also peace with myself. I had become a journalist because I wanted to make an impact on the world for Jesus, but I had spent most of my career writing about the problems of the privileged, like high property tax rates or Not-In-My-Backyard real estate squabbles. I envied these Catholic Workers, helping people who actually needed help. My writing had helped poor, hungry, alienated people, too, here and there. But I felt like my hands were too clean. Spending time at Nazareth House got me closer to the action—maybe even closer to God. The name "Nazareth" had symbolic power: Being from Nazareth made Jesus an outcast in Jerusalem. North Carolina's abolition movement, led by Duke Divinity students and the grassroots People of Faith Against the Death Penalty, liked to remind the public that Jesus himself was the victim of capital punishment. Like so many who die on the death row, he was from a backwater ghetto, lacking money or cultural status.

Langley and Sheila were the kind of people who skipped showers and fueled their old Benz diesel with recycled vegetable oil. On the day they met, they were both on CNN after getting arrested in D.C. protesting U.S. military aid to Colombia. A little sign in their bathroom said, "If it's yellow, let it mellow. If it's brown, flush it down." Hanging out with these Catholic Workers was part of my search for spiritual identity. Being near people who were radically following Jesus in lives of sacrificial love—well, maybe they'd rub off on me. They were teaching me to speak up for environmental protection, oppressed workers, and a robust pro-life platform to include opposing war and the death penalty. I'd watched them cull from dumpsters to feed themselves, distribute food in the streets, and go to jail for what they believed in. They were my heroes.

I figured if Jesus had given me this platform to reach tens or hundreds of thousands of people with my writing, the least I could do was to use it to amplify the voices of the poor, the mourners, the meek, the hungry, the merciful, the pure-hearted, the peacemakers, the persecuted—all those people Jesus had called "blessed" in his Sermon on the Mount. Jesus, after all, had been a prisoner himself, and he counted prisoners among "the least of these" we Christians ought to visit. If you end up on death row—as most murderers don't—you were probably too poor to afford a good defense. If you love a man on death row, you go broke paying for lawyers, hotels, travel, and meals: You're not only in mourning, but you're poor and you're hungry. And if you love people who love people on death row, you've got to have the most merciful and pure of heart, because you're inviting no great joy into your life—more often, it's devastating sadness. And, on top of all that, you're asking for persecution. Case in point: Over my several months of traveling back and forth from our home in Chapel Hill to watch these Catholic Workers doing their work, Lily had the same message for me:

Why are you wasting your time? Killers deserve to die.

Of course, she had some precedent for saying such a thing. We'd both grown up in churches that taught us Moses's "eye for an eye" but not Jesus's "turn the other cheek." I had come to think the latter was the one that really mattered, and she hadn't. I had twin callings: Compassionate journalism and compassion for my wife. And they were at war with each other. I was at war with myself. I would return from writing a story about energy-efficiency with free samples of compact-fluorescent bulbs, and Lily would complain about the quality of light they gave out. I would proudly pedal my bike back and forth to work, or ride Chapel Hill's free buses that stopped every fifteen minutes near our house, or write a column about how weaning ourselves off Middle Eastern oil might help make the world a more peaceful place for our girls, and Lily would complain about not having a second car.

We had moved to North Carolina two years earlier. On one of my first visits to our Episcopal church, I had struck up a conversation with a middle-aged woman. I told her I was worried—about our second daughter then in Lily's womb, about my demanding independent journalism project on Latino immigrants, about living in a new place, far from anyone who knew us.

"We're going to need some help from this church," I told her.

"Well, I don't have time to get involved with anything else right now," she said, "but I'm sure you'll find someone who can help you."

And, in fact, the church's Sunday school director had cared for three-year-old Aurora overnight when we'd gone to the hospital, an assistant priest had visited there us after Rowan's birth, and a few women had delivered meals as Lily recovered. But after that, we were alone. That had been the choice we'd made. It had always been that way. Lily had never adjusted to the cold, hard winter, nor the cold, hard temperament of my native New England—the place she'd hoped would impress her estranged mother, a native Appalachian who had given her up at six months old to jetset from Boston to London to Los Angeles. Lily's mother had bequeathed to her a genetic thirst for Cambridge degrees, Nordstrom fashion, Bombay & Company furniture, and a house bigger than the dingy apartments or basement condos we could afford on my writer's wages. I relished bargain shopping at Goodwill and cast a judgmental eye toward wealth, so I wasn't exactly predisposed toward patience with her.

When I would suggest inviting friends over, Lily would say we hadn't the room to entertain. Which meant we had few friends. I'd turned down a reporting job in Florida, where my parents, three younger siblings, and both our sets of maternal grandparents had moved—Lily's having relocated from the childhood home they'd shared with her in the mountains of eastern Kentucky. Lily had wanted to get away from our families—to have a state all to ourselves.

For my part, I'd been drawn by the same impulse that had led me to these anti-death-penalty activists: to get to Duke Divinity School, which had trained so many of Langley and Sheila's comrades to live out an ethical, political faith, pursuing peace and justice in the world. Along with potential opportunities at UNC, nearby newspapers, and a thriving music scene, the move to Raleigh-Durham-Chapel Hill felt like seeking God. I'd been hoping my grant-funded writing project would still leave time and a flexible schedule to study at Duke's seminary and UNC's journalism school, to think through how to use journalism to serve God. I was struggling to find a place in this world for my particular gifts and passions. I thought this move might help me figure out where I belonged.

But I'd been scared. We hadn't known anybody. I hadn't known the South. An only child bickering with both my mom and her own grandmother, Lily had needed me—a twenty-four-year-old kid who happened to have four younger siblings—to teach her how to care for baby Aurora back in New Hampshire. Could I expect much different with Baby No. 2 in the lonely South? My work was to write about Latino immigrants in North Carolina. I didn't know much about immigration and had only been learning Spanish for a few months. This fellowship would demand as much energy as I could give it. And so would Lily.

A month after St. Patrick's Day, I would sit on my friend Cooper's porch, across the street from one of Chapel Hill's big, old Victorian mansions that caught Lily's eye. Cooper was another grad student who went to our church, one of the few people who resembled a friend during our first couple of years in North Carolina. He and I had talked at church every now and then and had met for lunch a few times. We shared an interest in spiritually aware music that didn't fit the mold of the Contemporary

Christian Music we'd grown up with. On this night, we had gone to The Cave—"Chapel Hill's Oldest Tavern"—a basement bar with low ceilings and tight walls decorated with rough stucco to look like the rock walls of an actual cave. As was often the case at The Cave, we and a few of Cooper's friends made for the entire crowd of about seven people. Bill Mallonee, a friend of my and Cooper's favorite band Over the Rhine, was on tour promoting his solo album, *Permafrost*, and its songs of what he called "suburban angst." I could relate to his lyrics:

> You're on your way to somewhere else
> just like everybody else

Where was I going?

I had biked to Cooper's house, and we'd walked to The Cave together. As usual, on those rare occasions when I went out, Lily had stayed home with the girls. She always said she didn't trust babysitters. When Cooper and I got back after midnight, I lingered on his porch, longing for someone to talk to, someone who would understand me. Cooper was a Christian college kid just like Lily and me. He was studying to be a sociologist of religion and knew the tensions of trying to do secular work from a religious perspective. That winter, I'd gone to Charlotte to interview with the local alternative weekly *Creative Loafing* for an editing job that turned out not to exist. Since I'd come to North Carolina I'd been reading magazines like *Mother Jones* and *The Atlantic* and *Harper's* and dreaming of long-form, hard-hitting, in-depth storytelling that would reveal injustice and spark people to action. I'd just had a cover story in *Reason* magazine, telling the story of an immigrant Christmas tree farming family and how they were separated at Christmas time by the broken immigration system. Another story in *E: The Environmental Magazine* documented the long-term health risks to farmworkers from applying pesticides to the holiday trees. *Creative Loafing* had printed one immigrant's "Horatio Alger story" on its cover, my account of his harvesting the first crop of his own Fraser firs.

That paper would soon print another of my cover stories, "How to Survive an Execution," an inside look at Nazareth House and North Carolina's anti-death penalty activists. But these stories paid peanuts. I would spend weeks or months on one and earn a few hundred dollars—nowhere near enough to support my family. What would happen when my fellowships ran out? I was trying to pursue two vocations at the same time, truthteller and family man, and it wasn't going to work. I had thought that job in Charlotte might be an answer—a steady paycheck and the chance to write the kind of stories I wanted to write, with a brave, risk-taking paper in the tradition of *The Village Voice* or Upton Sinclair. But the editor didn't have the money to pay me for the job he'd all but offered—this is the reality for alternative newspapers, I would eventually learn—and he was soon gone too.

I'd been taking a j-school class in "Communication for Social Change," where I'd analyzed several years of death-penalty coverage in *The News & Observer* and *The Independent*, Raleigh-Durham's alternative weekly. I'd found the latter gave voice to the *people*—victims but also defendants and their families—while the former tended to quote *institutions*—judges and prosecutors—and only sometimes victims' families or their lawyers. *The News & Observer* was by far the most reputable and best-paying print journalism job in North Carolina's Triangle region. It had won Pulitzers and earned the nickname "Noise & Disturber" for watchdog government reporting. The professor I assisted with research and grading had recently left *The N&O*. He had been helping me place freelance stories and could help get me a full-time job there.

But I feared getting on the wrong side of power. Hadn't God called me to give voice to the poor? It was one thing to hold powerful people accountable, but that also meant admitting that earthly power not only *mattered*, but generated the *most important* stories to tell. Would I get caught up in endless government meetings, rubbing shoulders with men in suits and trying to make sure the *taxpayers*—not "citizens," not "community members," but "taxpayers"—didn't get screwed by their backroom wheeling and dealing? Did bumbling, inefficient bureaucrats really represent "the principalities and powers" waging war on the Kingdom of God? Or was that war being fought elsewhere, at Nazareth House, in migrant farmworker camps? Would I have to ignore that war, in fact, in order to maintain the veneer of objectivity that could keep me in power?

"When I came to UNC," I told Cooper, "I said I didn't ever want to work for the corporate media again."

Cooper just listened. What could he say?

"Now, I don't know what else to do. I've tried everything to make Lily happy. I just need a good job, and maybe I can get her the house she wants."

Catholic Worker founder Dorothy Day herself was a strong, faithful woman who gave up the comforts of marriage, gave up a partner in raising her daughter, in order to pursue a Christian vocation of hospitality. Yet in her autobiography, after decades of simplicity, social activism, and sacrificial sharing alongside both men and women, this is what she wrote:

> I am quite ready to concede now that men are the single-minded, the pure of heart, in these movements. Women by their very nature are more materialistic, thinking of the home, the children, and of all things needful to them, especially love. And in their constant searching after it, they go against their own best interests.

I did not want to believe that. Were Lily and I really that different? Yet all around me was evidence staring me right in the face. Day's words were more true than false, at least in my own living room. I was single-minded, for sure, though anger and self-righteousness marred the purity of my heart. My idealism and Lily's materialism were ever at enmity. I had watched Lily sabotage even her own dream of a charming antique house through wasteful spending—never mind the dream of saving for Aurora and Rowan's education that we were supposed to have in common. Lily managed to undercut even her own self-interest. Yes, she was selfish and short-sighted, but I knew women about whom Day was telling a terrible lie. Look at Sheila. Look at Roberta.

"Community only becomes a community when the people living together come together for a purpose above themselves," Sheila had told me one afternoon, painting their new bedroom at Nazareth House. She and Langley had first opened the Catholic Worker house in a tiny bungalow in a gentrifying neighborhood a few blocks from Central Prison. But in February, just weeks before Patrick Moody's scheduled execution, their ministry partners Scott and Roberta had purchased this sprawling two-story stone house in a poorer section of Raleigh to expand the work. Langley and Sheila had bought cheap paint from a Habitat for Humanity Re-Store and were mixing whites and yellows, experimenting to get a shade they could live with.

"If we all live as equal with each other, we can all reach our God-given potential," Sheila went on. "For us to be truly human and to be the greatest of who we could be involves serving other people. I think that's what makes us truly human is when we care about other people."

"Does it have to be the right people?" I asked her. *Will I ever have that sort of community with my own wife?*

"I don't think that personally I would want to live in community with people I wasn't compatible with," she said. "I mean, I hope that I could."

"It's hard," Langley said.

"It is hard," said Sheila. "Like, part of me wants to say, 'Anyone who wants to join, come.' But there are people I know who really annoy me."

Please, Jesus

"What about when you have children?" I asked her. "Will that change the way you live?" She didn't yet know she was pregnant. *Surely you'll turn more selfish then.*

"I hope so, and I hope not," she said. "I hope that doesn't stop us from still being able to take risks and challenges and go to prison or risk that. Even if I personally am not going to risk that right now, part of my community is, so I still am part of that. We know so many people who have kids and live in a Catholic Worker house. One of the spouses is in prison or they share a home with homeless people. I think it's great for kids to see their parents caring about the world and trying to change the world. If we had a baby, the baby would have two parents home most of the time. If anything it would lead to more family time and community time than a normal child would get, although I think there's many great ways to raise a family, that's for sure."

Sheila wasn't there to judge me and Lily or anyone else. If she only knew the truth of it. My marriage was *my* problem, and I kept it hidden from my friends at Nazareth House. They had their hands full taking care of Patrick Moody's family.

On the night of the execution, his mother Rondelle sat in her wheelchair, picking at Bojangle's biscuits and bite-sized pieces of fried chicken that Roberta had skinned and cut from the bone. It was going on midnight. Patrick's death was scheduled for 2 a.m. Half the house was asleep. Sheila was in her bedroom upstairs, while Langley was in a jail cell downtown. She'd skipped the night's peaceful collision with local police to protect her queasy stomach and the baby inside her. Her mother-in-law Mary, who'd traveled from Texas to cheer on Langley, slept in a nearby bedroom. Rondelle's brother-in-law Larry had also turned in for the night. He told his wife Lou he wanted to leave at 4 a.m. for the next day's eleven-hour drive back to Canton, Ohio. Rondelle's oldest living son Jason soon retired to another room. But first he gave his mom a tiny digital radio with earbuds, so she could try to hear the news of Patrick's death when it was finally over. Rondelle's most vivid memories were from Patrick's early childhood, before his father gained full custody. The witnesses just outside the execution chamber were from his father's side of the family. Rondelle was here, three miles down the road, waiting for a radio newscaster to say that her son was dead.

Midnight ticked by, and Patrick's aunt Lou tried to stay awake for her sister. Every now and then, she would say she was going to bed. "I doubt I'll be able to sleep," Lou would say, over and over again.

"I can't believe this is happening. What a nightmare. It's such a waste," Rondelle said at one point, speaking to no one in particular. This would be one of a few moments of clarity to punctuate the meandering monologue of a woman at once trying to deny and to accelerate the inevitable by talking about anything but . . .

After munching on marshmallow Rice Krispie treats donated by some friends of Nazareth House, Lou finally succumbed to sleep, joining Larry in the bedroom just across the dining room from the kitchen where we sat. Half an hour later, around 1 a.m., Rondelle's husband Ellis retired to the bedroom next door to Lou and Larry's. The family had done just about all it could do for Patrick. The only thing anyone could do for him now was to stay awake until his death. Rondelle would spend the last hours of Patrick's life with Scott, Roberta, and me, a complete stranger.

Rondelle sat at the table in the middle of the kitchen in the back left corner of Nazareth House, her face toward a window at the rear of the house, with the dining room to her right and the kitchen sink to her left. I sat across from her, with my back to the window and the back door off my right shoulder, a vase of wilting daisies between us. Scott, still wearing his olive green twill jacket and New Balance runners from the chilly protest, sat backward on an oak chair, set back a couple of feet from the table on my right and her left, leaving just enough room to open the back door. Roberta was dressed in a heather gray North Carolina State veterinary school sweatshirt, black turtleneck, Tar Heel Blue slippers, and jeans with their cuffs turned up. She stood off Scott's right shoulder near the sink, her perpetual post, ready to meet any need for food or drink.

Rondelle was a large woman, age sixty-seven. She wore a black fleece cape that covered her upper half and part of the wheelchair. Underneath she wore a bright pink polyester blouse with a stylized flower pattern from the 1970s. Her eyes were barely visible through her large, single-vision lenses, tinted to match her pearly gray plastic frames. Her shoulder-length hair was gray and straight, bangs falling to her nose, so she'd occasionally push them away from her sagging face. She talked almost non-stop, thank God, because I, for one, had no idea what to say.

A former country-club couple seeking a life of radical simplicity, Scott and Roberta had only recently joined Langley and Sheila in this ministry to death row families. For a couple of years, they'd been feeding the homeless from their home in downtown Raleigh and had just bought this 5,000-square-foot, ten-bedroom, ramshackle house in a poorer neighborhood to make room for Langley, Sheila, death-row visitors, and anyone else who might want to join the Catholic Worker community. Over the previous several years, the younger couple had been befriending death-row inmates from New York to Texas, but now Sheila was in bed, and her husband was in jail. Scott worked as a family counselor and Roberta as a veterinarian, so they were experienced caregivers, but this was on-the-job training in the extreme.

Rondelle talked about Patrick's childhood, how he used to bring her peanut butter toast in bed and make her cupcakes in his EZ Bake Oven, forgetting to grease the muffin tins.

You'll have to eat it with a spoon, he'd tell her.

My memory could only capture so many details, so, after several balks, I worked up the nerve to ask her permission to take some notes and record the conversation. That was okay with her, as long as I sent her a copy of anything I published. Control of the conversation was suddenly in my unwilling hands. I wanted to witness her grief, not interrogate her. But Rondelle looked for my cue, so I asked her what her week had been like.

"Nightmare," she said. "It's like walking into a vacuum and something that's sucking you right on in and down."

She talked about another son and two visiting nurses who'd tried to cheer her up at home. She'd only recently told them about Patrick's impending death.

"I would bust out crying, and they would never know what was wrong," she said.

She talked about her other children: Steven, in and out of jail; Jerry, the first-born son, dead; Jason, the good uncle, who took in his big brother's orphan. Inescapably, her monologue returned to death.

Her father died in 1960. She was twenty-one.

Her first husband died in 1965. He was twenty-eight. She was twenty-six.

Jerry died in his early twenties, she couldn't remember exactly how old.

Speaking in dialogue, Rondelle relayed a conversation she'd had with Jerry's son Israel, a few years after his daddy's death. He had been seven months old when Jerry died.

"Grandma, do you know where my daddy is?"

"Yeah, honey, I do know where your daddy is."

"I do too. Would you like to go with me sometime when I go over there and talk to him?"

"You go and talk to your dad?"

"Yeah. He's over in the cemetery in a box."
"Oh, did your mommy tell you that?"
"Yes, she did, and I don't like it."
"What don't you like about it?"
"'Cause he ain't just in a regular box. He's in a nice box. I asked my teacher. She told me my dad's in a funeral casket, and he's in there where nobody can get to him, and that's all right."
"Well, when you go up there and talk to your daddy, what do you ask him?"
"Anything I want to know."
"Well, does he answer you back?"
"No, but he listens good."

My only acquaintance with death was my great-grandmother when I was about ten years old. I'd been spared so far, but couldn't tragedy strike at any moment? Was Rondelle any different from me? Jesus said the Father sends warming sun and quenching rain to both the just and the unjust. But I was trying hard to be one of the just—you know, in case it might make a difference.

"I just can't believe this," Rondelle said.

She sighed heavily.

"I can't believe it's almost all over.

"I . . . I can't believe this happened.

"It's hard to think about him," she said, whispering.

"It's hard to think that he's never been married," she went on, her voice crying though her eyes stayed dry for the moment. "He's never got to do things that other guys do."

"His dad made sure of it whenever he had him around him," she added, her voice turning bitter.

Patrick's father Dick gained custody when he and Rondelle divorced in 1970. Patrick was four years old. Rondelle blamed her ex-husband for the way their son turned out. At the prayer service held for Patrick at Pullen Memorial Baptist Church, the theme had been the abuse that Patrick suffered at the hands of his family. The atrocious stories came from an interview Patrick gave to the alternative newsweekly *The Independent*. A clipping sat on the table in front of Rondelle. In it, Patrick told of eating his meals in a separate room from his step-siblings; staying home while they went on vacation; watching them receive allowance while he got none; being locked in a room, beaten with two-by-fours and wrenches, and run over by his family's truck.

Please, Jesus

Early in the article, Patrick was quoted saying that both his parents hated kids. From the context, it appeared that he was talking about his father and his stepmother, but Rondelle took it personally.

"I never so much as ever smacked Patrick in his life, and he put in that paper that his parents were cruel to him," she said. "He only had one cruel parent, and that was his father, 'cause I don't believe in hitting kids. As a matter of fact, I love kids to death."

I didn't want to ponder how she must have felt. I'd gotten up at 3 a.m. for bottle feedings. I took Aurora to father-daughter classes in tumbling, soccer, basketball, and baseball. At eighteen months old, she'd led me around Waterfront Park in Newburyport, Massachusetts, begging food off friendly picnickers during a Bruce Cockburn concert as only a toddler can do. Two-month-old Rowan had sat in my lap those nights in the fall of 2004 when my beloved Red Sox were coming back on the Yankees and then winning their first World Series in eighty-six years. I jogged the two girls around Chapel Hill in our double-stroller. We walked to the playground. I prayed with them every night at bedtime. Could things really turn as bad for us as they had for Rondelle and Patrick? How could I ever let them out of my sight, even for a couple of nights a week? *Custody.* That word and everything it represents sounded like a curse word to me. Lily and I just had to make this marriage work.

Rondelle talked about the seven teenaged boys she had taken in over the years, in addition to her own nine children.

"I just can't believe on top of everybody else, I can't do nothing for mine."

She couldn't protect Patrick from a lifetime of abuse. She couldn't protect him from himself. And now she couldn't protect him from the state of North Carolina. At the time of the murder, Patrick was having an affair with his victim's wife, and they conspired to kill the man for a $5,000 insurance policy.

"I can't hardly believe it, all that stuff that they say he done," she said, emphatically. "It's hard to believe," she said, more softly, "... that he did it," she continued, more softly still. "I don't think he did," she added, almost inaudibly, as if trying to convince herself.

Waking from her innermost thoughts, Rondelle quickly changed the subject. She commented on the cold weather and how she prefers marshmallow treats to a bowl of plain Rice Krispies. But older, wiser, family-counselor Scott, unlike me, knew she should keep talking about Patrick, not repress her suffering.

"When's Patrick's birthday?" he asked.

"Fourth of July. I told him, I said, 'Here you are born on the Fourth of July, you know, big celebration, and here they are, gonna kill you on St. Patrick's Day, still another big celebration.'"

She told how Patrick's aunt Audrey, her only friendly contact on his father's side of the family, wrote a petition and collected signatures to keep Patrick from being executed on St. Patrick's Day. Patrick had told the freelance *Independent* writer, who also happened to run another Catholic Worker house with his wife, that executing an Irish-American on St. Patrick's Day was like executing a black man on Martin Luther King Jr. Day. In fact, North Carolina's last most recent execution had been Perrie Dyon Simpson, an African-American, a few days after the MLK holiday. On that day, Langley and the other protestors had called themselves "The Martin Luther King Jr. Affinity Group," invoking the civil rights leader's name because the death penalty is so much more likely to be used against blacks than whites. On this night, they trespassed on the prison grounds in honor of Patrick, the patron saint of Ireland, who said, "In Christ, there is no killing." But no signed petition or 1,500-year-old moral proscription would stop this killing. A judge and jury had found Patrick Moody's crime worthy of death.

"My daughter died when she was fourteen-and-a-half hours old, so this makes three of my children," said Rondelle. "Dead. I've had so much death around me . . . It just seems like a dream sometimes, but after a while you don't wake up."

"I can't hardly believe it," she whispered, barely moving her lips, almost mumbling.

The kitchen was silent for several seconds until time grabbed Rondelle and dragged her back into the present.

"What time is it?" she asked with urgency in her voice. "Does anybody know?"

Roberta, who had gone from standing, to sitting cross-legged, to stretching her legs out on the shiny gray-checked vinyl floor, rose to a stooped position, legs straight, bent at the waist, high enough to crane her neck around to her right and look at the clock built into her brand new, white electric stove donated by some local Quakers. Roberta never fully stood but instead leaned her head and shoulders forward toward Rondelle, as though trying to look into a child's eyes while breaking some bad news. Roberta's lips were pursed, and the skin of her forehead scrunched together, slanting her eyebrows upward. She had worn this devastated look throughout the night, even at the vigil when she was merely *preparing* herself to comfort this grieving family.

"About 1:20," said Roberta, in a voice higher and more earnest than her usual measured drawl. Forty minutes to go.

"Oh my," Rondelle cried.

Silence.

"Oh, Patrick," she moaned.

"I loved my baby so much," she said, her pitch rising and falling, like singing.

She told of asking each of her boys, before she gave birth to the next, if they wanted her to go to the hospital to get them a little baby brother to play with.

"They all loved each other so much. Each one of 'em took care of their baby. I don't know how all this time, and even after my boys got men, they always looked out for each other. Patty left home, and he left home with nobody. It just makes me so sad. I can't believe this.

"Anything but this!"

"How do you really ever say goodbye to somebody like this? I thought it was hard when my husband died, but it's not as hard as it is when you're child dies. It's harder, and since I've had both of it happen to me . . . I can't believe it. I just can't believe it. It didn't have to end this way."

"I don't know what to do about his funeral or memorial services or nothing. I'm not even sure what kind of religion he was at this time. I know he was Catholic for sixteen years. I can't understand what he is now."

Silence.

Scott: "Did he talk, did Pat talk any about the funeral, or . . . ?"

Rondelle: "Yes."

Scott: "I thought I heard you or Lou or somebody talking about where he wanted his ashes or something like that."

"Yeah, he told me. He was supposed . . . his ashes were supposed to go to his dad, they told me. And I said, 'Pat, do you really want your dad to have your ashes?' And he said, 'No, he ain't bein' near my ashes.' And I said, 'Well, I hate to tell you, honey, unless you make some arrangements, he's gonna be right at the middle of your ashes.' [Patrick's father] told his sister to tell me that he's putting them on his flowerbed in the backyard and he's putting some at Rick's house and some at Gary's house and his, and if there's any more, I just might get some. And he says, 'I'm not being in his backyard or Gary's backyard or Rick's backyard.' He said, 'I really don't care what they do with 'em, Mom, but they better give you more than half,' and I said, 'No, that ain't necessary.'"

This Littler Light

Geez. How could a family get to point where you were fighting about where to put your son's ashes after a lethal injection? Could that happen to Lily and me?

"I just couldn't believe when they told me that he'd been arrested, and that he'd been arrested for murder. Sometime I wondered whether he even knew what murder was. He told me, he says, 'Mom, I want you to tell Rick, that Rick, you get half of them, and you get the other half, Mom.'"

"Well, I'd put 'em up on a mantle if I had one," she said.

Every so often, Rondelle's speech had been slurring ever so slightly, her sentences trailing off, her arms falling limp at her side. Scott noticed this before anyone else and looked at Roberta and me to see if we were concerned. We weren't, but he subtly slid his chair an inch or two toward Rondelle in case he needed to catch her falling out of her wheelchair.

"Now I want to thank you both for your hospitality these last couple of days," Rondelle said.

"Rondelle, would you like to lie down?" Scott asked.

"No. It wouldn't do any good if I laid down," she said with a hint of embarrassed amusement in her voice. "It would just be worse. I'm having little seizures."

Scott: "Yeah, that's what I was wondering if it was something like that."

Rondelle: "Yeah, I have 'em. I get 'em about twice a day, especially when I get really worried. I don't know, I just seem to can't, can't cope with the rest of it. Everything around me just seems to bring 'em on. And I can't help stop 'em, and my doctor don't know what to do to stop 'em."

Good Lord! Would Lily or I one day get this old and sick and sad? Is this what happened when your marriage went bad? Was that the path were were on?

Scott pointed out a Rice Krispie crumb that had fallen out of Rondelle's hand and onto her lap during one of these seizures. Rondelle began to explain the diet and medical regimen she keeps in order to control her diabetes.

"Oh my," she said suddenly. "I'm keeping everybody up!"

"No!" said Scott and Roberta in unison.

Rondelle kept talking—about the strength of German coffee, the virtues of the self-cleaning function on Roberta's new oven, the death of her first husband, the death of her mother. She started talking about the tribulations of dialysis when Patrick flashed through her mind. It was 1:55 a.m. She stopped in the middle of a sentence, silent.

Please, Jesus

"Is it 2:00 yet?"

Roberta, softly: "No, ma'am, not yet."

Scott: "Almost."

Roberta: "Almost."

Rondelle: "Is there any way we can find out when this is . . . done?"

Scott: "It's, um . . . usually they're right on schedule at 2:00."

Rondelle: "Yeah, but when they do that, when they, when do they announce it to the public?"

"Uh . . ." Scott wasn't sure.

Roberta: "When the witnesses come out after . . ."

Scott: "Yeah, they don't . . . they have a press conference afterward but it's not usually carried until the next morning, like the 6 o'clock news, that kind of thing. It's in the morning."

Rondelle: "How come they don't tell it?"

Scott: "I guess they figure that, uh, I mean, they tell it, but they just don't broadcast it. I guess they figure that most folks are not up for it."

He doesn't share his theory that state officials schedule executions for 2 o'clock in the morning precisely because they don't want anyone paying attention to them.

"I've never been to no prison and seen anything like this happen or anything," said Rondelle. "I don't know nothing about it really. I don't know nothing about jail. My kids do, but I don't."

Earlier that day at the prison, Rondelle said she had reminded Patrick what she'd taught him: how to make beds, clean house, and wash dishes.

I didn't teach you how to go to jail, and how to kill somebody, or anything like that. I'd like to know how you got down that road. I just can't believe that this is . . . you're my baby and that you're doing this.

"I've never been able to figure out all this stuff," she told us in the kitchen.

Scott: "It's one of those things that don't seem to have answers."

Rondelle: "I can't understand how it happened in the first place. What was there to make Pat go this way? I just . . . I don't understand it." But if you read Patrick's story in his own words in the newspaper article, you had a pretty good idea. Lily herself was worried our girls would turn out like her—clinging, materialistic, dependent. She used to tell me I'd have to make sure she wasn't too controlling when they got older. What if we split and I wasn't around to check her impulses? What would happen to them then? And, marriage or no marriage, I had to get my anger in check, or I was going to pass it on to them.

At 2:15, Rondelle's thoughts, like mine, returned to the abuse Patrick had suffered at the hands of his father. The 2 o'clock hour had begun without her noticing. Scott interrupted her.

"I think it's pretty safe to say that things are finished now," he said. "Patrick is at rest."

"Well, can we find out for sure?" she asked. "Can we call the prison?"

Scott went into the dining room to make the call. After a couple of minutes he returned with no news. He retreated to his office to see if the outcome had been posted on the prison web site. Still nothing. He telephoned the prison again and returned quietly to the kitchen.

Rondelle: "So what's happened?"

Scott: "He said it's over."

"Oh no!"

Scott placed his right hand on her left shoulder.

"Thank you," she breathed.

Her left hand curled into a fist. She put it to her lips. A tear ran down her right cheek.

"Please, Jesus," she whispered. "Please take care of him."

Please, Jesus. Please take care of us. This love business, this family stuff, this romance and marriage and child rearing could go spectacularly, explosively, murderously wrong. Sometimes I thought maybe I was in the right. Maybe I had the moral high ground. But who cares? What good is being right when your marriage is at stake? When your five-year-old and your two-year-old need to see that their parents love them and love each other? When, if we don't, they might end up on death row some day? How badly was I screwing them up? Dorothy Day had this much correct: This man could claim "single-mindedness" for himself. "Pure of heart", though, was a stretch: I was agitated, angry, and irritable. I didn't want to love my wife the way she was. I wanted her to change.

This is a story about expectations—how they haunt you, oppress, and control you while at the same time presenting the illusion that you're in control, that cause and effect operates in the moral universe like $1 + 1 = 2$, that you can dream dreams and live up to your dreams and that if you don't, then someone is to blame. This is a story about working my way toward righteousness, trying to do the right thing, trying to make the world a better place, trying to build a life that pleases God, and finding that all of these efforts can actually drive us farther from God and from the people we're supposed to love. It's about fundamentalism as a habit of the heart, whether you're threatening violence on homosexuals or heaping scorn on those who don't recycle. It's about how we tamp out the moral ambiguity that permeates our homes, our workplaces, our entire lives and replace it with a Great Rule-Maker in the Sky who has designed for us perfect little lives if we will just follow the instructions.

It's about how living by these rules casts implicit judgment on others, how trying to keep all these little commandments we think God has for us can keep us from keeping the two Greatest Commandments: to love God and neighbor. It's about learning that God does not need me to stand up for her, to protect him, to show the world how good I am, so the world will know how good God is. This story is about learning that my neighbors—including my wife and children—need my love and acceptance a whole lot more than they need my moral example.

It's a story about my refusal to fail, a refusal often praised as meritorious, but which, in truth, doubles as a refusal to accept my place as a creature, with limits; if you refuse to fail at a badly mismatched relationship, there's a good chance you'll have to deny the identity of one or both of the people involved—to struggle, perhaps for decades, against your own God-given uniquenesses. I fought for my marriage because I believed in the sanctity of marriage, not because Lily and I brought out the best in each other. I was probably fighting for the wrong reason.

And doing the right thing for the wrong reason is not doing the right thing at all. So this is a story about the discovery that doing the right thing and being right before God are two very different things. Being right before God is a posture of receiving grace in the midst of perpetual failure, and if we think we're capable always of doing the right thing, there's not much room left for grace. I am the Prodigal Son, not the Older Brother. I am no Good Samaritan, but the man lying robbed, beaten, and bloody by the side of the road. As the prophet Isaiah said, "All our righteous acts are like filthy rags."

In the end, this is a story about how grace can break through our failures, and sometimes even break through our successes, to show us the most fundamental truth about ourselves: We are creatures of a caring Creator, sustained at every moment by no power of our own—foolish, incompetent scaredy-cats always trying to prove we're something more, yet constantly accepted and embraced by Love. If God needs me for anything, it is as a child on which to lavish love. If I have any light to offer the world, it is as a tiny moon reflecting the brilliance of the sun. This is a story about discovering our limits, our weakness, our inability to save ourselves. It's about forgiveness, and how the most important kind might be forgiving ourselves, which can only come after we find that God has forgiven us. It's about the God who doesn't promise a perfect life, but promises to be there when it goes bad. It's about the perpetual prayer on the lips of those who know God: *Kyrie eleison.* Lord, have mercy. Please, Jesus.

2

Love Not the World

> There is nothing wrong in America that cannot be cured by old-fashioned preaching.
>
> —Brother Jack Hyles

When I was seven years old, Mom started taking my brother Marco and me to Grace Bible Baptist Church and School in rural New Hampshire. We'd pass by all these well-attended, high-steepled liberal churches to worship in a squat, utilitarian building hidden on a back road in the woods, with a congregation of thirty or forty strong: The Moral Majority. There were Ronald Reagan posters in the lobby. We'd listen to sermons about "back masking" and the Satanist propaganda you'd hear if you played rock records backwards. One week, we came back to church every night after school to watch Russell Daughten's four-part 1970s *Rapture* movie series, the original *Left Behind*: Polyester pandemonium.

A guy named Jack Hyles in Indiana was like our pope, and sometimes we'd listen to his sermons on tape at church. The real Pope might have been the Antichrist; we weren't sure. We were pretty sure the Roman Catholic Church was "the Whore of Babylon" from the book of Revelation, leading our neighbors to hell, with a stop at the corner bar on the way. (We stuck with grape juice.) Until I looked it up just now, I had always thought Hyles was from Denver; I must have confused him with the Broncos quarterback, our pastor's other big hero. Some things were certain: Reagan and Hyles would save us from the Communists and Catholics, and John "The General" Elway would lead a fourth-quarter touchdown drive to beat the Browns in the playoffs.

One time a singing group from the pope's college in Indiana came to our church for a concert. It was an unaccredited college because Hyles, like our pastor, didn't want any bureaucratic meddling. It was bad enough that Gorbachev and the United Nations were conspiring to form the "One-World Government" and that Mom and Dad's credit-card company was an accomplice, stockpiling our personal information so they could link it to the Mark of the Beast in the run-up to Armageddon. The Hyles-Anderson Singers were a barbershop-gospel quartet. They did the old folk song, "This Train," the bass rumbling and the high tenor soaring about the "righteous and holy" who'd get on that train, the liars, gamblers, hypocrites, and midnight ramblers who'd be left behind. They sang a verse added by Woody Guthrie in the 1950s: Cigarette smokers were his target. Bad news, because Dad liked his Winstons. No wonder he didn't come to church much. The Hyles-Anderson Singers even got creative with the lyrics:

> This train is bound for glory, this train.
> This train is bound for glory, this train.
> God made Adam and Eve,
> God didn't make no Adam and Steve
> This train is leavin', get on board.

The pastor presided over both the church and the school with absolute authority. He identified us as "independent," "fundamental," "Bible-believing," and "Baptist," in that order. Calvary, a competing Christian school from which I would eventually graduate, used the same words, but it wasn't strict enough for this pastor, and he would constantly bad-mouth it as "liberal." The Rolling Stones' swaggering frontman Mick Jagger, fifteen years past his prime even then, was one of his favorite villains: something about his "prancing around the stage." Smoke machines were meant to make a rock concert look like hell, he'd tell us. He forbade Mom and the other church ladies from wearing slacks or cutting their hair short; that would make them too much like men. Likewise, earrings and long hair were off-limits for men. Brother Starch, aptly named, wore dark, double-breasted power suits, shiny black cowboy boots, his black hair slicked back, and a thick, Magnum P.I. moustache. He taught me a firm handshake, saying limp wrists were a symbol for gay men, though I wasn't sure why; didn't their arms work like everybody else's?

One morning during our weekly chapel service at school, my friend Sean threw some pocket change toward the pastor as he entered our classroom to preach. It was an innocent gesture: Sean must have seen video footage of Catholics throwing flowers in front of the Pope or heard the story of Jesus entering Jerusalem over a path of palms. "You DO NOT throw things at the man of God," Brother Starch barked.

Anybody, even Dad sometimes, could come to church on Sunday mornings, but Sunday night at 6 o'clock was the time for the true believers. We didn't miss it. Mercifully, when our hometown Patriots got beat 46-10 in Super Bowl XX, Brother Starch had been taping the game so we could watch it after the service in the fellowship hall that doubled as our school classroom; we didn't have to see the massacre on live TV. One Sunday night he announced he had never been "saved" in all those years he'd been leading the church and that only days earlier had finally accepted Jesus as his personal savior. I wasn't sure why he told us that, but it caused me to doubt my own salvation, surely an effective means of control. If you couldn't have faith in your own faith, there might be hell to pay.

Brother Starch would convene us every Sunday night to boast to one another about how many souls we had won the previous week. "He that winneth souls is wise," he'd always say, quoting Proverbs 11:30. Winning souls was never about anything like, say, convincing a man to stop beating his wife or to start serving at a soup kitchen. It was about keeping people from eternal damnation. One lady, Miss Beth would come reporting she'd won seven or eleven or seventeen souls in any particular week. Nobody, not even Brother Starch, ever came close to beating her.

We were supposed to hand out "Chick Tracts," these little comic books a guy named Jack Chick wrote against Catholics, Mormons, and evolutionists, trying to get people saved. Every tract ended with four steps to salvation, a pattern prayer asking Jesus to save and a reminder to "Read your Bible (KJV) to get to know Jesus Christ better." We were to believe that the King James Version of the Bible, translated in seventeenth-century England, was the only version that had come down through history untainted by human error. One tract, "Back from the Dead," showed a guy with a Luke Skywalker haircut having a near-death experience, going to hell, and then reviving in the emergency room and screaming for a preacher to tell him how to get to heaven. Another tract, "A Demon's Nightmare," had a guy in a nice suit telling a teenage boy about Jesus while some Disneyfied devils try to distract the kid. The demons used the new believer's worldly family and friends to persecute him and tried to steer him toward a "wonderful little modern church" instead of a "Bible-believing" church that preached "the second-coming of Christ."

Our unsaved relatives weren't *supposed* to like us.
We were *supposed* to be different.
We were *supposed* to be weird.
That's how we knew we were right.

> The mountains and hills will burst into song before you, and all the trees of the field will clap their hands.
>
> —Isaiah 55:12

I'd gotten saved at an altar call was when I was four years old at a different fundamentalist church. The pastor's wife was waiting up front to lead me to the Lord. She was a nice lady who taught Children's Church in a room behind the sanctuary, and she smelled like flowers.

"Dear God," she said, her voice warm and motherly.
"Dear God," I said, in my tiny voice.
"I know I'm a sinner."
"I know I'm a sinner."
"And Jesus died."
"And Jesus died."
"To save me from my sins."
"To save me from my sins."
"I ask him to forgive me,"
"I ask him to forgive me,"
"And come into my heart,"
"And come into my heart,"
"So I can go to heaven,"
"So I can go to heaven,"
"And be with you when I die."
"And be with you when I die."
"Amen."

"Amen."

I didn't have much to confess. One time, I'd told Mom I'd eaten a banana but really I'd thrown it away. Another time, I'd filled her drinking glass from the toilet. It was all I could reach, and it seemed clean enough. Another time, I'd taken her giant wooden spanking paddle and thrown it into the fireplace. I don't think she had ever used it on me, but just the thought! And I liked to scare my little brother with a Batman mask left over from Halloween. He'd be squealing in our bedroom closet while the Dark Knight lurked outside.

But it didn't matter how big or little your sin was: You were either right with God, or you weren't. I needed forgiveness just like everybody else. There was a whole world out there that needed saving, and if I didn't get on board, who would tell them? We preschoolers would clap our hands and sing,

> Be a missionary every day
> Tell the world that Jesus is the way
> Be it in the town or country or a busy avenue
> Africa, or Asia, the choice is up to you

The pastor's wife gave us biblical heroes to imitate, in full-color felt on a flannel board: Abel who gave his best to God, murdered by his own brother; Noah, who seemed crazy to be building a giant boat, until God sent the Flood to rid the world of the wicked (like Dad?); Abraham, who trusted God so much he almost killed his own son; Joseph, sold into slavery by his brothers (could you really trust your family?) only to become a great leader in Egypt; Moses, separated from his family and not much of public speaker, whom God called to lead Israel out of Egypt; Samson, who had strength like Hulk Hogan, as long as he obeyed God; shepherd boy David, who killed the Philistine giant with five stones and a sling; Elijah, who outprayed the false prophets of Baal and called down fire from heaven; Daniel, whom God protected from the lions; Peter, who denied Jesus but later healed the sick, just like the Lord; Paul, who hated Christians but then became a great missionary.

Mom, too, used to sit in her bed and read Marco and me these Bible stories. The burgundy leather and gold edges of her King James Bible were worn thin. She read through the whole thing multiple times when I was a kid. She especially liked to read to us from Proverbs, I guess because it taught us how to live: share with your neighbors, make peace, tell the truth, be faithful to your spouse, work hard, plan ahead, show mercy, keep confidences, guard your tongue and, most of all, trust God. Mom would also read to us about George Mueller, who ran an orphanage by praying to God, so that free milk or bread would just show up on the doorstep to feed the children.

We, too, could do great things for God. It wouldn't be easy, but we could do it, if we just put all our faith in Jesus. Whether they were brash and boastful like Goliath or Nebuchadnezzar, or cunning like Abel or Delilah, or sick like all those lepers Jesus healed, or cigarette-smoking heathens like Dad, non-Christians were all the same: they just needed Jesus—they needed to see that obedience made us happy, that prayer worked, that God could do things through us we couldn't do for ourselves.

When I was nine, Brother Starch dunked me into the baptismal waters, in a giant vat like an extra-deep jacuzzi, normally hidden behind a curtain at the back of the altar. My extended family was there to watch. They didn't believe like we did, but they came to support me. It was a good excuse to get them to our church to hear our preacher. How could they say no? Some of them had been baptized as Catholics, but that didn't count. You had to get baptized in your own faith, not your Mom's, and not sprinkled but immersed, all the way under. My chain-smoking Nanny, Mom's mom, raised an Irish Catholic in Manhattan, always said she didn't need a church to worship God. The church hadn't been much help during her marital strife or the sudden, inexplicable death of my twenty-year-old uncle in his sleep. But I didn't see any other way to know God, besides church.

"I baptize you in the name of the Father . . ." Brother Starch said, standing in his chest-high fishing waders and lowering me backwards into the chilly water.

"And of the Son . . .," he said, submerging me a second time.

"And of the Holy Spirit," he added, dunking me for the third and final time.

Nanny and her cousin helped Mom hold towels around me, in a makeshift changing room in the back of the church, after the pastor had dipped me and I'd had to walk back through the sanctuary, dripping wet. Your family could be nice to you, but that didn't mean they were saved. If I needed forgiveness for some toilet water, God must have had something on them. Rejecting Jesus alone was enough to send them to hell.

And that's where most of my family was going. Nanny, who bought me Luke Skywalker's X-Wing Fighter for Christmas, and even let me peak inside the wrapping a couple of weeks early just to make sure she'd gotten the right one; whose refrigerator always held Kraft singles, which

Mom never bought, and slow-cook chocolate pudding with the skin on top and Cool Whip; who melted margarine on my spaghetti because I was an Italian kid who didn't like tomato sauce. Mom's sisters, who always remembered my birthday and bought me G.I. Joe men and their expensive helicopters or tanks, even though they had kids of their own. Certainly Grumpy, Dad's dad, who had passed on his drug problem to my Uncle Eddie. I would pray for God to save them, but as far as I knew, they were still going to hell, forever, burning for all eternity. Dad's friend, who died of a heart attack while out on a jog in his early thirties? Bam. Hell. My uncle Steven, Mom's brother, who died suddenly in his sleep at age twenty, and had never known any faith but the Catholic one? Bam. "He's gonna split hell wide open!" as Brother Starch used to say.

I didn't want to believe that, but if I didn't believe it, I might go there too.

So I even had to believe that Dad was going to hell, if he didn't change his ways. Even Dad, who would play me Kenny Loggins's "House at Pooh Corner" on his guitar or take me on the Boston subway and share an Italian sausage sub outside Fenway Park before a Red Sox game. Dad, who would come downstairs early on Saturday mornings to watch cartoons and play with my Star Wars action-figures in the mountainous terrain of my favorite blanket piled up around me on the living room floor, breaking my rules by making characters fly who couldn't fly in the movies. Dad, who coached my baseball team and threw pass after pass as I practiced my zig-zag or hook-and-go routes in the backyard.

Dad was my hero and my anti-hero all at the same time. Dad was everybody's friend—funny, easygoing, not afraid to have a drink, but one of my earliest, haziest memories is of he and Mom throwing dishes and saltshakers at each other across the kitchen. Whether it was running off with his old high-school gang to watch football or gamble—or worse—he seemed to make Mom sad a lot. He'd been a star pitcher, third-baseman, and tennis player as a kid, but when I was about four years old I heard him yelling from the garage behind our house and ran out there to find him stumbling around, blinded by the chemicals he used to refinish furniture. He ended up being OK, but I couldn't shake the feeling that Dad wasn't quite as invincible as I wanted him to be.

The furniture business was just one of many jobs Dad did to try to support us while hanging onto his real vocation as a musician. He drove a cab, just like Tony the boxer in *Taxi*, one of our favorite TV shows. He even looked the part with his long, reddish-brown curls tumbling out of his tweed driver's cap. He delivered for a Greek pizzeria, bringing Mom fresh baklava and pizza for all of us; the gross fishy taste from his anchovies always ran onto my plain-cheese half. These seemed like dangerous, manly jobs: working with wood, driving all over town, playing electric-fuzz guitar through speakers bigger than me.

Dad had his music studio in the basement of our 100-year-old duplex in Lowell, Massachusetts, an old cotton-mill city on the Merrimack River. Sometimes I'd go down there to listen to him practice. He liked to read to me from *The Hobbit*, so I recognized his poster of Bilbo, Gandalf, and the dwarves climbing the Misty Mountains. Dad was working on a rock opera based on Tolkien's story. That and the fieldstone walls made the basement feel not just creepy but mysterious and ancient—a real man cave. I remember my uncle Eddie rolling papers down there.

"What's that?" I asked him.

"Oh," he said, "we're just making our own cigarettes."

When I was a baby, Dad had been able to earn most of his living with just music. In fact, on the Saturday night of my birth, Dad had been playing in his duo, The Fabulous Linguini Brothers, at The Alewife, a bar in Somerville, Massachusetts, owned by one of his cousins. Dad and his partner Bob Gentile were out four or five nights a week, playing cover songs in restaurants, bars, and hotel lounges all over New England. He'd come home late from a gig the night before, but I woke him and Mom with pregnancy pains at 5 a.m. Saturday morning. They'd slept at Nanny and Poppy's house that night, and they stayed there with my grandparents all day until Dad had to leave for The Alewife.

Mom called the bar around 11 p.m. to say she was in labor and Nanny and Poppy were taking her to the hospital. The bartender told the waitress, who whispered in Dad's ear right in the middle of Simon and Garfunkel's "Cecilia." Dad stood up and knocked over his microphone stand, filling the room with ear-splitting feedback before he could pick it up.

"My wife's having a baby," he announced to the full house.

The crowd cheered.

Dad left his rock star life in the middle of a set, to come to the maternity ward. That was 1977, and fathers were just being allowed into the birthing room. Dad put on green scrubs, a surgical cap, and mask, and stood near my aunt Lori, who was filming as my head crowned. Dad can't handle much blood, and he walked up near Mom's face, to hold her hand. But that still wasn't far enough away. He started to lose his balance, and Mom ordered him out.

In the waiting room, another father mistook my green-scrubbed father for his own wife's obstetrician.

"What's happening?" the worried dad asked, as my Dad sat bent over with his head in his hands.

"I'm losing it, man," he said.

So Dad wasn't perfect. He played rock 'n' roll and gambled and drank and smoked whatever it was they were rolling in the basement. God hated those things, and so I understood if God wasn't too happy with Dad. But wasn't he at least trying to love Mom and us kids? And didn't that count for something? It was easier not to think about that, to try and think happier thoughts about God.

I didn't have the word for it then, but *beauty* is where I felt closest to God, especially singing Christmas carols. I was a big brother (Marco was born when I was three and a half and Katie when I was nine), and I knew babies were something special. But all the power of the universe wrapped up in those swaddling clothes! A star shining just for him, beckoning those Wise Men from a faraway land! The angel choir! Mary's love, Joseph's devotion. The gentleness of "Silent Night" or "Little Town of Bethlehem." The high, sustained notes of the human voice on "O Holy Night." The exuberance of "Joy to the World" or "Hark, the Herald Angels Sing." God appeared at Christmas like no other time of year. I guess that's why we call it the Incarnation. Mom's faith and Dad's music came together in Christmas carols like nowhere else.

The only thing that compared to Christmas was skiing. Dad had gotten into real estate by the mid-'80s. When business was good, he'd take us to the slopes a few times a year. He'd always tell us how he'd first gone skiing when he was seventeen, and his friends pushed him down a black diamond trail at Loon Mountain before he knew what he was doing. It took him hours to creep his way down, slow turn by slow turn. Dad let us learn on the green-dot trails, but it wasn't long before I conquered that same black diamond.

When I raced down Loon or Cannon or Bretton Woods, wary of the trees and chairlift towers and other skiers who could kill or maim me with any wrong turn, there was fear and power, anxiety and excitement, frostbite, adrenaline and sweat, all wrapped into a singular experience of the present. It was uncomplicated: You were riding on the back of something much bigger than yourself, just trying to hang on.

My favorite part, though, wasn't the speed, or even the movement. It was sliding to the top of a trail, after the slow, boring climb up the lift, where you saw the mountain up close and only a little bit of it at a time, only to turn and face downhill, across a valley to the opposite wall, miles away yet so close you could reach out and touch it, a vast forest cascading far below the end of your own sight line at the near ridge and looming high above, touching the sky, a mass of earth taken in one big gulp, like God was a kid in the sandbox saying, "Look what I made!" When the weather was cold enough and the snow fresh enough, it clung to the balsam firs, a diamond crust coating the verdant needles, still green with life even in the middle of a five-month winter. God spoke most audibly when new powder silenced the swish of my own skis, like I was riding wind through the clouds.

I had to be sure not to worship nature itself; that was New Agey. But if that beauty reminded me of God the Creator, then I was still saved.

> Love not the world, neither the things that are in the world. If any man love the world, the love of the Father is not in him.
>
> —1 John 2:15 (KJV)

The first time I ever went to public school was my freshman year in high school. I'd had to leave my friends at Victory Christian, my school after Grace, because Mom was trying to extract us from fundamentalist faith. Mom, of course, had already started questioning the strict legalism during our time at Grace Bible Baptist, and then when the principal at Victory had spanked me and kicked me off the school basketball team for a minor childhood prank (more on that later), she couldn't take it anymore. She found this honors program at Memorial High School in Manchester, about twenty minutes from where we lived in the country. In junior high, I'd been a decent guard off the bench, a good defender on the soccer team, and held my own in schoolyard football and backyard wiffleball. But at Memorial I was a nerd. All these kids knew each other from eighth grade, and the only kid I knew was one of the nerdiest nerds whose mom had told mine about this honors program. In the cafeteria, I could sit with him, or by myself. Either way, I felt like an alien. In my computer programming class, there was this girl who always wore floor-length hippie skirts and cardigan sweaters over black concert t-shirts for bands like The Cure

Love Not the World

or Morrissey. One day, she called us over to see the message she'd coded her computer to write: "ENTER MY VAGINA." Was I the weird one? By December, I'd just started to get to know some kids in my classes and had a crush on a Christian girl, Kelly, who lived not far from my house. She was one of those "charismatics" Brother Starch had warned me about, probably speaking in tongues or raising her hands in church, but I didn't care. I liked her. I didn't really know her. Just had a few classes with her and admired her from a distance. I had some friends on her street, so I rode my bike to see her one afternoon. We talked for a few minutes on her doorstep. I wasn't sure if she was happy to see me.

Mom and Dad were having trouble paying their bills, and we had to move into a house half the size of our other one—Mom, Dad, Uncle Eddie and five kids, all squeezing into about 1,000 square feet, with two bedrooms and a closet-sized nursery Dad had built by adding a wall and carving off part of the living room. Marco and I had to share a bedroom with Eddie. He'd lived with my paternal grandparents, Nana and Grumpy, into his thirties. But Nana had had enough of his addictions, and he'd had enough of living with his parents. Mom was trying to get him clean because that's what she did: She took care of people. She didn't care so much about who smoked or drank or cursed or listened to rock 'n' roll; she didn't like those things, but she was more concerned about helping people. All my life I'd been watching her as she nursed an elderly woman with multiple sclerosis in her home or ours, or mentored young mothers through the Salvation Army, or cared for kids with disabilities, or took in a string of Dad's drug-addict tradesmen friends. Sometimes it seemed like she was taking care of Dad too.

We moved from one small town to another, just fifteen minutes east on Highway 101, but I had to change schools in the middle of my freshman year. I wanted more than anything for Kelly to hug me goodbye. Neither she nor anyone else knew me well enough to miss me. I'd gotten used to this, having gone to five different schools since kindergarten. I'd always been able to make friends, playing sports, or making jokes. But I was certain the same rules didn't apply at public school.

I transferred to Exeter High School. You might know the name "Exeter" from Phillips Exeter Academy, one of the most prestigious prep schools in the country. Novelists Dan Brown and John Irving, publisher Alfred Knopf, Jr., Arcade Fire frontman Win Butler, and Facebook founder Mark Zuckerberg all graduated from there. It sits in the center of this quaint little town, with Ivy League brick buildings, wide green quads, and the eight-story Exeter Library, one of the biggest high school libraries in the world and an icon of modernist architecture. I didn't go there. I went to the public high school down the street, in a brick neo-Colonial building, pretty in its own right but with aging innards and surrounded by a sea of asphalt. I was a double-misfit: Christian in a public school, public school kid in a prep school town.

At Exeter, most of my classes were with sophomores. One guy had a Beatles haircut and couldn't stop talking about U2's new album, *Achtung Baby*. I knew I wasn't supposed to care about things like that, but he seemed really cool. I did meet one other freshman honors kid who became something like a friend. I don't remember his name. He had a pudgy baby face, wore his pants too high, and had bangs cut straight across his brow like Jim Carrey in *Dumb and Dumber*. He loved baseball. We would trade cards at lunch. His favorite was Mike Mussina, a young Baltimore Orioles pitcher with a nasty curveball. It was like I was Kevin and he was Paul in *The Wonder Years*; at the very least, I thought, I was cooler than him. I'm not sure anyone else noticed.

Once, a skinheaded senior walked up to us at the lunch table. He was going into the Marines that summer and wore a muscle shirt and black cargo pants before they were fashionable. He threatened to beat us up if we didn't go over to a hot blonde and tell her he wanted to kiss her. He had at least fifty pounds on me, but I had enough pride to refuse. He left us alone after that.

After a couple of weeks, another freshman from my French class invited me to sit with him and his friends in the cafeteria. Maybe it was community service to impress a girl. I don't know. A few months later he asked about the small indoor racquetball club my parents ran as a side business, so maybe he just wanted free admission. Anyhow, he had dirty blond hair lighter than his ruddy skin, played lacrosse, and was built like Adonis. His was the popular crew in the class of '95. I started eating with them everyday because I wanted to feel like I belonged somewhere. One day at lunch, Adonis' girlfriend and another girl were talking about douching.

"She doesn't have to," Adonis announced with a sly smile. "I do it for her ... with my tongue."

His girlfriend gave him a playful slap on his burly chest, and I sat quietly. I was a sheltered little boy who had gone to independent, fundamental, Bible-believing Baptist schools all his life. I was different. God had made me that way, not just in my height and my smarts, but in the moral code I thought I was to live by. I'd never, ever thought about oral sex. Gross.

Love Not the World

I don't remember what happened to the Mike Mussina kid. I think we still hung out in the cafeteria between our biology lecture and lab. He and I and the U2 kid had these two straight periods with the big, jolly science teacher. He loved telling us about the student who drew cutaway pictures of male and female genitalia in the act of intercourse for an assignment on the reproductive system. He was also some kind of Buddhist, urging us to meditate at our desks during breaks, the sort of public school teacher I was supposed to fear.

I rode the bus back and forth with the other kids from my rural town. I didn't talk to anyone, just sat there minding my own business and trying not to be noticed. They'd sing the Red Hot Chili Peppers' "Under the Bridge" like a screaming, off-key choir. My aunt Peg, who went to one of those New Age "Unity" churches, had their album. All I knew was, I was a Christian and didn't listen to that kind of music. One day a kid belched in my face, just for the fun of it, I guess.

In my French class, there was a beautiful girl, tall, slender, blonde, and blue-eyed. I didn't know her real name, but the teacher named her Hélène. I was Jacques, and that's what Adonis called me, even in the cafeteria. One time I was staring at Hélène, and she shifted in her seat and flashed my eyes with her black underwear. That's my first memory of lust. Something more to feel guilty about, as if failing to make more friends or failing to keep them out of hell weren't enough.

I played on the JV tennis team. Mom came to watch me practice one time. I was matched against a teammate, and he hit a ball close to the baseline. I called it long. I probably should have called it in. He knew it, Mom knew it, and I knew it too. He yelled something about my being too cocky to handle losing and having to cheat in order to win. Mom must have agreed because she mentioned it on the way home after we gave him a ride and dropped him off. I blew up at her and said she never took my side and the ball was in and that kid was always trying to cheat and she should mind her own business.

I thought not being "of the world" would give me acceptance from God. But I wasn't feeling it. I wasn't into drugs or sex or the devil's music, but I was curious, at least about the latter two. Mom sometimes hinted at the mess drugs had made of her and Dad's life before I was born, and I could see Uncle Ed and Grumpy hadn't exactly prospered under the influence, what with my underemployed uncle still living in his boyhood bedroom and my grandpa sleeping in the basement with the washing machine and the dented cans of Sunkist Nana had salvaged from the supermarket clearance rack.

This Littler Light

I didn't want any part of that, but I wasn't clean either. Throughout my childhood, I'd been hearing pastors judge men for gawking at women or listening to pop radio or being too afraid to witness to the unsaved. Check, check, and check. I didn't fit in with the world, and I didn't fit in with God either.

> When Israel was in Egypt's land, let my people go
> Oppressed so hard they could not stand, let my people go
> Go down Moses, way down in Egypt's land
> Tell old, Pharaoh, let my people go!
>
> —Traditional black spiritual

Summer came. I could play wiffleball and Nintendo with my church friends. I didn't have to feel guilty about letting the Exeter kids go to hell or stupid about not knowing who U2 or the Chili Peppers were. The month of July was the best. I could go back to Mountain View Bible Camp in Dublin, New Hampshire, near the Vermont border, where I'd been going since I was ten.

At fifteen, I knew it was my last year as a camper. I was still small for my age, but maybe I was more coordinated than a lot of the kids. For whatever reason, I played really well in the afternoon games: Inner-Tube Tug, Dodge Ball, Capture the Flag, and an obstacle course with tennis balls being fired at me. I memorized my Bible verses and I guess I showed some sort of spiritual leadership. I won Camper of the Week. Nobody knew about the nerdy kid I had pushed into the pond, still wearing his pants and shoes. Why couldn't regular life be more like Mountain View Bible Camp?

I went home to my whiny four-year-old sister Suzanne. I don't remember what she did, but I was in the house only for a few minutes, and I snapped, yelling and screaming about people in my space and messes they made.

"Things were great here until you came home," Mom said.

"I'm going back to Dublin, and I'm staying there," I shouted, feeling both guilty and self-righteous at the same time: you know, the status quo.

Mom knew exactly what I meant. See, Mountain View used the dorms, the dining hall, and the rest of the campus at Dublin Christian Academy during the summer. DCA was a good school with a reputation for turning out good Christian kids. I was just being dramatic, trying to let everyone know how much I hated being home. I thought everyone should know that. Mom's reply floored me.

"Ok," she said.

Mom decided, on the spot, to go back to work and build up Dad's real estate appraisal business to pay the $8,000 tuition so I could go to boarding school. Mom, whom I had fought with and yelled at for what seemed like a year straight... Mom, who was raising five kids through foreclosure and bankruptcy... Mom, who had just lost the dream farmhouse she and Dad had renovated and had her minivan repossessed... As an only child for my first four years and the firstborn grandchild in Mom's extended family, as an honors student with piles of academic trophies, I suspected I was special, maybe even worthy of love. But nothing communicated that to me like Mom's sacrificial act. When I was little, I'd watched Mom and Dad fight, held her hand when she was sad. I thought she needed me, but now she was letting me go. I wasn't rich enough or smart enough or special enough to go to Phillips Exeter Academy, but now I was going to boarding school. Like *Dead Poets Society*—boarding school!

I went from one of the worst years of my life, to one of the best. Dublin had a soccer team that traveled all over New England, beating up on other little Christian schools with scores like 11-0. I earned a starting midfield position. We had cute cheerleaders who screamed your name when you scored; they did a lot of screaming. At halftime during one of these blowouts on our home field, we were up 5 or 6-0, and I said it might be nice to "get Jesse a goal."

"Let's get the team a goal!" one of the captains shot back. As usual, he'd scored most of the goals and had the cheerleaders screaming his name.

"The team has plenty of goals," I said.

Of course, if you know anything about team sports, you know I didn't win that argument. I soon found myself beginning games on the bench, but it didn't matter much to me. Somehow I figured out that my attitude stunk and the coach was doing me a big favor; I guess that's grace, God's light on our paths. The Lord chastens the ones he loves, say the writers of Proverbs and Hebrews. I still got plenty of playing time that fall, scored some goals, and felt like I was getting good at something other than school. I played the brash young lover Ambrose Kemper in *The Matchmaker*, a non-musical version of *Hello Dolly*. I joined a touring drama team, playing the older brother in *The Prodigal Son*. Mom signed me up for voice lessons. I made the school choir. We toured the East Coast and won awards at the American Association of Christian Schools fine arts competition at Bob Jones University. We sang the black spiritual "Go Down, Moses" in hushed intensity, our director's eyes wild with mystical reverence.

> No more shall they in bondage toil
> Let my people go
> Let them come out with Egypt's spoil
> Let my people go

I'd escaped from public school, but America had bigger problems. Bill Clinton had just been elected, another Pharaoh oppressing God's people. We were the Moseses who had to change that. Our choir director, also the voice and English teacher, was always telling us to "be real," which meant reading our Bible and trying to live its teachings, not just singing songs about it. She told us to search our hearts and make sure we were really saved. I guess I didn't show enough passion for her. "What does it take to get you excited?" she asked me one time. Feeling a little sad seemed normal to me, and it frustrated me when someone made a fuss about it. The people in the Bible didn't seem happy or excited, just obedient, and not always that.

Our Bible teacher made us read through the entire Old and New testaments that year. I often knelt by my dormroom bed, in a posture of worship, immersing myself in stories, poetry, and prophecy I didn't understand but still revered. This is what Mom did, even when no one was forcing her. As much as the words shaped me, so did the discipline. Daily prayer, after all, is what had gotten Daniel thrown into the lions' den—and what saved him. "Quiet time," we called it.

Soon, Mom told me I couldn't go back to Dublin for my junior year. She couldn't afford it, and she wanted me home. By then, she was going to Calvary Bible Church, which had a school where I'd be going and eventually graduate. Calvary was the biggest fundamentalist school in our area, the place Brother Starch had bad-mouthed because the kids there allegedly drank, had sex, and listened to rock 'n' roll just like kids at public school. I didn't want to go. Once I got to Calvary, I kept in touch with a girlfriend back at Dublin. I even drafted a letter to Nana and Grumpy asking them for the money to go back for my senior year. But I never sent it. Mom wanted me home, and I at least owed her that.

Before I switched schools, I arranged to go back to Mountain View Bible Camp that summer to work as support staff. I didn't want to leave the safety, the quiet time, God's shelter. We replaced siding on a dorm, repaired bunks, washed dishes, and helped the counselors manage the kids. The camp had nightly sermons, and the preacher that summer came to speak about the evils of rock 'n' roll—not just secular bands like the Chili Peppers or U2, but Contemporary Christian Music artists like Amy Grant.

Love Not the World

She'd had an affair with fellow CCM star Michael English—proof, in this preacher's mind, that rock drumbeats reveal poor character and lead to extramarital intercourse.

After one of these sermons, my funny, light-hearted brother Marco, then twelve years old, went forward to "get saved" and "dedicate his life to Christ." In the fundamentalist lingo, these were two different events; one kept you out of hell, and the other changed your life here on earth. Marco didn't see any reason to waste time between the two. Later that night, he came to my room and told me what he'd done.

"Do you think I need to give up my music?" he asked. *Dad's music* was implied.

Friends at public school had turned him onto the Spin Doctors and Boys II Men. We staff members didn't have any bedframes, so I sat low on my mattress, in the middle of the floor, like some kind of spiritual guru.

"I don't see any other way," I said.

That was my job, you know, as a past Mountain View Bible Camp Camper of the Week, assistant counselor, and ascendant "spiritual leader."

3

God's Work and the Good News

> The sons of Issachar ... understood the times, with knowledge of what Israel should do.
>
> —1 Chronicles 12:32 (NASB)

A reporter stopped me on my way from the gymnasium at Calvary Christian School in June 1995. Dressed in a royal blue robe with a mortarboard atop my mushroom fade, I'd just graduated first in my class. The writer wasn't from the dinky little *Derry News*. He was from the big-city *Eagle-Tribune* across the border in Lawrence, Massachusetts, where there was no shortage of grisly crime or government scandal to occupy his time. Yet he wanted to interview *me*.

I hadn't given the valedictory speech, an honor laid out for me since elementary school. I'd always been the smart kid seeking popularity through sports and pretty girls and humor. It wasn't the speech that mattered; my classmates had already voted me most likely to succeed, and I didn't want them to think of me that way. It's just that I knew "valedictorian" meant something out in the real world, and that's where I wanted to make my mark. At school, I wanted to be a regular kid, accepted, normal. Our principal had called me into his office a few months earlier to break the news of a technicality: I couldn't be valedictorian because I'd

God's Work and the Good News

transferred to Calvary for my junior year, and you needed five semesters, not four, to be eligible.

Instead, they'd given me something called the President's Award for Educational Excellence. Any school could give this award to any A student. They could have given it to a few of my classmates, or nobody at all. It wasn't an award I'd ever heard of, being that fundamentalist Christian schools normally kept government paperwork to a minimum. Mom had been upset about the valedictorian slight: Maybe they wanted some excuse to call me onto the stage, to salve the sting? This award came without the $250 check and with an ink-stamped signature from Bill Clinton, that liberal who wanted us to pay for universal healthcare and abortions.

Our principal had been teaching us about socialism in a senior "Bible" curriculum called *Understanding the Times*. He was a bespectacled lumberjack of a man, with lined flannel overshirts and a chinstrap beard like the one evangelical brainiac Francis Schaeffer wore as he did battle with the Communists and the humanists in *A Christian Manifesto*. I'd watched the Berlin Wall fall on CNN. I knew which side we were on.

For one essay test, I explained the rationale for this Bible course, citing the Old Testament prophet Daniel, who refused to eat the meat or drink the wine of his captor, the Babylonian king Nebuchadnezzar. Daniel and his friends, who had been called to the palace as the smartest, healthiest young men among the conquered Jews, asked instead for vegetables and grains, with only water to drink. After ten days, the king could judge their health. "And in all matters of wisdom and understanding . . . the king found them ten times better than all the magicians and astrologers that were in all his realm."

We Christians too were captives in a welfare state of public sex-ed, progressive tax policy, and "abortion on demand." We true believers—not liberals or Catholics, and certainly not those New Age astrologers and Pentecostal magicians, but we fundamentalist, Bible-believing, born-again Baptists—we had to stand up for abstinence, the free market, and *life itself*. It was us against the world. We just had to win, for God's sake. Karl Marx, that founder of Communism, was one of our Nebuchadnezzars.

"Marxist-Leninism is one of the greatest persecutors of Christianity; thus we must be able to defend our faith in front of Marxists," I wrote on that Bible exam. "As Daniel stood for his faith by refusing the king's meat and proving God's way better, so we must understand other worldviews to defend Christianity."

On another test, I quoted the Apostle Paul in his second letter to a church in Thessalonica, in first-century Greece: "'If a man will not work, neither shall he eat.' . . . Under socialism, people can live by leeching off of others. This contradicts the Bible's teaching."

The reason for "understanding the times"—and for the entire Christian school movement, which I'd been part of since preschool—was not only to keep us true to the faith, but also to train us to influence society with biblical truth. I was a top prospect. "The answer is to fight fire with fire," I had written in a paper for Bible class:

> Humanism has for much time used the news media to promote its liberal agenda. Christianity must now use the press to get Humanism out of our schools and out of our government. The ultimate decision regarding the methods and morals of a child's education still belongs to his parents. However, most parents are blinded by the liberal smoke and mirrors of Humanist teachers and school boards. We must use the newspapers and television stations of America to educate our nation's parents and remove Humanism from our educational system.
>
> The Humanist agenda has long controlled American government. Legislators, executives, and judges have bowed to the pressures of Humanist special interest groups for years. Christians must use the media to apply a little pressure of our own. We can force government to change by attacking the liberal biases of the media. The various methods of proclaiming the news could be a powerful tool in fixing the problems in America's schools and government. Christians must seize the opportunity to remove Humanism's rampancy from our nation and to make America great once again.

Years later, when I was covering Board of Education meetings and classroom projects for newspapers, I would come to see that teachers and school board members are just people, trying their best like most everybody does. But back in high school, I guess I thought I understood people better than they understood themselves. In that same Bible class, I gave a speech on one of our heroes, William Jennings Bryan, the creationist lawyer in the Scopes Monkey Trial. Coming of age in the Culture War, I envisioned my life in the public sphere, writing, and speaking against evolution, welfare, abortion, and homosexuality, maybe even running for office. I was vice-president for a class of twenty-six, after all! Our principal/teacher—let's call him Mr. Chinstrap—humbly and unselfconsciously reminded me that teaching might be an option if punditry or the White House didn't work out. And, truth be told, my essays were all theory: I was terrified to try and gain worldly power. In an English paper, I said I might run for President some day only "if I knew that I could not fail . . . As Bill

God's Work and the Good News

Clinton has changed our government for the downside, so could God use me to have a positive effect on America."

Here was my chance—the chance to speak Bible truth to 50,000 readers. I had never imagined it would come so soon. Was I ready? The *Eagle-Tribune* reporter's request for an interview came with another complication: The reason he had sought me, in particular, was that one of my teachers had told him I might become a pastor when I grew up.

That's the way it was: The smartest, most articulate kids, the student-leaders at a Christian school, were supposed to become pastors one day. Even this secular journalist knew it. Sure, there was power in government or media, but the pastor's job—like Mr. Chinstrap's job—was to equip people to witness for Christ wherever they worked. The pastor knew the Greek and Hebrew of the original Bible, he had the answers, he knew the truth. He was the one who studied secular ideologies so he could explain why Christianity was better.

As far back as I could remember, I had stood out from my peers. I wore a three-piece gray pinstriped suit to my first day of kindergarten. Mom swears it was my idea. From second to fifth grade, I won trophy after trophy for getting the best grades at Grace Bible Baptist Church and School, where kindergarteners through twelfth-graders learned in a single classroom, at desks that folded out from the outside walls like Murphy beds. There was no teacher standing at a chalkboard. We'd work through activity books on our own, and the headmaster would circulate through the room offering help, more like a tutor than a teacher. Good grades earned us extra recess. There were many afternoons I can remember playing alone in the sandbox because everyone else was stuck inside studying.

At the end of each day, we'd set goals for the next day on little paperboard calendars, and the principal would sign them. I'd normally race through page after page, but if I discovered I wasn't going to reach the page number I'd predicted, I could lick an eraser and surreptitiously alter the digits I had inked. I figured it wasn't cheating since I had set the goals to begin with. I still felt a little guilty, but getting caught in failure, even a small one, seemed worse than getting caught trying to avoid it.

It wasn't just my academic achievements that put me in this spot, talking to this reporter. It was my piety. Fundamentalist culture had a tier system: The most righteous young men, the super-Christians, became pastors or missionaries, and everyone else supported their work. What stuck with me from the song "This Little Light of Mine" was the "mine," not the "little." The song set us up more for a competition to see whose star was brighter than for a communion of candles each doing its part. There was no concept of "calling"—the idea that particular gifts were suited to particular tasks and how you did your job mattered to God, whether as a pastor or something else. The important thing was that you used your position to convince people to believe and obey. There were plenty of dissenters along the way, but this tier system had deep roots in Christendom. Way back in the fourth century, in the first Christian autobiography, St. Augustine couldn't imagine how he might use his gifts as a public speaker and rhetoric teacher for the cause of Christ, unless it was as a preacher. As he saw it, he faced either the pulpit or a life of promiscuity; there was no middle ground. Upon his conversion, he "notified the people of Milan that they must find another vendor of words for their students, because [he] had chosen to be [God's] servant."

Being a good carpenter, guitar player, or bureaucrat didn't matter for its own sake, because God didn't care much about beautiful woodwork or music or road maintenance. We never heard much about the craftsmen who built Solomon's temple in Jerusalem, or the poets who wrote the Psalms. What mattered was Israel's *morality*: the Ten Commandments, rules about sex, an eye for an eye, that sort of thing. These showed people how sinful they were and how much they needed Jesus's saving power. What the world needed was for us to preach this truth of human sin and eternal salvation and to live morally clean lives so as not to undermine the message. Whoever did these things best should be pastors. When you conceive of salvation as a free pass into heaven when you die, there's little use for dentistry, motherhood, or business-consulting aimed at cultivating human society under the lordship of Jesus. Why recycle if this world is passing away? What's important is preaching the Word and living lives that testify to it. This calling is the same for everyone. Pastors just do it better than anyone else. A successful writer or a movie producer had cultural power that could convince people to believe, but a pastor might influence a congregation of influencers plus write his own letters to the editor, lobby the legislature, and give interviews, to try to get prayer back in schools, get people following God again.

Some of my teachers thought that would be me. I had been a soccer captain in the fall. On a five-hour trip to play against his old school in Maine, Coach had me lead a team devotional, talking about how Jesus was selfless, how he'd want to pace his team in assists, not goals. The world needed to see us practice this Good-Samaritan morality so they would know the Jesus we followed was the way to God. In an Easter play, I had

God's Work and the Good News

the lead of Judas Iscariot going insane after the betrayal; you could never lead a good, peaceful, happy life if you turned your back on Jesus; it would make you sad, lonely, maybe even crazy. Our choir director sometimes asked me to give mini-sermons during our concerts. She tasked me with a dramatic monologue as an unbeliever facing The Judgment, begging God to let him into heaven.

"Where's Your love?" I whimpered before The Judge. "Look at me through the eyes of grace!"

I didn't like to think of God holding back some of his love, just because someone didn't trust in Jesus before they died. Nanny's and Dad's lives were at stake. But that was the only God I knew. For as long as I could remember, I'd been going forward at the altar call, to rededicate my life to Christ, to make sure I was saved. "Every head bowed, every eye closed, no one looking around," the pastor would say, while the pianist played "I Surrender All." *All to thee, my Precious Savior//I surrender all.* "Hallelujah, I see that hand!" the pastor would say. "Come forward, repent of your sins, and the Lord will forgive you."

Knowing I had lust and pride and anger in my heart, this was the Psalm that played in my head, over and over again:

> Create in me a clean heart, O God
> And renew a right spirit within me
> Cast me not away from thy presence
> Take not thy Holy Spirit from me
> Restore unto me the joy of thy salvation
> (Ps 51:10–12 [KJV])

I wanted to be one of the pure, one of the holy, someone who blessed others' lives. My senior yearbook is full of "thank yous" from my friends for my "listening ear." "Whenever I've had a problem, I always knew I could count on you to give me advice, whether it was what I wanted to hear or not," wrote one girl. "I'm so happy . . . that I've been able to trust you enough to talk and confide in you. . . . I really do appreciate your honesty," wrote another. "You have been a good example to me," wrote the valedictorian.

These friendships shaped my understanding of myself as a mentor, counselor, and truth-teller. But a pastor?

"Actually," I told that reporter, "I'd kind of like to do what you're doing."

That wasn't the answer he was looking for. I was scared but also intrigued by cultural power, such as I thought I might have as a journalist or a politician. The pastors I'd known had power over their little fiefdoms—a church and maybe the Christian school attached to it. But they didn't have much influence beyond that. Also, fundamentalist pastors, at least those not named Falwell or Bakker, didn't make much money. I'd seen their ramshackle homes and the second jobs they worked to support their families and their ministries. Infiltrating the newsroom seemed more subversive, more exciting, and probably more lucrative. Plus, I wasn't sure I was a super-Christian.

Earlier that spring, some friends had passed around a notebook of sperm cartoons—teachers and celebrities caricatured as human seed, your run-of-the-mill teenage boy humor. I was supposed to stop it: throw it away, give it to a teacher, something. Instead, I joined in. Someone drew "Sperm Madonna," with pointy cone boobs and a long wiggly tail. I was no artist, but I added a caption I'd seen on Comedy Central, mashing up Madonna and Forrest Gump: "I am like a box of chocolates. Lick me."

Predictably, Mr. Chinstrap got hold of the notebook. "Do you know that's talking about oral sex?" I'd been through this in junior high, having tricked a schoolmate into sitting on a pat of butter and ruining his pants; my punishment then had been sitting alone in Victory Bible Church's closet-sized audio-recording booth for five hours, surrounded floor-to-ceiling by the pastor's sermons on cassette, not even remembering my crime from a week earlier, while the principal interviewed the witnesses against me, then getting spanked with a paddle the size of a racquetball racket and kicked me off the school basketball team. Now the stakes seemed even higher. I had lost a measure of respect from a mentor and friend.

My teachers expected more from me. Needless to say, I didn't get the year-end senior spirituality award, and that hurt as much as not being valedictorian. I'm sure Mr. Chinstrap saw this as a learning experience, but it felt like an epic failure. How was I supposed to purify the world, when I couldn't even keep myself pure, let alone have courage enough to share my faith?

> Purity of heart is to will one thing.
> —Soren Kierkegaard

Thinking about what I wanted to be when I grew up hadn't always been so complicated. Like a lot of boys, I had dreamed of a career as an athlete. For a kid growing up in New England, it was the Red Sox. Sure, as

God's Work and the Good News

a nine-year-old, I'd seen the Patriots go to the Super Bowl and the Celtics win the NBA Finals in 1986 before Mookie Wilson's slow roller and Bill Buckner's error cost the Sox the World Series that fall. I was small and quick like the Giants' Dave Meggett, and my junior-high friend Josh, an all-star linebacker, was always trying to get me to play football, but Pop Warner teams played on Sunday, and Mom forbade me. I might have made a decent point guard, but when I was first learning to dribble and the ball bounced up and hit me in the nose, I told Dad I hated basketball, in my hot-blooded way. (My parents used to call me Mr. D for Dramatic.)

No, I was a second baseman, like the Sox' Marty Barrett. He wasn't the best hitter, but he was a slick fielder, and he was smart. If a pitcher threw wide of the catcher with two strikes, Barrett would swing and miss on purpose, just so he could steal first base. (For readers who have no idea what I'm talking about: The catcher has to catch a third strike; if he misses it, the batter can run, and the catcher has to chase down the ball and throw it to first base before the batter gets there. I never saw it happen, but my Poppy swore Marty did it). I knew I wasn't the best athlete, but I would outthink 'em and outhustle 'em. In the late '80s, I'd stay up late listening to the Sox on WRKO, in a cave/bed Dad built for me with a mattress on the floor beneath Marco's bunk and a little round door and three portholes cut through a thin plywood wall.

In 1989, I hit .321 playing second base for the Brentwood Angels Little League team that won one game all season. I was always the smallest kid—on my teams, at school, everywhere. I remember hitting a double over the center fielder's head at Hampstead. An extra-base hit. Wow. That was big. Did I do it twice that game? It gets bigger in the nostalgia. Dad, an assistant coach, was running late and missed it. "No way!" he said. I remember better another game against Sandown, backpedaling into the outfield on a high pop fly. It kept going higher and higher, and I misjudged it. I didn't get back far enough fast enough, and it dropped behind me as I dove backward into right-center field. Error (E-4, if you're scoring at home). That same game, I pulled a ball down the left-field line that would have gone for a double or a triple if it had stayed fair. Coulda, woulda, shoulda.

I was twelve years old, and that was my first year of baseball. Dad had thought I was too clumsy, so he didn't push me to play at nine and ten like most kids. The next spring I joined a Babe Ruth league for thirteen-to-fifteen-year-olds. With my brother starting Little League, I noticed how small the fields suddenly seemed. Dad was coaching Marco's team that year. One Saturday, he left my little sisters, who were probably five and two years old, playing on the swings near the field. A neighbor lady came over and started yelling at him for leaving them alone. I didn't like someone judging my family. *We* were the good Christians. Not Dad, exactly, but he was one of us. The next year, that lady's son stole Marco's limited-edition Doug Drabek special-insert card, worth $100, and I went to their house and shamed him into giving it back. He wouldn't even come to the door, made his little brother hand it to me. Vindication.

I told Dad if I just had one more crack at Little League, I'd be hitting home runs. But, instead, I slogged through two seasons of Babe Ruth and the humiliation of the curveball, hitting a lone ground-ball single up the middle and batting under .100 each year. In the majors, going 1 for 11 is a mini-slump, but when you're a kid, that can be your whole season. As a short guy with small strike zone, I walked a lot. I also struck out a lot, a few times to Chris Carpenter, who became a star pitcher with the St. Louis Cardinals. At age fifteen, he was throwing 86 m.p.h., they told us. He'd also mash balls into the boundless outfield of our home diamond. I played center field, not second base, and had to chase them down. My coach had put me out there because I used to make all these circus catches in practice, leaping, diving, sliding, and almost always coming up with the ball. But in one game on the road, a batter lined a bullet over my head. I raced back and leaped for it, but it just kept going, almost to the steep, manmade hillside that served as the home run fence at Auburn's field. Back in the dugout, coach glared at me. "I'm not Ken Griffey Jr.," I told him.

The worst, though, is when I swung at a third strike in a home game, and it skidded past the catcher. I just pouted back toward the dugout. Coach was yelling at me, but I didn't notice him until the catcher had almost retrieved the ball. He'd thrown me out by the time I got halfway up the first base line. Marty Barrett would not have been proud.

That summer at age fourteen, I stood throwing baseballs off the bounce-back net in my backyard, wondering why I wasn't playing second base. "I'm never going to play for the Red Sox," I thought. But I was beginning to think I was a pretty good writer, and I knew Boston had a rich history of sportswriting. Maybe I could be the next Bob Ryan or Dan Shaughnessy. I'd never play for the Sox, but maybe I could write about them.

My last year of Babe Ruth wasn't so bad. I hit .285. I ran down a short liner and caught it sliding across the left field line at Deerfield. I even started at second base for my high school team as a junior. But my coach started hassling me for ignoring his signs after I stole second and then third in the same inning. Plus, he had us praying The Lord's Prayer. I knew Jesus himself had written it, but it was one of those rote prayers the Catholics prayed, not from the heart. This coach was just one of our pitchers' older brothers, and he didn't know any better. Besides, the soccer team had some cachet at Calvary, but baseball was just there so athletes would have something to do in the spring. I decided to quit and focus on choral ensemble and the play I was in. I'd never quit anything before. It felt weird, but I knew baseball wouldn't take me anywhere. If I was going to be a public face for Jesus, it wasn't as an athlete—maybe I would be an actor or a singer or a writer.

> It was my ambition to be a good speaker, for the unhallowed and inane purpose of gratifying human vanity. The prescribed course of work brought me to an author named Cicero, whose writing nearly everyone admires, if not the spirit of it. The title of the book is *Hortensius*, and it recommends the reader to study philosophy. It altered my outlook on life. It changed my prayers to you, O Lord, and provided me with new hopes and aspirations. All my empty dreams suddenly lost their charm and my heart began to throb with bewildering passion for the wisdom of eternal truth.
>
> —St. Augustine, *The Confessions*

I had been planning to go to Bob Jones University with my best friend Mike because they were serious Christians there, they had a journalism program, and it was cheap—something like $5,000 a year. Mike was going there because his brothers and parents had gone, and that's the only school they would pay for. Then in May of my senior year I'd suddenly changed course. Cedarville College was another fundamentalist school but more open-minded: You could listen to Christian Rock, whites and blacks (if there were any) could date one another, and girls could swap their skirts for pants (in the winter).

Cedarville offered me lots of scholarship money and invited me to enroll in Making of the Modern Mind (MOMM), an honors program that covered history, philosophy, and the arts, alongside whatever your major was. *Understanding the Times* had been my favorite class in high school, and this sounded like a beefed-up version of it. I figured this was the type of class that prepared you to do battle with the evolutionists and Buddhists and secular humanists, whether you were a pastor or a TV pundit or whatever. I told Mom I wanted to write, and maybe this program would give me something to write about. Our philosophy professor, Mr. Mills, was an environmentalist who zoomed around campus on his twelve-speed road bike, his nappy, receding red hair steadfast, unmovable. We called him the Red-Haired Firedemon.

On our first philosophy exam, we had to write about Socrates' influence on Plato. We'd read about the Socratic method and Plato's Allegory of the Cave—the idea that human wisdom is but a shadow of true reality. I thought I could coast by on my basic knowledge of these men's lives and what they taught.

I had always studied just enough to get the A, and that usually wasn't very much. In junior high, Jon Webster and I had been the smart kids in our tiny class at Victory Christian School. I remember telling Dad one night about how Jon always read ahead in our history textbook.

"I don't know why he does that," I said.

"For love of learning," Dad said.

Dad must have known that I studied for the grade. I had trophies and plaques for my elementary school exploits, and I liked them. Reading ahead might have helped Jon get better grades, but I knew just how much effort I needed. Essay tests were my specialty: I could usually write my way around some facts I might have forgotten. I glided through high school this way.

The Red-Haired Firedemon gave me an F on my test. I stared at that red letter in disbelief. I'd never seen one on my work before. I'd never even seen a C, at least not on anything as big as a mid-term exam. Clearly, I wasn't the smart kid I thought I was. Clearly, I had been nothing but a big fish in small ponds all my life. Suddenly, the pond was an ocean. He couldn't have given *everyone* an F. In fact, I was sure that most everybody had done better than me. Not only was I not the smartest kid anymore; I wasn't even sure if I belonged in the same classroom with them.

From then on, I consulted Mr. Mills before every exam and asked for feedback on my papers before they were due. I'm not sure I became a lover of wisdom right away, like Jon, but I wasn't going to let the subject beat me. I ended up with a B in the class, which would have been a disappointment if I didn't know where I'd come from.

I liked to think the difference between me and Jon was insignificant: We both learned the material, we both got the grades. What did it matter if he read about the Battle of Waterloo while I watched *Baseball Tonight* on ESPN? I would learn whatever I needed to know about Napoleon in time for the test.

But Mr. Mills asked more of me. He wanted me to work for it, and there was more than just grades or even knowledge at stake. Spiritual writer Simone Weil has written that intellectual rigor is training for prayer—for paying close attention to God. Ours was a young professor who didn't even have his PhD yet, but maybe he knew I needed to work hard, struggle, and still not get the results I wanted. Maybe he'd read Weil:

> If we have no aptitude or natural taste for geometry, this does not mean that our faculty for attention will not be developed by wrestling with a problem or studying a theorem. On the contrary it is almost an advantage... It is certain that this effort will bear its fruit in prayer ... Students must therefore work without any wish to gain good marks, to pass examinations, to win school successes; without any reference to their natural abilities and tastes; applying themselves equally to all their tasks, with the idea that each one will help to form in them the habit of that attention which is the substance of prayer.

This was not why I'd gone to college. I needed knowledge so I could get results—good grades, yes, but ultimately *influence*, the ability to change the world for Jesus. I wasn't interested in studies or in spirituality that didn't get me anywhere. I wanted to win. And if I couldn't win, then I didn't want to play. I fought against prayer that might express hope—longing for a brighter future I couldn't control. I felt both compelled and defeated in my prayers, like that Nanny would get saved or Grumpy would get clean. Dad was always showing some spiritual interest and then falling away. I knew Jesus's brother James had written, "the effectual, fervent prayer of a righteous man availeth much." Maybe I'd never been effectual, fervent, or righteous enough, but I feared that prayer aimed at dreams fulfilled couldn't help but disappoint me. In prayer and in life, I didn't want to just pay attention to God; I wanted to accomplish something.

In a way, that's what had kept me from embracing my uncertain call to the pulpit. I wasn't sure I was worthy, but also, what if it didn't work out? If I took another major, other than "Pre-Seminary," at least I'd have something to fall back on, something of significance outside the church. What if the gospel turned out to be a sham? I'd chosen Communication Arts because it was the closest thing they had to journalism, and wouldn't communication skills translate into any business, even if it turned out I wasn't going to change the world? Now the Firedemon had thrown down the gauntlet: What if I was made to be a philosopher, a lover of wisdom for its own sake, a curious seeker, with no perfect knowledge to gain or recognizable path to employment upon graduation?

Rhetoric might make me an effective communicator but philosophy could give me something to say. Communications might give me a job, but philosophy could give me a purpose. My moment of decision, during my freshman year at Cedarville, was not so clear a choice between light and darkness as Augustine's lust and chastity—at least I did not see it that way. Tugging on my soul were my high school teachers, who saw my future in the pulpit, and my own twin (competing?) desires to make an impact on the wider world as writer—"for Christ," I thought—and to achieve more financial freedom than my parents had. I never wanted money issues to force my family to move or change schools. I wanted to pay back my student loans one day.

That winter, I played in a fantasy basketball league. The way it works is each participant drafts real NBA players and then gets points corresponding to his players' statistics: baskets, assists, steals, blocked shots, etc. You draft a starting five plus a few players for your bench, in case someone gets injured or you find a late-round sleeper who's outperforming your higher picks.

A couple of months into the season, I was in second or third place and decided to take a risk. I had some bench players who were scoring really well. (The LA Clippers' Loy Vaught was one of them, I think.) I made some trades to try to assemble the best starting five in the league, even if I didn't have any good back-ups. I ended up with an All-Star team: Penny Hardaway, Alonzo Mourning, Grant Hill. My team looked so good that people started getting suspicious.

Half of the guys in the league were at Cedarville and half were at the University of New Hampshire. I hadn't known any of them back home, but I had met this guy Jamie at Cedarville who'd also grown up in New Hampshire, and they were his high school friends. Anyway, they started accusing my trading partners of purposely stacking my team so we could split the first-place prize, which might have been $50 or $100. That wasn't it at all. I knew I was convincing my friends to play for second place, but I probably would have beaten them anyway, so this way we'd both benefit—assuming none of my starters got hurt, in which case I would lose. I felt like I was taking a big risk and deserved a big return; I thought, player for player, the trades were fair. I certainly didn't feel like I was doing anything wrong.

But the UNH guys retaliated by actually doing what they were accusing us of doing. They started trading all their good players to one team, not just emptying their benches of talent but making clearly lopsided trades.

I fired off an email late one night calling them all cheaters. But I couldn't just leave it at that.

"I guess I can't expect anything better from people who don't know Jesus," I wrote.

Two could play at that game.

"You, my friend, have sinned," one of the UNH guys wrote back. "And you need to repent and ask your Lord to forgive you."

This sent me into a whirlpool of self-loathing. What did I expect? An apology? "You're right, Jesse. We're cheaters, and God will judge us." Instead I had to search myself, like I had been taught to do before taking the Lord's Supper, to make sure I was right with God. I wrote back and confessed that I had pressured my friends into making trades to give me the best starting five. Looking back now, I'm not sure that was true or that I did anything wrong. But I felt so bad about communicating a Christianity of judgment, rather than love, that I had no choice but to admit having done something wrong. I couldn't just let my moral superiority stand.

Here, I think, my fundamentalism began to fissure. Not only didn't I want to act better than other people; I didn't want to *be* better than other people. I didn't want that kind of enmity with the world, that alienation. Paul said, "Love not the world," but Jesus ate with prostitutes and sinners. I had understood the "light of the world" and the "salt of the earth" to mean Christians were supposed to influence the rest of the world. With our help, people would come to Christ and stop lying, stealing, cheating, killing babies, and sleeping with people who weren't their husbands or wives. If they weren't ready to get saved, we were at least supposed to show them how much they needed Jesus by raising up a moral standard that would make them feel like the sinners they were. But if this is how that felt, I wasn't sure I wanted to be a part of it anymore.

Before this ethics scandal rocked the northeastern quadrant of the United States, I wrote about that fantasy basketball league for *Cedars*, the student newspaper. The story was my idea, and that was before millions of white collar workers started playing fantasy sports on their computers at work. It had the important news value of novelty, but it just didn't seem all that important. I'd also written another fluff piece on one of the varsity athletes. I had no role models for what revelatory, investigative journalism might accomplish. Administrators did not allow the paper to question their decisions, which is a key role for any campus paper, but I didn't even recognize this as a shortcoming. I just concluded that journalism was insignificant, mere word-vending. Faced with both the impotence of journalism and the psychological risks of trying to impose Christian morality on the world, I began to question my career ambition.

And so, mentored by Mr. Mills and other scholars who listened to Christ in conversation with Plato, Marx, and Derrida, I followed Augustine in pursuing the life of the mind. As a sophomore, I would enroll in Mr. Mills' ethics course and add philosophy as a second major. I contemplated dropping Communication Arts because, though my ambition had been for serious journalism, I found the major was perceived around campus as "cake." "I can speak and write, read and count, and I want these things to be used to serve [God]," Augustine wrote, and I believed this about myself. "[Speech] studies taught me many useful words, but the same words can be learnt by studying something that matters." What sort of career philosophy would yield, I didn't know. It was a path of seeking truth, not making a living, but a path I had to take.

In the midst of all this confusion, my thoughts went back to that day in my backyard, taking grounders off my pitch-back net and wondering how I could use my gifts at Fenway Park. Confined to our dorm after a 1 a.m. curfew, my hallmates and I had been playing a lot of Monopoly, and I had been doing a lot of winning. Between that and my fantasy-basketball wheeling and dealing, I thought maybe I was a businessman. Maybe I could be the general manager of the Red Sox.

I was reaching, grasping for a sense of purpose, a career, but something more. Into this crisis of calling, God spoke.

I was alone in my dorm room, an eight-by-six-foot cell in a former Army barracks physically relocated onto the campus. I knelt on the rough, short-pile carpet squares, reading through the book of Romans, as I'd been doing for my quiet time. I came to the same passage in chapter 10 that Augustine quoted on the first page of his *Confessions*: "How, then, can they call on the one they have not believed in? And how can they believe in the one of whom they have not heard? And how can they hear without someone preaching to them? And how can they preach unless they are sent? As it is written, 'How beautiful are the feet of those who bring good news!'" It might have been a burst of adrenaline at finding an answer, or heartburn from the cafeteria, but I was sure I heard the Holy Spirit that afternoon, as never before and never after. Wasn't this the same message delivered by that reporter back on my graduation day from my teachers—that I was supposed to bring good news?

Like Augustine going to his friend Alypius after the voice told him to "take it and read" from that same book of Romans, I announced in my classes the next week that God had called me to be a pastor. It felt like a true calling—but also a retreat to the safety of preaching the Good News to people who were already eager to hear it. I'd forgotten the hopes for Christian journalism I'd had back in Mr. Chinstrap's class; it didn't even occur to me that "good news" might have anything to do with newswriting.

4

Girls and God

> Therefore I must be intimate with you, and lie in your bed with you. Daughter, you greatly desire to see me, and you may boldly, when you are in bed, take me to you as your wedded husband.
>
> —God's voice, portrayed in
> *The Book of Margery Kempe.*

One night in the spring of my junior year, a bunch of us drove over to Young's Dairy Bar in Yellow Springs, Ohio, home to the radical Antioch College. The town itself may as well have been Red China for all the fear-mongering and evangelistic scheming it inspired at Cedarville. But Young's was just outside Yellow Springs and pure Americana. It was on a farm and made its own ice cream. You could get hot fudge sundaes, baskets of fries, or battered jalapeño poppers filled with cream cheese. At the gift shop, you could buy a cow magnet, or a rubber udder, or a little bike license plate with your name on it. It was like a Cracker Barrel prototype, with pine floors and paneling and a wide front porch.

The sky was dumping rain, one of those torrents that used to soak my khakis (no jeans allowed!) on campus because western Ohio rain goes sideways and umbrellas are futile. We tiptoed through the downpour, dodging puddles up to our calves, and hunkered down around a picnic table on Young's covered porch. After a while, the rain stopped, and we guys tried to wrestle each other into those pothole ponds in the parking lot. Down near the entrance to the restaurant, thirty yards away, we saw a guy doing the same with his girlfriend: Being a good foot taller than her, he'd raise her arms up above her head so she was off-balance on her tiptoes, and he'd pull her backward and try to sit her down in the water. We talked about how that wasn't very nice and just stood there watching.

Then Marjory spoke.

"Get him!" she yelled.

Marjory was a year ahead of me at Cedarville. She led a campus women's organization called Prayer Force. They were spiritual Amazonians; instead of seizing men as sex slaves, they used their collective intercessory powers against abortion doctors, the Chinese Communists, Bill Clinton, Slobodan Milosevic, hypocrisy, singleness—whatever threatened God's good plans for the world.

I didn't think about it at the time, but Marjory reminded me of Mom. One time we heard ambulance sirens while sitting in the cafeteria. Marjory urged us to pray for whoever was in trouble—and shook her head at the kids who kept their eyes glued to the O. J. Simpson trial on TV through it all. Marjory helped me organize a youth group at a dwindling Baptist church where the old women were happy just to have some people under age thirty in the pews. One of them almost killed our friend Kevin with some undercooked chicken wings. Marjory and I laughed together when we found out our pastor had a thing for *Xena, Warrior Princess*.

Marjory was the first girl I wanted to marry. She had compassion, spunk, and a sense of purpose. I'm calling her "Marjory" because she exists in my memory less as a real woman and more as a type: The She-Mystic. And she brought out the mysticism in me—what she called "intimacy with God." She used to raise her hands above her head during the praise choruses in Cedarville's daily chapel services; she was practically a Pentecostal. Come to think of it, she had a pixie haircut, just like Kelly, my charismatic crush back at Memorial High. And you know those come-hither cartoon eyes on Faline, Bambi's girlfriend in the Disney movie? Those big kaleidoscopes that make him trip all over himself? Yeah, Marjory had eyes like that in real life.

I spent a lot of time on my knees and in my Bible during those two middle years in college. Marjory showed me this pretty grove of trees out behind Cedar Lake, a manmade pond on the backside of campus. It would have been a great place to make out with her, but she just thought it was good for intimacy with God, so I'd go out there for quiet time. Marjory even got me to fast a few times; that's when you don't eat so you can concentrate on your spiritual hunger—at least, that's the idea. I mainly concentrated on the gurgling in my stomach. This intimacy with God seemed to come easier for Marjory, compared to my chronic low-level sadness.

"What can I say to encourage you, my brother, except to point you to God our Father?" she wrote to me in a note, like one of the Apostle Paul's letters, an Epistle to Jesse. "Sometimes I get overwhelmed and realize that I haven't been taking time to meditate on how incredible God is. So I decide to take the time out and spend an hour with Him, expecting to feel better, to feel peace when I'm done. . . . There is nothing more satisfying than pure worship. . . . I write this in faith that I am only encouraging you in what you are already doing."

What I was doing wasn't enough.

My buddy Kevin had pretty blue eyes and Jude Law looks that earned him the nickname "Mr. Beautiful." He'd gone to public high school, seen a girl naked (he would never elaborate), gotten drunk, and introduced me to bands like REM and Toad the Wet Sprocket. Kevin was something like a man of the world in Cedarville's Bible-camp environment but now pursued God through reading and prayer with a voracious kind of discipline—Marjory's type of guy. He'd unsuccessfully tried to parlay their illicit swing dance in the balcony of the old Cedarville Opera House into something more. His roommate Mick, tall, dark, handsome, and good at everything he tried, did actually date her, briefly, while our friend Ben and I nursed crushes on her. We never talked about it because, well, our friendships were at stake. Still, we all loved her.

In my own head, at least, I had an interest in girls that was a little stronger than other guys. Marjory was the quintessence of what interested me. I knew most CEOs and pastors and politicians were men, but it seemed to me that women had the real power, a kind of magic that transcended earthly authority.

First off, Mom wasn't the only one dragging her husband to church; there were a lot of families like that—like the wives had more access to God or something: They were the Sunday school teachers, they had the answered prayers to announce in church—"Grandma got saved!" "Vernon got healed!" "We made rent this month!"—they were the spiritual ones. There were always lots of single women in church, but hardly ever any single men. If you didn't have to marry a girl to get the inside scoop on God, you at least had to listen to them.

Girls and God

But you did want to marry one, because you wanted to have sex, and it's just what you did, and you wanted to have sex. And that brings me to my second point about women having the real power. I mean, winning a girl's heart was like a trump card in the game of life. You might not be the best athlete, or the best looking, or the tallest, or the richest, or come out on top in any other way against the male competition, but if you got a nice, beautiful girl to like you . . . well, you were the King of the Hill. Marrying the right girl was the key to happiness, and it didn't depend on the same things that made you successful in other areas. Girls didn't always value the same things that guys used for one-upping one another and making the global economy whirl. It could almost seem like girls had evened the playing field; at least, that was my working hypothesis. If you could make them laugh, make them feel beautiful, write them sweet notes, give the right gifts, flowers, chocolates, just listen to them, protect them, lift heavy things for them, give them your jacket in the cold or rain—it was simple, really, if you could pass the physical attraction test. Only she could decide if you won or lost. If she let you inside—her heart, her mind, her body—you were a winner, even if you were a loser in every other way.

And that was the thing: They were a lot easier on us than we were on them, in that regard. What did physical attraction even mean for them? Did they actually desire our bodies? Or was sex just something they traded so they could get what they really wanted? It was a mystery, hidden up under their skirts, behind all those layers of lace and cotton covering their skin: bodices, blouses, camisoles, princess lines, sweetheart necks, empire waists, demi cups, strapless, underwire. We just had pants and shirts. Everything that mattered about them, even the core of their physical pleasure, was hidden. Our genitals, like our intentions, hung there, masters of the obvious, mindless, pitiless, bulging through our pants, uncomplicated—alternatingly stiff, standing at attention, or slack, indifferent. Our objectives—physical pleasure, conquest, status—seemed so crass, so basic, compared to whatever it was they wanted. It was like they knew us better than we knew ourselves, knew what we *really* wanted, if they could just coax it out of us.

Or did they even *know*, in the sense of an idea you could explain? They talked about it in their impregnable huddles, in the ladies room, at the lunch tables, on the sidelines, but there were forces at work beyond words. PMS, the orbit of the moon, gentle as the tide, until the waves came in like a tsunami, emotions you couldn't predict, like they were connected to some unseen world of angels and demons, spirits whispering in their ears so the scent of a wildflower smelled different than it did to us, a

This Littler Light

gesture or a facial expression sent messages that went right over our heads. Women had secrets—secrets you wanted whispered in your ear, even if all you could offer in return was, "Mmm."

I thought Marjory had gone overboard when she said God told her to break up with Mick; it's kind of like all these politicians who claim God told them to run for office or go to war. Are they too insecure just to admit that it's what they want to do? Margery Kempe was a medieval mystic who lived apart from her husband because she thought God wanted more devotion from her. Does God really move in such ways? Maybe so, with women, or just certain women, like Marjory.

She was never interested in me, but my interest in her helped to shape me: She showed me that I didn't want what the fundamentalists called a "help-meet"—a contraction of the Genesis description of Eve: "a helper, meet for him," that is, suitable for Adam, which I understood to mean the submissive, self-effacing sort of wife whose identity would be wrapped up in mine. I'd watched Mom try to be that wife for Dad, even though he wasn't leading her anywhere. Mom wasn't the type of person to be led, but she'd tried to follow anyhow, because that's what our churches had taught her to do. Dad wasn't really the type of person to lead, but that's what she wanted from him, and she was always disappointed. It didn't seem fair to either men or women. I wanted a partner whose goals I could help advance and who could help advance mine—not a helper: an equal. I wasn't too sure I was Marjory's equal; she couldn't stop talking about her ex-boyfriend, Trey, a backup wide receiver who was "discipling" his teammates on the University of Florida football team, long before anyone had heard of Tim Tebow. A Florida Gator and a man of God: Who could compete with that?

By then, I was studying guys like Marx and Nietzsche with a teacher, Mr. Mills, who didn't just want to prove them wrong but to engage with them from a Christian perspective and learn from what they had to say. Marxism didn't seem so bad, once you got past the stuff about religion-as-the-opiate-for-the-masses. Wouldn't Jesus side with the poor, oppressed workers rather than the rich, entitled capitalists, just like he sided with the outcast prostitutes and not the insider Pharisees? As I wearied of the world-blind piety of my upbringing, I daydreamed about co-pastoring a nice liberal evangelical church with someone like Marjory.

"Chivalry is not dead!" she shouted.

We charged down the parking lot, Kevin, Ben, Mick, and I, six of us in all, screaming like William Wallace's army. The girl backed away in fear as we tackled her boyfriend onto the wet pavement. Within a second or two we retreated back toward our table, trying to figure out what the hell had just happened.

"Guys!" Kevin cried. "Help!"

Mr. Beautiful was on his back, with the guy kneeling over him and his fist poised to strike. We lurched back toward them, and the guy let Kevin go.

A few minutes later, the barbarian walked over to our table.

"Why?" he asked us, his voice cracking. "Why?"

Why, indeed. We just stared at him, speechless.

Why? Because Marjory told us to. She talked with God, after all.

> Solid food is for the mature, who by constant use have trained themselves to distinguish good from evil.
>
> —Hebrews 5:14

I spent most of my four years at Cedarville thinking I would go back home to New England after graduation to study at Gordon-Conwell Theological Seminary. My Calvary classmates had gone to fundamentalist colleges like Bob Jones and Falwell's Liberty University. Teachers had told me mainstream evangelical schools like Wheaton, Calvin, or Gordon College were so liberal I might as well go to a state university. But after visiting those places while at Cedarville and meeting other kids who went to them, I craved a more freethinking atmosphere. I had gone to Cedarville because they'd offered to pay most of my freshman tuition, and GCTS likewise had a big scholarship program for students planning to become New England pastors once they graduated.

One of my writing professors, who moonlighted as a pastor, round and tousle-haired like a hobbit, told me to watch out for the feminists and baby-baptizers at Gordon-Conwell because they threatened the authority of scripture. If Luke was wrong when he said baptism should come *after* belief or Paul was wrong when he said women shouldn't preach, how could you trust the Bible on any subject?

"I'm just trying to learn," I told Mr. Baggins.

"Oh, 'I'm just trying to learn,'" he mocked. "What a conceit!"

Gordon-Conwell was no Harvard or Dartmouth, but it seemed to me like a step toward intellectual respectability. It was also friendly to the

Reformed theology that was taking hold of me. By the time I was a senior, I got a morning job at Chuck's, the Cedarville cafeteria named for its longtime manager, so I wouldn't have to go to the daily chapel service. The contemporary worship of the evangelical "seeker" movement made me feel manipulated toward the "intimacy with God" that Marjory seemed to conjure on her own. A band would lead songs from the chapel stage, using the dynamics of rock 'n' roll with repetitive refrains like "Lord, you're beautiful" and smoky-voiced alto beauties to try and make us swoon. It was as if there was only one appropriate emotional response in worship, ecstasy, and if you didn't feel it, there was something wrong with you. I wanted to ground my faith is something more solid than my own inner emotional experiences, and I wasn't alone. I remember hearing how songwriter Rich Mullins had a fan tell him she felt the presence of the Holy Spirit at a certain point in one of his songs. "No, that was just where the kick drum and the bass came in," Mullins said.

Mullins managed to be in this evangelical world, but not of it. One time at a concert, I heard him talking about a friend's struggle with alcohol. "Don't get me wrong: I like beer as much as the next guy," he assured us. Mullins was not only a holy man, living in solidarity with poor Native Americans, but also a rebel. I couldn't help but like him. I'd recently heard that my old high school principal, Mr. Chinstrap, enjoyed a pint or two from time to time. That seemed to fit with his Francis Schaeffer look and refined manner of speech that set him apart from the "pahk ya cah in Hahvud Yahd" of the New England middle class. I couldn't imagine him drinking a Bud Light, but maybe a Guinness. It was good to see some true believers challenging a central piece of fundamentalist morality that seemed at odds with Jesus, who turned water to wine.

The Cedarville pulpit was a turret in the Culture War. In the run-up to the 2000 presidential election, James Dobson's disciple Gary Bauer was our man. He was the longtime head of the right-wing Family Research Council and would go toe-to-toe with gay rights activists, stem cell researchers, global warming conspiracists, and the easy divorce culture. We stood against Postmodern Relativism and for Absolute Truth, which encompassed, "He who will not work, neither should he eat," but not "Sell all that you have and give it to the poor." I was starting to feel like I was on the wrong side.

Postmodern philosopher Richard Rorty seemed to call people to greater compassion than these Baptist preachers did. Meanwhile, Marx and Nietzsche had persuaded me that too many Christians were just trying

Girls and God

to avoid hell and that their hope of heaven anesthetized them against the suffering all around them—suffering they should have been salving. I was starting to believe the government needed to provide social welfare where the church had failed and that "Love your enemies" was incompatible with war and capital punishment. A one-man play by a gay theater major at Antioch made me ashamed of how the church had treated other human beings in its defense of biblical inerrancy. So what if homosexuality was a sin? Weren't we all sinners?

Rodney Clapp's book *A Peculiar People* convinced me that theology, ethics, Christian politics, even the question of which texts belonged in the canon of scripture itself, had always been worked out by the living church in its historical context. If there was any absolute truth, we'd been dancing around it for thousands of years, like angels on the head of a pin. If I was going to become a leader in the church, I needed to learn to do it among people willing to explore the many versions of Truth embraced within the universal church, not among people who already thought all their answers were the right ones.

That brings me to Heloise. After Marjory, I spent much of my sophomore year chasing this smart, tall philosophy major with blonde hair in tight curls: The Sexy Scholar. Consider the New Testament archetypes for evangelical women, the resurrected Lazarus's two sisters: Mary, lavishing expensive perfume on Jesus's feet in intimate worship; Martha, toiling behind the scenes, setting tables, baking cookies, that sort of thing. Heloise was a Martha—an intellectual worker bee to Marjory's prayer warrior Mary; where Marjory heard God's audible voice, Heloise searched for God in what the church and scholars had been saying about God for centuries.

The Apostle Paul and some ancient Greek philosophers had led me to Calvinism, a sixteenth-century theological system that offered rational coherence and an honest grappling with the Letter to the Romans' teaching on predestination I thought the Baptists didn't want to deal with. When I found John Calvin, the French Reformer, there was Heloise, the French beguiler. She had this porcelain skin, a button nose, and a crooked, omniscient smirk, like she knew things we guys could only dream of. In a boys club of intellectual arm-wrestling, where our attention both flattered and embarrassed her, it was like she'd inverted the old speech class coping mechanism: Behind her shy smile, she imagined *herself* naked, in complete control, with us staring at her while she turned in another A paper. With Cedarville's modest dress code leaving everything to the imagination, her faith seeking understanding was a turn-on. I would be her Abelard and she my tutor, reverse roles foreshadowed when I arrived daily from my job in the cafeteria and delivered apples to her desk in Mr. Mills's "History of Ancient and Medieval Philosophy."

> Young teacher, the subject
> Of school*boy* fantasy
> He wants *her* so badly
> Knows what *he* wants to be
> —The Police (sort of)

For my junior year, I was appointed class chaplain. It was normally an elected position, but no one had run for it. I had struggled to decide between running for vice president or chaplain; I had chosen the former and then dropped out when I heard the latter was unclaimed. In making my initial choice for VP, I think I had just wanted to win an election—the acceptance of my peers. From rejection on the kindergarten playground to the alienation of my freshman year in high school to my status as an honors student, an intellectual, I'd always felt a little different. Does everybody feel like that, for one reason or another? I don't know, but trying to get elected to a position of spiritual leadership felt too much like a referendum on my faith and my personality. How does one campaign for such a thing? Can you mix faith and ambition? That's what the Moral Majority had taught me to do, but I wasn't sure I had it in me.

I had run for class president as a freshman. I had a lot going against me: I'm a short guy, not particularly gregarious, and I'd been assigned to Bethel, the smallest men's dorm on campus with guys who stayed real tight among themselves and were perceived as a little weird by the rest of the campus. Instead of trying to meet my classmates and get them to like me, which scared me to death, I tacked giant cardboard letters you could read from hundreds of yards away, spelling out "JESSE 4 PREZ," on the side of the centrally-located dorm. Mass Communication for Dummies. I built a six-foot sandwich-board sign, put it outside the chapel one morning so students could see it on the way out and then got a friend to help me move it near the cafeteria so they could see it again. One of the most pathetic memories of my short-lived political career was our scurrying with that sign just ahead of a crowd walking across campus. The most pathetic was me down on one knee, proposing to "marry" my freshman class during a campaign speech. I was literally begging for love.

A year and a half later, when I realized my class needed a chaplain, I thought I'd made a terrible mistake opting for VP, and I tried to correct it. Having little understanding or respect for procedure, I pestered the campus elections officer to try and get on the ballot after the deadline. I thought I had a calling, but instead of pursuing it confidently, I chased it in desperation. It was one thing to think I'd been called by God, but I still needed other people to validate me.

After the election, the new class officers appointed me chaplain out of an interview process. Over the summer, I met with my Baptist pastor back home for mentorship. I faithfully had my quiet time, feeling like I needed to practice Marjory's intimacy with God if I was going to lead my classmates. I've never been as earnest in prayer and Bible study as I was when I felt like it was my responsibility. I got ready for my first sermon, when I talked about Abraham begging God to spare his cousin Lot in the judgment of Sodom and Gomorrah and how praying for others is more important than trying to solve their problems for them.

That fall, I read Hebrews 5, with its diet of "solid food," which resonated with Heloise's Calvinists and their preference for serious doctrinal theology. I opened my winter chapel service playing a recording of the Christian folk band Caedmon's Call's song "The Truth" over the chapel speakers. "The truth's not contingent on me," songwriter Derek Webb sang, making his case against an experiential, postmodern sort of faith. As Mick later pointed out, I literally preached with my Bible in one hand and *Made in America*, Michael Horton's book criticizing anti-intellectualism among evangelicals, in the other. Horton had been associated with the Alliance of Confessing Evangelicals, guys like John Piper, John McArthur, Al Mohler, and Gordon-Conwell professor David Wells, who were trying to push conservative churches toward their historic Reformation roots with doctrines like original sin, predestination, and the sovereignty of God. Rather than defecting to the other side of the Culture War, I was trying to climb to the Christian Right's ivory tower, to try to see if I could trust the man behind the curtain. Citing Horton's critique of highly emotional evangelical worship, I reminded my classmates that Jesus was not a "crazy uncle," swinging them around by their arms like a helicopter. It makes me cringe to think about it now. What a downer of a message: Jesus is not Fun! He's the Savior of the Universe! Now think about that! Harder!

The class chaplain only preaches three times the whole year, so I only had one chance to redeem myself. The result was a spring sermon something like a thirty-minute apology for my winter sermon. I wasn't just feeling bad that I'd spoiled my classmates' morning. I was at war with myself. I had already begun to suspect that Calvin had wrapped up divine mysteries a little too neatly. Philosopher Ludvig Wittgenstein made a compelling argument for how truth works: It's built on a set of fundamental assumptions that help us make sense of our world, not a set of facts indisputably connected to ultimate reality. Soren Kierkegaard showed me that Christian life is a leap of faith—a sort of Heroic Assumption. Absolute Truth is not a category of Christian faith. God exists, God created the universe, God came to earth to redeem us: these truths, we have to take by faith and build our lives around them. This perspective made for a messier way of believing than even most Calvinists—intellectually honest as they seemed to be—could accommodate.

In that last sermon, I talked about the prostitute who crashed a Pharisee's dinner party with Jesus. The Lord raised her up as a symbol of faith because she had received forgiveness and responded to it by loving others. My friend Shawn, who'd been our freshman chaplain, had told me my previous sermon had been nothing but the same message my intellectual elitist, philosophy major friends were trying to foist on the campus. That hurt. In response, I told my class that theological reflection was just one way we can relate to God; maybe some of us do it through emotional worship or service to others, and it wasn't for me or anyone else to judge another's paths to God. I confessed the ways I had sometimes looked down on people I thought were worse sinners than me: gays, lesbians, drug addicts, Antioch College students. That wasn't love, I told them.

I had stumbled upon that story in Luke just by reading the Gospels afresh, but the impulse to figure out who belongs and who doesn't belong at Jesus's dinner parties was one rooted deep in my psyche. I had been trying all my life to figure out how the same God could relate to Mom in her mysticism, Dad in his vices, or Nanny in her doubting. A couple of years earlier, Nanny had replied to my letter asking questions about her beliefs, urging her to trust Jesus. Matriarch to six children and ten grandchildren, rising four feet, eleven inches off the floor, Nanny had command over some of the best life had to offer: kind blue eyes, a cabinet full of sugary cereals, terrific back rubs, and handbreaded chicken cutlets fried in butter. Yet I had something she needed: Jesus.

"The difference between being old and young is the young are idealists and the old are realists," she'd written to me. "I was there, once. Life, if you pay attention, changes you. If it doesn't, then you haven't grown. I know you think I'm probably going to hell for the way I feel. It's OK for you to feel the way you do. It's also OK for me to feel the way I do. My heart and soul is in God. I don't need Jesus. Jesse, you have to understand that that's OK. Think of me as a Jew. Your uncle Mike's mother was a Jew. Does this mean she didn't go to heaven when she died? No. It means if she was strong in her faith, it led her to heaven."

"Jesse, there are no masters. There are no idols, no icons. Why should I believe in the son when the father directs and guides me?" she wrote. "God is there, so is Santa Claus, so is love. God to me means I love you, I will never hurt you, I will always help you, I will always be there for you. I love you dearly, Jesse, and would never want to cause you concern. Please accept that I'm very happy in my faith, even though it may seem different from yours. I have no intentions of going to hell, even though I like the heat. And, Jess, another thing: You could never offend me by being honest, but closed-minded is something else. Always remember yours is not the only point of view. Yours is not the only religion, and yours is not the only way of life. Open up your heart and accept all. Just accept. It doesn't have to change you or them. God made all of us. He has his reasons. In our lifetime, we may never understand what they are. But we do know he made all of us, he gave us different thoughts and different religions. None of us know his plan. So just accept. I love you, Numero Uno.—Nanny."

I'd never heard such complicated theological ideas from Nanny before. I counted on her for instant apple cinnamon oatmeal packets and Marshmallow Fluff. Was there something to this? Could it be that the differences between people, even religious differences, were somehow grounded in Creation, God's stamping on us his own image? Even St. Paul said, "What may be known about God is plain to [nonbelievers], because God has made it plain to them. For since the creation of the world God's invisible qualities—his eternal power and divine nature—have been clearly seen." Now, of course, Paul was arguing that non-Christians like Nanny were responsible for their sin because they know of God's holiness, and they still do wrong. But didn't that describe all of us, Christian or not? If being responsible for our sin means rejection by God, then we all stand condemned. Maybe the same God who created us in all our diversity also saves us in all our diversity? *Think of me like the Jews*, Nanny said: The Jews, whom God has bound "in unbelief, that he might have mercy upon all" (Rom 11:32). The Jews thought they could see the path to God—their morality, their ritual sacrifices, their faithfulness. No, Paul said. It's about God's morality, God's sacrifice, God's faithfulness. And what if God has been faithful to all of us, in Christ, even to those who don't believe? Maybe Nanny was wrong in suggesting that all paths to God are equally good. Maybe they're equally bad, yet Jesus's wounded back is broad enough to lift up the whole world, dead-end paths to God and all. Nanny made me think, but I didn't let go of my wheat-and-tares theology.

This Littler Light

I ran for Advisory 7. On paper, this was the group of seven guys who led the Sunday night worship services on campus for people who didn't go to churches off campus. Symbolically, this election was another spiritual popularity contest. It was where your faith got evaluated and stamped with approval. "I got me an Ad 7" was how you might hear young ladies discussing their new boyfriends around campus. In my election speech, I talked about how we needed to dig deeper into what we believed, just like in my inflammatory Michael Horton sermon.

Golden-Boy Mick had the same message, but, playing off other candidates who'd given their conversion stories, he said he was saved 2,000 years ago on the cross. He didn't mention that he'd stolen that turn of phrase from Karl Barth; few would have known whom he was talking about, and those who did would have been suspicious of his "liberalism"—meaning anything we disagreed with—even though Barth wrote fiercely against liberalism. Barth's neo-Orthodoxy is among the most Christ-centered of the twentieth-century theologies, but the potential for universal salvation entailed by his cosmic reading of the Atonement makes conservatives nervous, even though it's found in Paul's letters to Rome, Corinth, and Colossi: God is in Christ reconciling all things, giving mercy, righteousness, and new life to all people. Barth, a Swiss theologian who'd been forced out of his job at a German university because he resisted the Nazis, hoped the cross just might be powerful enough to save everyone, in spite of themselves. Even someone like Nanny, even if she denied Jesus right up to her death, even if she never repeated a prayer at an altar call like I did. Maybe Jesus's death and resurrection were powerful enough even to save Hitler and comfort his victims at the same time. Anyway, Mick had managed to talk in a deeply theological way—to take the focus off humans and our own inner experiences for a moment—without anyone really knowing that's what he was doing. He got elected, and I didn't.

That year, I also ran for class president and student body chaplain. I didn't win either one. The guy who ended up replacing me as senior class chaplain veiled a critique within his campaign speech: If he was elected, he wouldn't tell us stories about his own life but would try to tell us what the Bible said. I'm not sure I had ever decoupled those things in that way. Yes, Jesus had saved Mick 2,000 years ago on the cross, but it was still Mick who had been saved. If God's story doesn't confront our human stories, how can we reckon with it? In my sermons, I had talked about how I was more inclined to try and mentor my little brother than to pray for him; to use prayer and Bible study to seek answers to my own questions instead

Girls and God

of seeking a deep and pure knowledge of God for its own sake; and to judge people for not being as intellectually curious as I was, rather than respecting our differences. My successor planted a seed of doubt in me: I had figured that talking about my own struggles was the only honest way to lead people in faith. I knew I didn't have all the answers, but maybe we could find some together, if we talked about our experiences with God. Did I have the wrong approach to being a pastor?

Contrary to what you might expect, none of this had any impact on my sense of calling. I still felt that if I weren't going to pastor a church, then I would teach theology at a seminary or college or would write books or articles to build up the church. Cedarville was full of Bible majors and future pastors, and they couldn't all be class chaplains or Ad 7 members. Plus, I still had seminary ahead of me and lots of time to figure this stuff out.

In the fall of my junior year, I had gone with Heloise and some other girls to a party at the closest thing Cedarville had to a frat house. The guys that lived there were known for their booze, drugs, sex—all the things that normal college students did but that made you an outcast at Cedarville. Their ringleader had shoulder-length hair, a scruffy beard and wore loose pants, flannel shirts, and faded sweaters like Kurt Cobain. He looked more like my mental picture of Jesus than anyone on campus, and he was always on the edge of expulsion: The Prodigal Son. One of his roommates had a cover band. That night, they played Edie Brickell's "What I Am," which became one of my favorite songs.

Heloise and I had already gone on a date earlier that fall. Still a growing boy, I'd wanted to go to Olive Garden for their bottomless pasta bowls, but she said she wasn't that hungry and wanted to go to a fancy café in Yellow Springs for something light. Then we got there, and we were both pretty hungry, it being dinner time and all. She ordered something called *tapas*. Sixty dollars later we'd eaten a gourmet meal I would never have dreamed of buying, given that I could barely pay my tuition and all. But, still, I hadn't given up on Heloise and was happy to be going to this party with her.

The thing is, I never saw her the whole night. She disappeared, so I spent most of the night talking to a petite brunette with big brown eyes like Marjory's, the kind that inspired Van Morrison. I'd seen her at a meet-and-greet for new honors students a few weeks earlier. So began a year and a half of romantic torment. Michelle would go on dates with me and then give me a dirty look if I tried to help her as she struggled to get her coat on.

Anyway, back to Heloise. I drove home from the party with her and two other girls.

"So, you were talking to Cobain-Jesus for a long time," one of the girls said to Heloise.

"Yeah, and he asked me to spend the night with him."

"He did?!"

"What??!!"

"Yeah," she said, "and I sooo wanted to."

"Heloise! I'm glad we got you out of there."

I went back to Bethel Hall, and Josh talked me out of going back to fight this Long-Haired Lover-Boy. He hadn't really disrespected me; Heloise wasn't my date. But I felt he had disrespected her and in the meantime lowered my estimation of her. I was personally offended. My beautiful Christian intellectual girl had a capacity for lust—and not toward me!—that I thought was off-limits. It was the sort of sin I was constantly beating myself up over, and to voice it in mixed company! Josh didn't have such a prudish view of the whole thing.

As freshmen on tour with the men's glee club a couple of years earlier, he and I had struck up a conversation with the pretty girl selling Dippin' Dots at Stone Mountain in Georgia. Well, Josh did. I just sort of stood there, dumbfounded: dumbfounded that he could flirt with a complete stranger at an ice cream stand hundreds of miles from home, dumbfounded that he rolled with the conversation even after she suggested we should meet up at Hooter's later that night. Josh didn't need approval from the Shiny People, Cedarville's mainstream, in their pleated khakis and polo shirts while he wore his baggy cargoes, big ringer t-shirts, and a goatee that made him look like Darius "Hootie" Rucker. He was honestly trying to figure out what he believed and to live it. He spooned with his girlfriend, whom he'd met online, when she drove down from Moody Bible Institute in Chicago and we went to visit her friends overnight in Cincinnati. They'd just *slept* together, but it still scandalized me. The only reason Josh came to Cedarville was because his aunt and uncle were paying for it. He embraced his outsider status, writing a regular column for *Cedars* called "The Masked Democrat," arguing for things like social welfare, abortion rights, and why Bill Clinton might not be such a bad guy. I wasn't nearly so comfortable with the great, big world outside the Christian Right.

With Heloise's fall from my perfect little pedestal, my Calvinism suffered another crack, but it held. As a senior, I would drive forty minutes on Sunday mornings to attend South Dayton Presbyterian Church, part

Girls and God

of the Presbyterian Church in America, a denomination connected to Michael Horton's crew and Westminster Theological Seminary. I'd already visited the main Westminster campus, along with Trinity Evangelical Divinity School, on trips to visit friends in Philadelphia and Chicago. On Christmas break that year, I went to Horton's Westminster-West satellite outside San Diego and also Talbot School of Theology at Biola University near Los Angeles. I was still leaning toward Gordon-Conwell because it seemed to balance Reformed academic rigor with open-mindedness, but I had never visited Cedarville before I arrived as a freshman, and I guess I wanted to make a more informed decision this time around.

Regret over my college choice simmered on the back burner. Dad and his side of the family had seen me as a smart kid (Grumpy called me "The Professor") and pushed me to go to Dartmouth. Not realizing I had always been just the big fish in small ponds, I assumed I could have gotten into the Ivy League if I'd tried. But Mom had insisted that I go to a Christian college; she was convinced that homosexuals and atheists would belittle my faith, though she was praying hard for someplace more freethinking than Bob Jones. Trying to steer me in another direction, Mom's sister Lori had suggested Duke, which was Methodist like her church. But I'd grown up hearing that liberals like the United Methodist Church didn't really believe the Bible. My aunts were some of the most loving people I'd ever met, but somehow their faith and good works didn't count because they didn't believe the same as we did. They'd grown disillusioned with the Catholic hierarchy of their childhood just like Mom, but they chose the liberal Protestants, and she chose the fundamentalists. Cedarville had been a last-second compromise, and Aunt Lori had still lost, badly.

For the second half of my Christmas break, I flew back across the country to Lori's house on St. Simon's Island, Georgia. I had been traveling with Mom and heard about all the fits my eleven-year-old sister Suzanne was giving her: hanging out with the wrong friends, listening to the wrong music, showing too much interest in boys. I pondered the Calvinist doctrine of election, the idea that God had chosen some people for salvation and others not. What if my little sister, the little girl who had wept for me at her bus stop on the morning I left for college, was one of the people God had not chosen? What bothered me wasn't the notion that salvation depended on God's free choice, completely independent of human will. That actually made a lot of sense. The free-will-minded Baptists had always assured us that mentally disabled people and young children couldn't be held accountable because they didn't have the capacity to choose for or against

Jesus. But that seemed strange, having one theology for some people and a different one for others. What about people like Nanny? What about Dad? What about addicts, or kids who grew up surrounded by adults who modeled Nietzschean will to power, preying on others through violence or thievery or drug-dealing? Did they have the ability to trust in another way of salvation? Faith seemed to come easy for people like me and Mom. It certainly felt like a gift, not of my own making, when I looked at how hard it was for other people to believe. Was I just naturally humbler or more contrite, more apt to trust someone else to save me? I doubted it, but even if so, why? Hadn't God made me this way, put me in these circumstances, and others not?

When I wasn't sure if Suzanne believed, it was too much for me to bear. Plus, Lori talked about her job as a pediatric ER nurse, and how she'd come to think abortion could be the compassionate choice in some cases because she'd seen such horrible cases of child abuse by unfit parents. That Christian love, not self-centered "choice," could lead someone to support abortion was a fatal blow to the faith I knew. *We* were supposed to be the compassionate ones.

I went into what my professors called "an existential crisis." I'd already had one faculty member call me a heretic because I'd written of Calvin's "dual election" in a book review in the student newspaper. This professor would have had us believe that predestination to heaven for some did not also mean predestination to hell for others. But how could I see it any other way? And how could I love such a God?

Our honors program director, an Old Testament scholar, told me to read the Psalms, and that was some comfort. King David sure didn't seem to have everything figured out. Maybe this conflict between human free will and God's sovereignty was one of the contradictions we just can't resolve, a mystery I just had to accept. David's favorite prayer wasn't, "God, help me to know the truth," but, "God, turn your face to me."

> He who finds a wife finds what is good
> And receives favor from the LORD.
>
> —Proverbs 18:22

Meanwhile, my adolescent male ego had also been suffering some serious blows. In the spring of my junior year, Michelle of the Doe Eyes had said she'd go with me to the Junior-Senior Banquet—"The Social Event of the

Year." This is what Christian high schools have in place of prom, and it just continued at Cedarville. After the banquet, a bunch of friends were going up to Gull Lake in Michigan to stay at someone's vacation house for the weekend. A couple of weeks before the banquet we sat in the cafeteria, with Michelle nervously circling the rim of her drinking glass with her finger, 250 revolutions a minute, round and round and round and round.

"I didn't know we were going to the lake after the banquet," she said.

"What do you mean?" I said. "We've been talking about that since the beginning. Chad and Kim are going."

Kim was one of her best friends, Chad one of mine.

"I don't want to go," she said. "I'll still go to the banquet with you."

"But the weekend's the part I've been looking forward to. Hanging out with our friends. I don't even care about the banquet. What's this all about?"

"I just don't want to go. I didn't know that was part of it."

"Well, forget it. I'll just find someone else to go with."

But it wasn't that easy. For what seemed like a week straight—no, three years straight?—I got rejection after rejection, until finally Marjory found one of her Prayer Force girls to go with me. This was the second year in a row that Marjory had had to help me find a date for the banquet. Pathetic.

The guy who was hosting us that weekend at the lake had a girl named Alli as his date. She had pulled a Michelle in the fall of my sophomore year, saying she'd go with me to Homecoming and then telling me a few days later she wouldn't; someone better had asked her. I'd been assigned to write about that event for *Cedars*, so I'd had to go by myself. I suffered a reclusive depression that fall. This suffering was all my fault: I'd broken up with my gorgeous high school sweetheart midway through my freshman year. We'd only ended up dating because she flirted with me after my friend Mike had told her I was too intimidated to ask her out. As a freshman, I thought I could play the field and started chasing the hottest girls on campus, but it didn't turn out so good for me. I got turned down by at least three beautiful girls that year, and those were just the ones named Rebecca. When Alli went out on a Ski-Doo at the lake, bashed her face on the steering wheel, and spent the weekend with a big fat lip, I'm ashamed to admit, it felt like poetic justice.

Josh and Ben had a band, OSHA, named for the federal Occupational Safety and Health Administration because they wanted a political name, "but not too political." When I was seventeen and wanted to impress my girlfriend, I'd tried to learn Richard Marx's "I Will Be Your Man" on Dad's guitar, but I quit because my fingers hurt. I had learned to play bass a little since then, but Ben played bass, so I was just the comic relief. Sometimes I would open their shows with a mock workplace safety presentation. I'd wear a hardhat I got from the campus grounds crew, and I'd point to a sketch of a worker falling off a ladder I had found online and blown up with a photocopier. As I lectured about the importance of ladder harnesses, the band would get louder and louder until they drowned me out, and I was screaming, red-faced.

In the fall of our senior year, OSHA played at a friend's harvest party in a barn at a local farm. I sang some back-up vocals and held Josh's lyrics when he needed them—pathetic, wannabe rock star stuff. After that party, Mick's new girlfriend Lindsay, the daughter of a seminary president, who used to recite entire books of the Bible from memory on the chapel stage, told Mick, who passed on the message to me: "Jesse needs a girlfriend." Thanks for the newsflash, Lindsay. I really hadn't thought of that.

Around that time—gosh, was it the night of that same party?—Michelle and Kim came over to the big farmhouse I rented with Josh, Ben, Mick, Kevin, and Chad. The cornstalks were still tall in one of the farm's giant fields, and Chad and Kim, who'd been dating for three years, ran off into the moonlit rows. Michelle was there in the yard with us, and I grabbed her hand to follow them, but she jerked it away. I really wasn't thinking about romance, just the exhilaration of running in the dark, but she couldn't have known that. She'd already had me drop her off one night after a date at the apartment of one of my friends she was also seeing. She hurt me all the time, but I wanted her to like me, so I never complained. I'd get to her somehow, my Michelle.

Our farmhouse, with its big kitchen and giant living room lined with four couches and a few easy chairs, served as an off-campus social nexus in our one coffeeshop town. One time Michelle planned a "Praise Party" at our place without telling anyone. I was home with gentle Ben, a tall, big-boned Michigan boy who liked to drive to Dayton just to sit alone among the abandoned mills on the bank of the Great Miami River. When all these strangers started walking into our kitchen with hand-drums and guitars, Ben stormed out the back door and drove off in search of personal space. I wasn't into Praise Parties, but Michelle's spirituality was compelling, like a substitute Marjory, especially since she was an honors student with Heloise's smarts. She'd close her eyes and raise her hands in worship and volunteer mentoring high-school girls through Young Life. "I hope

Girls and God

God has knocked you out of your rut," Michelle had written to me that summer. "Get in the Word, brother! . . . I will pray for you. I'll pray that you do things in God's strength and not your own and that you'll take time to know the difference. Because His strength is perfect!" Maybe a She-Mystic was better than a Sexy Scholar, after all.

That fall, Chad, Kim, Michelle, and I drove through Indiana for simultaneous events at Wheaton—the girls for a worship conference, Chad and me for brainy theology stuff. On the six-hour drive to Chicago, Michelle made a comment about how she thought parents who couldn't afford to send their kids to college just shouldn't have kids. She didn't know that both Chad and I needed student loans to get through school. That was finally the end of my self-inflicted torture. I could never be with someone so devoid of compassion, I thought. I knew she wasn't such a bad person, but it was what I needed to tell myself, to reclaim my self-respect.

Emerging from my winter blues in the spring of my senior year, I had a new aspiration. Mick, who had introduced me to so many of the authors who were shaping my thinking, returned from a spring-break visit to Yale Divinity School. He'd met with Reformed philosopher Nicholas Wolterstorff and learned that two up-and-coming evangelical theologians might be joining him at Yale. The possibility of an apprenticeship with three orthodox scholars in an Ivy League setting sounded like a perfect way to stay true to my roots yet pursue my academic ambitions and maybe please the family members who'd wanted me at Dartmouth or Duke. The pastor at Calvary and the principal at Dublin both tried to talk me out of Yale. "They'll turn your brains to mush!" But coming through my crisis over predestination, I wasn't afraid of theological ambiguities; wading into them seemed like the only path to truth. What scared me was anyone who said the opinions of another Christian would turn my brains to mush.

I started reading Yale Divinity scholars Hans Frei and George Lindbeck. Frei called for reclaiming the Bible from the "historical critics" who wanted to prove (or disprove) the claims of scripture by external research in science or history, and giving it back to the church, where we use it to orient our lives, whether or not we believe every jot and tittle. Writing *The Nature of Doctrine*, Lindbeck followed Wittgenstein in describing theology as "the rules of a game" or a "grammar" that sets boundaries for our thinking but also gives us freedom for creative experimentation. When a Crusader screamed, "Christus es Dominus!" while hacking off the head of a Muslim, those words he uttered were not true, Lindbeck argued. And so, "Christ is Lord," becomes not a proposition of truth but a "rule" that must be made meaningful through experience in community. In other words, "By this shall all men know that you are my disciples, if you have love one to another" (John 13:35). These postliberals, I wrote in one of my senior papers, understood Christian faith as "adopting a whole new way of life and thought by entering the community of Christ-followers." What matters for the kingdom of God is not what we believe but how our lives point to the cross and the empty tomb—God's presence in suffering and the hope of Resurrection.

In my paper, I made what I thought was an uncontroversial statement: that God had "inspired his servants to write" the text of scripture. But handing back my work, the honors program director wrote in the margin: "Inspiration applies to the text, not the author." You see, Cedarville has a fourteen-point doctrinal statement, including biblical inerrancy, six-day Creation, and individual Christians' duty to be "soul winners." I remember parroting the idea that you had to believe the Genesis creation story was literal fact or you couldn't trust the Bible; Mattman, an honors student who was a year ahead of me and wore a black trenchcoat everywhere he went, had said simply, "No, you don't." Cedarville had people like Mattman and Heloise and Mr. Mills who made me think, but my budding postliberalism was a threat to the overall theological status quo. Our honors director wrote, "You have demonstrated that the postliberals do have a valid point to make. At the same time, what they say could easily swing the pendulum into a mirror image of the abuses that they decry."

I suppose he meant that abandoning doctrinal truth claims could unmoor the church from anything solid much as the liberal critics had. But I figured practices like sharing the Lord's Supper, bearing one another's burdens, and caring for the poor would anchor us to Christ more than any doctrinal statement would. Postliberals were also called "narrative theologians," and as a writer, I felt drawn to the story, the narrative of the Creator sacrificing his only Son to express love for his creatures, the Son invading the danger zone of earth to rescue those he loves. The gospel continued to woo me, almost twenty years after I had decided to believe, not because it was true—who really knows?—but because it was beautiful.

So now my heart was open to someone who was not an intellectual like Heloise or a mystic like Marjory or even a combination of the two like Michelle. I was ready for a romantic, a girl who might not always know why she believed this or that but who appreciated and incarnated a beauty of body and a beauty of soul. I first met Lily after she asked Mick on a TWIRP (The Woman Is Required to Pay) date on the night so designated

Girls and God

by Cedarville's social calendar. Mick had since broken up with Lindsay the Bible Memory Queen. He brought Lily back to the farmhouse briefly, and I think I was the only one home. Anyway, I came downstairs to say hello, and she'd later make fun of me about it, saying I just stood there staring at them.

I only remember thinking she was beautiful that day, but I knew that already. Mick had gotten to know her because she attended the Ad 7 services he helped to lead on Sunday nights. Before the Sadie Hawkins date, they'd often say hello around campus, and Mick and I had taken to calling her "The Eastern European Figure Skater Girl" because of her thin frame, long, dark hair, sharp facial features, and elegant style. I concerned myself with the spiritual life, the intellectual life, the higher things, but I still had an eye for a cute girl and prided myself on my thrift-store fashion. I was like the underpaid, bookish lawyer Lawrence Selden in Edith Wharton's novel *The House of Mirth*. Lily loved Victorian lit, and this was at the top of her list. In this story, Selden's romance with the big-spending Miss Bart seemed impossible to both of them. Selden had

> the stoic's carelessness of material things, combined with the Epicurean's pleasure in them. Life shorn of either feeling appeared to him a diminished thing; and nowhere was the blending of the two ingredients so essential as in the character of a pretty woman.

TWIRP night fell near the end of the winter trimester, and I thought about Lily all through spring break. I asked, and Mick said they hadn't really clicked, so I should go for it. I saw her in the chapel before a special service one night in March, walked up, and asked her out. A few days later, we went to a recital in the music department and then for dessert at The Winds, that fancy café where Heloise had tricked me into buying her dinner. Lily talked about playing tennis and how she'd wanted to go off to Cambridge in England or medical school at the University of Kentucky or to become a fashion model but her mom had made her stay near home at Marshall University before she transferred to Cedarville. I don't remember what else she said, but I do remember thinking she was not the Kentucky "trailer trash" that Ohioans liked to joke about but probably from a rich family that raised thoroughbred racehorses or something.

We met for lunch at Chuck's the next week, and then Easter break came. Mick and I went home with Kevin for the weekend, and I pressed them to help me figure out whether to keep after her. Was she trying a little too hard to impress me? Having grown up in New Hampshire, where

This Littler Light

Massachusetts friends thought we were "hicks" and would ask if we had Little League and cable TV "up there," I knew about having something to prove. Doesn't everybody try to put their best selves forward on the first couple of dates? She was smart—an English major and a writer, but not like me, less analytical, more artistic—a poet, maybe. So what if she fell asleep in Mr. Mills's philosophy class? Mr. Baggins, our writing professor, the one who warned me about the feminists, also warned me about her.

"She's a romantic," he said. "She'll rebel against everything, and then when there's nothing else left, she'll rebel against you."

If anything, that made me more interested. There was so much worth rebelling against in this world; couldn't we rebel together? At one point that year, I considered enlisting in military interpreter school to get my student loans paid off. Ben, who shared my room in the farmhouse, was maybe my least rebellious friend—six feet, two inches and 220 pounds of turning the other cheek. He talked me out of the Army, saying I could never put up with people telling me what to do all day. He knew me better than I knew myself.

The night I got back from Easter, I called and asked Lily to play tennis. She didn't want to play tennis but hinted she did want to see me. I didn't get the hint. I felt another rejection coming on, but a day or two later I found what would become the first of many notes in my campus mailbox. She'd write them on fancy stationery and include fragrant flowers she'd plucked from one of the campus shrubs. We did play tennis later that week, and I learned she really wasn't much of a tennis player. I played barefoot to try and even things out.

It was sitting in the grass out near those tennis courts on the edge of campus that I fell for her. I had dated some pretty girls in high school, but she topped them all: Round blue-gray eyes, dainty little nose, high cheek bones, and a long, regal neck put on display because she often wore her hair in a ponytail. Mr. Baggins seemed to think she had a future as a writer. She went to Bible study like a good Cedarville girl. One night around closing time at Meier grocers, I wanted to buy some sliced turkey at the deli, but Lily noticed the clerk was cleaning up to close for the night and suggested I get it another time. But it wasn't her beauty or smarts, her spirituality or kindness that captured me. It was her brokenness.

I learned that day in the grass that Lily's biological parents had given her up before she could talk. She'd gone to live with Bootsie, her maternal grandmother. Joe, Lily's step-grandfather, was "Dad" to her. Not only that, but Lily's real mom lived just half an hour away in Dayton, and nearly two years into her time at Cedarville, Lily still hadn't seen her. The mother had an on-again, off-again relationship with Lily's father, who was living in Kansas at the time. When they had given her up, they were both working for the defense department in Texas. They had jobs and money. They just couldn't handle parenthood, or didn't want to.

What amazed me, despite all this, were Lily's hope and enthusiasm, her humor and sense of wonder. If she was bitter at anyone, it was her grandparents, not her real parents. I wanted to understand. She'd worn way too much make-up to Chad and Kim's engagement party. What was she hiding? I couldn't imagine there wasn't real hurt somewhere deep inside her. I wanted to find it, and I wanted to heal it. I wanted to love her where her parents hadn't, to erase the sense of abandonment she must have felt. Not only that, I wanted to bridge the gulf between them, to help her repair the broken relationship with her estranged parents. Her mom was right there, just a short drive away. How could they not reunite? I felt what Selden felt toward Lily's pseudo-namesake, Miss Lily Bart, in whom my Lily saw herself and so did I:

> Hitherto he had found in her presence and her talk, the aesthetic amusement which a reflective man is apt to seek in desultory intercourse with pretty women. His attitude had been one of admiring spectatorship, and he would have been almost sorry to detect in her any emotional weakness which should interfere with the fulfillment of her aims. But now the hint of this weakness had become the most interesting thing about her.

It was messy, sure. But my life, too, was messy. I'd recently learned the real story behind why my parents had been fighting my whole life: Dad was a drug addict and had been since before I was born. I'd watched him let Mom down over and over again, and I'd held her hand to try and make it OK. Plus, God himself had gotten into the mess of humanity, sending his own Son to suffer rejection, persecution, and martyrdom. Lily had a story, and it might turn out to be a story of redemption, at that—narrative theology, in the flesh. I wasn't afraid.

I can't say Lily felt like a mission or a calling. She was a prize: brilliant, creative, attractive, compassionate, gentle, and fun. It's just that the depth of her wounds offered a kind of challenge—a call to love that seemed bigger than just winning her hand, a call to cradle her broken heart.

5

Making Love

We were cloaked in darkness, fifty yards off her family's desolate country road. Could anyone have seen us from her house, thirty feet behind me? I wasn't sure. I was afraid of getting caught, but that was part of the deal with teenage love. I was always afraid of getting caught.

Cari straddled my right leg as I sat on the edge of a bench shrouded in shrubbery in her front yard, our lips and tongues entwined, my hands wandering. This was a new technique for us, my knee meeting her intimate parts.

"I want to make love with you, Jesse," she whispered.

With. She had said *with*. Not *to*, like she just wanted to please me or be pleased, but *with*, like she wanted a real connection, a melding of spirits. She always wanted more from me: more hugs, more notes, more sweet words.

"Well, you know, you're a lot more stimulated than I am," I said, in that holier-than-thou tone of mine.

Stimulated, as though everything I knew I had learned in my freshman biology class. She was a good girl, who grew up in fundamentalist churches just like me. Maybe it was a difference between her, the charismatic, and me, the Baptist, but I had learned that my body was something I could and should control. "We're like a pretzel," she'd say as we cuddled after a nighttime make-out session. I thought we had an unstated rule that sex was off limits. That grand illusion came crashing down around me.

"I think you just need to calm down," I prodded, for good measure.

She had poured out every drop of love and desire from her seventeen-year-old soul, and all I could offer in return was moralism.

I can't remember the hurt on her face.

Making Love

When I was nine years old, an older friend had wanted to try to have sex and wanted me to try it too. He'd talked two girls into it, one for each of us. They were our good friends too. Our parents still trusted us to have a co-ed sleepover. We were all just kids. I didn't have enough testosterone to grow body hair or a peach-fuzz mustache. I had no desire yet, just peer pressure. It was nothing but a weird game of Doctor, which is good, because the real thing would have scared the shit out of me.

The fallout was bad enough, as it was. Not long after that, I started becoming aware of Grace Bible Baptist Church's rules about sex, which had never much interested me before.

It was bad.

Really bad.

Having sex with someone outside of marriage was the worst possible thing you could do, and there was hell to pay for it. It would ruin your life, her life, both of your family's lives, your church, your town, the United States of America—no one would escape God's wrath. I remember hearing the lyrics, "I want to feel your body" from Samantha Fox's 1980s song "Touch Me" on the radio in the Museum of Science in Boston and feeling dirty every time I thought about it.

Mom had come to this church looking for something to believe in. The last thing I ever wanted to do was to hurt her. I felt like I needed to take care of her, not hurt her. I felt guilty about playing Doctor with my friend. I wanted to tell Mom. But I couldn't. I sat under unspoken judgment from her, from my church, and from God.

As a reward for getting good grades at my school, I got to go out to lunch one day with Brother Starch in his Acura with the leather seats. I had never ridden in a car like that. No one else in the church had a car like that. He stopped at the Highland Country Store, I forget for what. At nine years old, my idea of humor was to replace the first letters of words to make new words.

"Highland Country Hore . . . I mean, Store," I said.

"Do you know what that word means, son?" the pastor asked, glaring at me.

"No," I said, shrinking into myself. I'd never heard the word *whore*.

"Don't you ever say that word again," he said. "That's a very bad woman."

Whoa! That sounded as bad as one of Dad's four-letter words! A year or so later, the pastor showed up with a brand-new white Corvette. People started asking questions. They discovered he'd been skimming the church treasury to buy the cars and renovate his family's home. Meanwhile, the staff nursery workers had gone six weeks without a paycheck, and the pastor's own wife had gone to the church's food pantry for peanut butter. Brother Starch had also been sneaking off with his secretary. The pastor warned us schoolkids not to listen to anything bad about him our parents had to say. We left the church, and it soon folded, putting an exclamation point on the pastor's preaching about the destructive nature of sex.

That church was called Grace.

When I came back from spring break that one year at Dublin Christian Academy, I found out my roommate, a senior, was getting kicked out of school just months shy of graduation for having had sex with his girlfriend. This was dangerous stuff, could turn your life on a dime. What bothered me most was that the school administrators thought expulsion, exclusion, *excommunication* would guide him back onto the straight and narrow. I'd heard for years that premarital sex would ruin your life, but here it seemed not my roommate's choice but others' judgment was ruining his life.

Such legalism wasn't confined to sex. God was an all-powerful, all-holy Judge who was keeping track of my every move, not to decide whether I would go to heaven or hell—Jesus took care of that on the cross—but whether I needed a carrot or a stick to guide me toward spiritual perfection and treasures in heaven.

When I was at Cedarville a few years later, I briefly dated this girl, a singer and guitar player whom I dreamed of making beautiful music with—one of the girls Heloise had told about Cobain-Jesus's sexual proposition, in fact. We walked to Marjory's grove out behind Cedar Lake and lay on a hillside looking up at the stars. I took her hand, and she said, in a flirty sort of way, that she was surprised that an RA, a good boy like me, would break the rules like that. Holding hands made me *dangerous*.

At twenty-one, twenty-two years old, my sexual peak, when other guys were sowing their wild oats, I was celibate. I wasn't any different from hundreds of thousands of kids at fundamentalist and evangelical schools all over the country. We were afraid of normal adolescent experiences, and we learned to hide them, to lie—to our parents, our teachers, ourselves, whoever might be disappointed. They told us sex before marriage would distort our expectations for our future spouses. It would be just perfect, as long as we didn't do anything to mess it up. So we stopped short of intercourse and orgasm—usually far short, trying both to become adults and to maintain spiritual purity at the same time. It was a tightrope, and one mistake could kill you.

Making Love

> How little that which thou deny'st me is.
> —John Donne, "The Flea"

About six weeks into our relationship, Lily and I shared a picnic out on a tree-canopied quad at Antioch College with Chad, Kim, Mick, and his new girlfriend Rachel, visiting from Bethel College, an evangelical school in Minnesota. We had crusty French bread, a cheese plate, and sun-brewed iced tea with fresh fruit floating in a giant glass jar—a classy sort of European lunch that made Lily really happy.

After lunch, the other couples started getting all lovey-dovey, so Lily and I took a walk. We hadn't ever touched each other yet. We strolled into a glade of flowering trees and sat in the grass. The sun filtered through the leaves, casting pretty shadows all around. I picked a wildflower from the ground and tickled Lily's face as we talked. She told me later she thought I was going to kiss her. I'd been too scared.

A week or two later, she slipped a note under the door of my study carrel in the basement of the campus library. "How is the Purple Book?" she asked me. That's what she called Hans Frei's *The Eclipse of Biblical Narrative*, the 400-page tome I'd been plowing through all spring term. The postliberal hermeneutic inside pushed me toward an aesthetic appreciation of the gospel. She liked the aesthetics of the book itself, like Miss Bart in Selden's apartment:

> She began to saunter about the room, examining the bookshelves between the puffs of her cigarette-smoke. Some of the volumes had the ripe tints of good tooling and old morocco, and her eyes lingered on them caressingly, not with the appreciation of the expert, but with the pleasure in agreeable tones and texture that was one of her inmost susceptibilities.

Her note invited me to go with her to Krohn Conservatory, a botanical garden on Mt. Adams, one of my favorite spots in Cincinnati. The night before, I bought fresh strawberries for our breakfast on the ninety-minute drive down there. We wandered the gardens all afternoon and ended up on a shady hilltop, where I read from a thick, hardbound volume of Anglican divine poets I'd borrowed from the library, lingering on George Herbert and John Donne. I took Lily's beautiful, elegant neck in my hand to turn her face toward mine, to kiss her. She stiffened in protest, and I let go.

"We should get some dinner," she said.

"Ok," I said.

A busy week passed, and we didn't have time for any long conversations. I picked her up after her girls Bible study on a Sunday night. I apologized for trying to kiss her. On our way back from dinner in Yellow Springs, we passed by a farm with a pretty little grove of trees and fallen logs we'd always admired.

"Why don't we stop?" she said.

"I might try to kiss you again," I said.

Instead, we went back to read in the farmhouse's little parlor with a marble fireplace. Its flue was cracked, so we couldn't use it, but it still charmed, like The Purple Book. Lily said she was sorry for making this so hard on me; she just wasn't sure she was ready. She went on for quite a while, and I got the feeling she was trying to tell me she really was ready. "I'm tired of talking about this," I said. I took her face in my hands again, and we kissed. There were many more kisses after that, including one in mystical Marjory's moonlit clearing behind the lake, where heartbreaker Michelle just happened to be out for an evening jog.

> He'd kissed a woman. He'd kissed her long, and he'd kissed her good.
>
> —The Sandlot.

For as long as we'd been dating, Lily had been complaining about her adoptive parents. How her grandmother had kept her from Cambridge and medical school and modeling classes. How she'd had to work for their business all through high school and her time at Marshall, riding along the mountain roads of Appalachia, restocking Dolly Madison snack cakes in supermarkets and gas stations. She was a bundle of contradictions: She made the early morning delivery route sound backbreaking and bleary-eyed, but the first time we made dinner together at the farmhouse, I had to teach her how to slice bell peppers for stir-fry because she said her grandmother never let her help in the kitchen. She was concerned for that deli clerk at Meier, but she demanded $7-a-tube Tom's of Maine toothpaste from her grandparents. She told stories of Joe taking her shopping to soothe any schoolgirl sadness, as though that were the most normal thing in the world, as though a new dress could heal what ailed her. "High Maintenance" was her family nickname.

Making Love

She didn't want to go back home for the summer, but she didn't know what else to do. We had met her biological mother that spring but found only the cordial distance of strangers. I don't think Lily even considered staying with her to work in Ohio. As usual, I thought I had a solution to her problem: She could come back to New Hampshire with me. After a couple of months of dating, I was starting to think she might be The One. We'd even talked about it in a quiet stairwell outside her parents' hotel room near Cedarville.

"I'm going to be a poor writer or a pastor," I told her. "Are you sure you want to live like that?"

She paused, thinking about it.

"Yes," she said. "I want to be with you."

My mind, though, filled in the blanks of the conversation, and it went more like this one between Miss Bart and Lawrence Selden at the Bellomont estate, where she had been ingratiating her rich friends and trying to catch a rich husband—where the topic was not so much would she *accept* a simple life but would she *choose* it herself? Would she see why it was better than a life ensnared by material things?

> "You despise my ambitions," she said. "You think them unworthy of me."
>
> Selden smiled, but not ironically. [Miss Bart still speaking:] "But isn't it possible that, if I had the opportunities of these people, I might make a better use of them? Money stands for all kinds of things—its purchasing quality isn't limited to diamonds and motor cars."
>
> "Not in the least: you might expiate your enjoyment of them by founding a hospital."
>
> "But if you think they are what I should really enjoy, you must think my ambitions are good enough for me."
>
> Selden met this appeal with a laugh. "Ah, my dear Miss Bart, I am not divine Providence, to guarantee your enjoying the things you are trying to get!"
>
> "Then the best you can say for me is, that after struggling to get them I probably shan't like them?" She drew a deep breath. "What a miserable future you see for me?"
>
> "Well—have you never foreseen it for yourself?"
>
> The slow colour rose to her cheek, not a blush of excitement but drawn from the deep wells of feeling; it was as if the effort of her spirit had produced it.
>
> "Often and often," she said. "But it looks so much darker when you show it to me!"

> He made no answer to this exclamation, and for a while they sat silent, while something throbbed between them in the wide quiet of the air. But suddenly she turned on him with a kind of vehemence.
>
> "Why do you do this to me?" she cried. "Why do you make the things I have chosen seem hateful to me, if you have nothing to give me instead?"

But I thought I did have something. My Lily was no orphaned debutante from the end of the eighteenth century, forced to trade her beauty for a man's provision, forced to turn her back on the bookworm she loved in order to pursue her own comfort. She was a smart, educated woman, needing only to summon enough internal fortitude to learn to take care of herself and to offer her talents to the world, rather than merely taking from it. And if I had anything in spades, it was internal fortitude. A biographer, rather than this memoirist, might call it stubbornness.

Before I'd met Lily, I had given up on finding a wife at Cedarville. It had been a hard pill to swallow, because where else was I going to find such a concentration of good Christian girls? Once you left the safe confines of a Christian college, it was a crapshoot, or so I thought. By then, I was hoping I would meet Miss Right at seminary. True fact: I'd come back early from Christmas break that year, and Mick had found me lying on my bed, in my boxers, eating a box of BonBons and reading *I Kissed Dating Goodbye*. Josh Harris wrote this book about how young Christians should avoid one-on-one dates with the opposite sex in favor of old-fashioned "courtship" rituals where the families can keep an eye on things. That book didn't have much to offer: I didn't think the women at Gordon-Conwell or Yale would have dad and their big brothers in tow. Then Lily came along, a Southern belle from the bluegrass fields of Kentucky (at the time, I didn't know that eastern Kentucky was mostly tobacco).

Yes, she would come back to New Hampshire with me. I'd never had any trouble finding a job, and it sounded like there weren't many options where she was from, even if she'd wanted to go back. My parents and her grandparents agreed, and the plan was set.

Lily took over Marco's room on the main floor of my parents' three-bedroom ranch house. Marco and I shared a carpeted room in the basement, which leaked in any heavy rain. My sisters and youngest brother, ages thirteen, ten, and eight, crammed into another bedroom. My parents had already turned the dining room, with double doors off the kitchen, into their bedroom. We had only one bathroom, which had exposed studs,

Making Love

broken sheetrock, and ceramic tiles missing as Dad was renovating it that summer. He installed an extra shower over a floor drain in the basement. It was a freestanding, rickety plastic thing fed by nothing but a hose running from a utility sink in the corner. Lily was in it one time when I came down the stairs and joked that I was coming to take a peek; she was so flustered trying to grab the vinyl curtain and hold it closed that she instead opened it, showing me all her glory.

My big, loud Italian family in this tiny house was a huge stretch for Lily. She'd grown up in a sprawling hillside home with three bathrooms, four bedrooms, an office, living room, family room, a great room they never used, two-car garage, a billiards room, and an in-ground pool with a big patio surrounded by a concrete wall topped with cast-iron fencing. Her grandparents' own kids were all grown by the time they adopted Lily, so she was an only child by both birth and rearing. The great room had a giant portrait of Lily her grandparents had commissioned. My parents barely had money for my senior photos.

We had differences to overcome, but it was a fun summer. My uncle David took a bunch of us cousins to see Barenaked Ladies at an outdoor pavilion south of Boston. Lily and I drove up to the White Mountains for a waterfall hike. We went to the beach and down to Springfield, Massachusetts, to visit friends from school. Mom and Dad had moved to this house in Manchester, New Hampshire's biggest city, while I was away at Cedarville. It was only about 100,000 people, but it was the biggest city I'd ever lived in. Lily and I went to a fancy new Italian restaurant in a converted rivermill building and strolled along the Merrimack waterfront. I'd (finally) broken the rules and tried a rum and coke and a homemade margarita hanging out with my housemates and some close friends during my last few weeks at Cedarville. I hadn't acquired much of a taste for beer, but in Manchester, Lily and I went to the Strange Brew Tavern a few times because it had live music and pool tables, and I liked to drink a bottle or two of hard apple cider.

Even as I opened up to the world, I was searching for God. I found an Orthodox Presbyterian Church congregation downtown. The OPC was a sister denomination of the PCA, the kind of church I had gone to in Dayton. The differences between the two are more aesthetic than theological. The OPC prefers weightier sermons and traditional Reformed hymns, while the PCA takes a more evangelical approach, often with practical sermons and contemporary praise choruses on overhead projectors. But they're both strictly Calvinist.

Though I was wrestling with Reformed theology after my winter crisis, these were still the churches where I felt at home. They weren't afraid of the wider culture. They didn't have hang-ups about alcohol or rock 'n' roll. They had faith seeking understanding. They didn't speak the evangelical Christianese of "prayer warriors" or "quiet time" or "getting saved." They talked about "God's sovereign grace": the love that God has shown us even though we don't deserve it. It wasn't just the particular grace by which God saves individual Christians from their sin; it was what theologians call "common grace": the goodness and beauty of God's creation that we all enjoy.

We met in a gorgeous blue Victorian building, its spacious sanctuary rising across the pews like a high sky over the Fenway grass. The pastor, a Westminster Seminary grad with a penchant for pipe tobacco and Red Sox radio broadcasts, had recently restored his own Victorian home a few blocks north. With his ornate pipe collection, his jealousy for (architectural) gingerbread, and his ear for the musical masters, the pastor embodied the maxim that Christians ought to enjoy all that God has created and called good. In every beautiful thing, he saw an earthly symbol of heavenly reality.

It was through this lens I viewed Lily. She was a gift, a treasure that God and Joe had entrusted to me, like Bishop Myriel welcoming the convict Jean Valjean into his home, risking his most precious possessions. We were both to take care of each other and lead the other closer to God. That was what Christian marriage was all about. Not only that, but I felt like I owed it to her parents to watch over her, and that meant finding her a job. Would I live up to the trust?

As soon as we'd gotten back to New Hampshire for the summer, I started working for Dad's real estate appraisal business. I would drive all over southern New Hampshire, taking photographs of houses and visiting town halls to copy tax assessment data. I would also take Dad's notes from his inspections and enter that information into his appraisal software. It was 1999, the economy was buzzing along, and he had plenty of work for me. The mortgage companies would pressure him to push a home's value high enough to justify the sort of loans that inflated the housing bubble and led to the Great Recession.

I got home from work one day and found the local Budweiser plant had called offering Lily a job. She'd been out going door to door filling out more job applications and was late getting home because she'd gotten lost. She had a terrible sense of direction and would often decide to stay home just because she was afraid. That always annoyed me a little bit, and then when I asked her about Budweiser and she said just hadn't gotten around to calling them back yet, I really started to get mad.

"What are you doing?" I pressed her. It was already July. We had two months before she had to go back to school, and I couldn't understand why she was running around filling out job applications when she already had a job waiting for her. Her grandparents had given up so much to raise her, Joe working into his seventies, after a heart attack, just so she could get through school and have her nice clothes and her $7 toothpaste.

"I don't know," she said. "I just thought I should put a bunch of applications out there."

"No!" I said. "You need a job! Your parents are counting on you to make some money this summer. It could be another month before any of these places hire you. Why wouldn't you just take the job that's right in front of you?"

She started crying.

"I'm sorry," I said. "I know you've had a hard day. I just want what's best for you. I love you."

It was the first time I'd said it.

Lily lasted only a few days at Budweiser. The specific job, it turned out, was shoveling beechwood chips out of their fermentation tanks. The work was too hard. Lily had been afraid they might give her this task from among a whole list of openings, which was why she hadn't called them back in the first place, though she hadn't told me that. My own self-possession and go-getter attitude had colored my expectations of her. I'd never had any trouble finding a job and doing it well, and I thought she could do anything I could do.

None of the other jobs were calling her back, either. Mom started paying her for work around the house: babysitting, cooking, cleaning, weeding, that sort of thing. She let my little siblings know who was boss around the kitchen, and I thought she might make a good mother for my own kids someday. Instead of seeing my vision of partnership slipping away, I adjusted my expectations. I never would have used the word "helpmeet" but I started seeing her as someone who might help me create a good life at home but maybe not much more than that. I was the one who had dreams about doing something meaningful out there in the world, and maybe that was OK. We would take care of each other, just in different ways.

This Littler Light

At the end of the summer, I'd planned to drive Lily back to Ohio. I told Mom I might ask her to marry me. Mom's response was tepid; she worried that Lily was too dependent on me. But I wanted a ring on her finger before there were 900 miles between me and the hordes of other eager bachelors looking for a good Christian wife.

On the day before we left, Mom wanted to take Lily out for a mother-daughter day: lunch, shopping, that sort of thing. Lily chose instead to come with me all day as I drove around taking photos of houses. Her decision didn't seem like a big deal to me at the time.

The next day, we made the thirteen-hour drive to Ohio. As soon as we got her things moved into the dorm at Cedarville, we drove over to Yellow Springs, to that quad where we'd picnicked with Chad, Kim, Mick, and Rachel. We walked hand-in-hand through that pretty glade where I'd tickled her face. Back at her car, I got down on my knee and asked her to marry me. She pulled out a poem she had written for this occasion. Its five verses describe me as her protector, approaching her with reverence, sympathy, and chastity. Here's one stanza:

> My lover, he cares for me, as has no other
> For with gentle instruction
> He guides me rightly through the questions and fears
> That would overtake my thoughts
> And overwhelm my hopes,
> Obscuring the truth of his love from me.

At the time, I thought I was capable of living up to these words. Now, it seems like you could honestly write them about God alone.

We stayed with her biological mother for a night or two that fall and told her we were looking for a ring. She suggested the jewelry counter at Nordstrom. I only had a few hundred dollars to spend. We drove to vintage jewelry stores all over Dayton looking for something old, with a garnet as the center stone: Our birthdays are two days apart in January, so that's our birthstone, and we knew it would be cheaper than a diamond. We finally ended up at Nordstrom and found an oval garnet bigger than a pencil-eraser, surrounded by tiny diamonds, with gold prongs that made it look like a crown. It was a big ring like you might see on a Medieval princess, but it only cost me $400.

Before school started, we drove Lily home to Kentucky. After a summer of domestic intimacy, we had nine months of distance in front of us. I flew back to New Hampshire alone, my tears and nose flowing for most of the flight. We were engaged, but we weren't planning to marry until

Making Love

the following summer, after Lily graduated. I had a job with Dad, and we didn't see ourselves staying in Ohio after Cedarville, so it didn't make much sense for me to try to get work there. Plus, Dad, Marco, and I had started playing music together, and I didn't want to give that up just yet. I took over Lily's room when I got home, and there the weeping started all over again. I was supposed to be a man. I wasn't supposed to cry. But I did.

I started building my life as an adult. I applied for a loan to buy a duplex where Lily and I could live or rent out as an investment if we moved elsewhere for seminary. By now I was a pastoral intern at the Presbyterian church. I prepared a sermon on the Lord's Prayer, highlighting the social dimensions of "forgive us our debts" and "*our* (not my) daily bread." Biblical scholars understand the prayer for "thy kingdom come" as a petition for the Jewish Jubilee, the fifty-year cycle when all debts are erased. The Lord's Prayer is a political statement in favor of what we might now call socialism: redistribution of wealth, universal healthcare, food sharing. Of course, this was still a conservative church, and I didn't spell out that connection for them. I just talked about how this kingdom demands that we share our bread and give away our resources without expectation of return. As I had arranged with the pastor, I announced we'd be opening a food pantry to help hungry people in the neighborhood. I asked the thirty or so members of the church to consider donating packaged food to get us started. I didn't bother to check and see if we might be duplicating services or if we could partner with other programs. I just wanted to feed people and didn't know how else to do it.

I also led a Bible study on Paul's letter to the Colossians. I'd been struck by the *cosmic* scope of Christ's reign described in the first chapter. Jesus is the "firstborn of every creature": Somehow all of us, not just humans, but *all creation* will participate in his birth and resurrection, the Incarnation of God, a New Heaven, a New Earth, a New Jerusalem. And even as we wait for that to happen, Jesus remains our Creator and Sustainer: The whole universe holds together because of his presence. He is in everything, and everything is in him. And where the universe appears to be at enmity with Christ, it will be healed. "It pleased the Father that in him should all fullness dwell, and having made peace through the blood of his cross, by him to reconcile all things unto himself; by him, I say, whether they be things in earth, or things in heaven."

To reconcile *all things*. Colossians challenged my self-centered view of salvation—the way I had learned in Baptist Sunday school to insert my name into John 3:16: "For God so loved Jesse, that he gave his only begotten son." According to Paul, the cross was only for me insofar as it was for everyone. When Jesus said "for God so loved the world," he really meant *the world*. Salvation was something bigger than just individual Christians knowing "beyond a shadow of a doubt" that they would go to heaven when they died. Salvation is all creation reconciling with the Creator. It is a renewal of God's original plan, where lions sleep next to lambs and humans remain innocent of the knowledge of good and evil, blindly trusting that Good is whatever God speaks. The church's job is to foreshadow that renewal: to live with one another in justice and peace, keeping sex within the bonds of commitment, holding our possessions loosely, speaking gently, transcending divisions of race, class, and culture, singing together, and deferring to others in our families and workplaces. Just as Jesus is reconciling all things within his power, we reconcile all things within our power. We don't send doctors and engineers to Africa or South America to meet physical needs just so they'll gain people's trust for sharing the gospel. We build sanitation systems and heal disease because that's making creation work for people as Jesus intends. We're ambassadors for Christ not just by sharing a message about him but by imitating his reconciling work.

Old Testament scholar Meredith Kline connected this imitation back to the creation story. My Cedarville hallmate Mattman had helped me to stop reading Genesis as a science or history textbook, but I didn't know how else to read it. Kline gave me an interpretive lens. My Presbyterian pastor was trying to start a seminary in Manchester, so he asked Kline to come to the church and teach a night class. Kline framed Genesis 1 as poetry meant to show God's kingship over all creation and how God shares that reign with humans. He described a crescendo of increasingly complex creation: water, light, air, earth, plants, stars, birds, fish, mammals, and finally Adam and Eve, equipped as co-creators in God's own image. The point of Genesis 1 is not to tell us precisely how the earth came to be but to show the relationship among God, humans, and creation. When God told Adam and Eve to subdue the earth, he was inviting them into the creative process.

As a writer and musician, I had a creative impulse, so this was good news for me. It opened the possibility of creating for creating's sake, not simply to get people saved, but to point my own little penlight at the beauty inherent in God's creation, to explore the depths of joy and suffering in human existence, to write about all the complexities of God without having to wrap them up in a neat little box called "gospel." God's revelations in

Making Love

creation and in Christ were complex beyond our understanding, so why should I try to simplify them? Why not, instead, imitate this author of paradox, this teacher of mysterious parables, this Holy One who ate with sinners?

The Calvinists had preserved my fundamentalist reverence for scripture but also deepened it. It was like falling in love with a woman for her beauty, reason, and kindness, only to learn to love her rebellion against patriarchal modes of beauty or her irrational passions. The Bible was not as simple to understand as I'd once thought, but more seductive.

Ironically, the deeper I fell into the complexity, the farther I felt from the Calvinists who had led me to it. I took another course from this new seminary, "The Word is Worth a Thousand Pictures," taught by the pastor. For him, the gospel was fundamentally a message—a collection of words about God that we needed to believe and preach to others. I suspected it just wasn't that simple. He was taking a stand against postmodernism and the "electronic age" where "image is everything." He thought the gospel could cut through the visual onslaught of television and the Internet to offer something solid: The truth about God to serve as an anchor amid the sea of competing images. That much I could accept, but his view was a two-edged sword. What was lost when you tried to sever the propositions of the gospel from aesthetic experiences like story? In a sermon, he could eloquently expound the doctrine of Christ's atonement, but with hundreds of carefully chosen words, he couldn't quite explain what I experienced whenever I knelt at the rail to receive the bread and wine: Yes, Christ is precisely that for which I hunger.

I loved the words of scripture, but I also loved the sacraments: physical experiences like baptism or communion that let me *live* the gospel, not just believe it. Lily and I were talking about receiving the bread and wine as part of our wedding ceremony, but the pastor said he wouldn't serve us. He argued that marriage was a secular institution, that since unbelievers also marry, believers should not treat it as a distinctly spiritual covenant. I believed the opposite, that Christian marriage was a picture of Christ and the church—a picture of how marriage ought to be—and therefore deeply sacramental. Why lower our expectations just because non-Christians didn't see marriage that way? We could *show* them, and the symbol of the Lord's Table could help us to strive harder for a good marriage.

In marriage counseling, the pastor had recommended lambskin rather than latex condoms and wanted to make sure we had common interests. I didn't stop to consider that such mundane concerns, and not my spiritual idealism, might make all the difference. This rather unusual conservative Reformed minister did see the value of celebrating Communion every Sunday, but he resisted because he wanted to offer a clear alternative for so many lapsed Catholics who lived in our city and wouldn't want reminders of a faith they had left behind. Such crass New England practicality, when there were ideals to live out!

> Behold, children are a gift of the LORD,
> The fruit of the womb is a reward.
> Like arrows in the hand of a warrior,
> So are the children of one's youth.
> How blessed is the man whose quiver
> is full of them
>
> —Psalm 128:3–5 (NASB)

I didn't leave the Presbyterian church over theology. God only knows how long I might have stayed at that church; maybe "the sovereignty of God" was their false crutch for surviving the suffering of the world, but these were good, earnest people. We only had about six months until Lily graduated, but on our phone calls she would cry and beg me to move back to Ohio. Staying in New Hampshire just didn't seem like an option. I'd gotten only as far as picking out a closet in the church to open my food pantry, and I had to go. It hurt too much to know she was unhappy.

Lily's grandparents arranged for me to stay with their daughter, Lily's mother, while I looked for work. Lily spent her Christmas break with me and my family in New Hampshire, and we drove to Dayton in early January. I moved into a guest bedroom, where her mother had never-opened boxes of Wedgewood china and Waterford crystal stored in the closet. In between her rants about the "stupid pigs" who worked in her pathology lab, she promised these treasures to Lily as wedding gifts. As Edith Wharton wrote of Miss Bart, Lily "knew people who 'lived like pigs,' and their appearance and surroundings justified her mother's repugnance to that kind of existence." Lily hoped that my New England pedigree would impress her mother, who talked so often of her transatlantic, *bon vivant* sojourns and her time in Cambridge, Massachusetts.

Lily and I were now thinking about moving up the wedding date to March, so we wouldn't have to pay room and board for her and rent

Making Love

for me in the spring academic quarter. Even if we'd considered moving-in together before the wedding—which we would have thought scandalous—Cedarville wouldn't allow it.

"So what are you doing for work?" asked her mother, a burly nurse who had a good thirty pounds on me and had somehow borne a daughter who had grown to only half her size.

"Well, I've got some interviews, but I'm not sure yet."

"And what if you don't have a job by the time you're supposed to get married?"

"I promise you I'll have a job by the middle of February."

I was planning to apply to Yale Divinity School for the fall, so I wanted a temporary job with a company (or at least new skills and experience) that might easily transfer to New Haven. I interviewed for a customer-service job with Progressive Insurance and then a sales job with Colorado Prime, a company that delivers meat and other food to your freezer once a month. Dad had bought from Colorado Prime when I was a kid, and I knew the food was really good. The company would set up appointments for me in people's homes, so it wasn't like cold sales. The customers were already interested. I would just have to show up and seal the deal.

I took the job, but before I started, I flew back to New Hampshire to get my car, clothes, and other things. I took my Colorado Prime paraphernalia with me so I could practice my pitch on my aunt and uncle. After an hour with them, I realized I wasn't a salesman. I couldn't talk people into spending their money. The meat was good, but it was very expensive, and I knew people didn't *need* it. I wanted no part of it.

The next day, I called the *Xenia Daily Gazette*, a small newspaper near Cedarville, just to see if they might have an opening for a reporter. They did. The editor, Nick Blizzard, told me to send him some writing clips from the campus newspaper. I found the pieces I had saved and visited the *Cedars* office when I got back to Ohio to find some more. I delivered my resume and writing samples in person, and then went back or called Nick once a week for the next three weeks. I had nothing better to do. The receptionist kept telling me he'd get back to me. "I didn't know whether to hire you or kill you," Nick later told me.

Finally, he gave me an interview. I didn't have much going for me. I had written a lot of soft stuff for the student newspaper: book reviews, concert reviews, human interest features, that sort of thing. The job was covering the local schools and city hall—mostly hard news about municipal budgets and development proposals. Nick asked me what I knew about the city manager form of local government. I took a guess and said the city manager is like the U.S. President—an executive who has to carry out the policies set by the city council, which makes democratic decisions like Congress.

"Sort of," he said.

"Well, if you hire me, I'll learn about it tomorrow," I said.

I got the job. I was going to be a journalist, just like I had told that reporter back at Calvary—at least for now, until I could go to seminary.

Lily's mother had been visiting her husband in Kansas for a few weeks, so Lily and I had the house to ourselves, me in the guest room, and she in her mom's. One night we invited Chad and Kim over to help us assemble our wedding invitations and watch a movie.

When Lily's mother got home a week or two later, I was making dinner in the kitchen, while the two of them talked in the adjacent living room. I overheard a word here and there and knew they were talking about the wedding.

"Jess, why *are* we moving the wedding date up?" Lily asked me.

I didn't have any context for the conversation. I could tell that Lily was just repeating her mother's question, and I knew that Lily already knew the answer: We would save a lot of money if we were married for Lily's spring term instead of paying double rent. But it wasn't an answer Lily was looking for. It was my protection she wanted. I just didn't realize that until it was too late.

"It just seems like a silly question," was all I said.

Sylvia stormed down the hallway and locked herself in her bedroom.

"What's this all about?" I asked Lily.

"She just doesn't understand why we're in such a rush," she said.

"We're not in a rush," I said. "I'll talk to her."

I knocked on the bedroom door and told her I was sorry. It wasn't a silly question. I just didn't understand where it was coming from. We could talk more about it if she wanted. She said OK. But she never came out.

The next morning, I awoke on the dining room floor (Lily had the guest room) and overheard the two of them talking. Apparently, her neighbor had accused us of having a "party" when Chad and Kim came over to make wedding invitations. Lily's mother had certain ideas about what kids from Cedarville were like. Lily was going to end up barefoot and pregnant, working in a convenience store or on the mission field in Africa. She was upset that I had tracked salt from the icy walkway onto the tile

Making Love

floor in the foyer. Why were we using the insurance payment from Lily's recent car wreck to pay her tuition? Lily could marry me if she wanted, but her mother wouldn't be coming to the wedding. This was her only daughter, the one she'd abandoned over and over again. "To Miss Bart, as to her mother, acquiescence in dinginess was evidence of stupidity." Lily couldn't convince her mother I was anything but dingy. To quote further from *The House of Mirth*:

> She was fond of pictures and flowers, and of sentimental fiction, and she could not help thinking that the possession of such tastes ennobled her desire for worldly advantages. She would not indeed have cared to marry a man who was merely rich: she was secretly ashamed of her mother's crude passion for money. Lily's preference would have been for an English nobleman with political ambitions and vast estates; or, for second choice, an Italian prince with a castle in the Apennines and an hereditary office in the Vatican. Lost causes had a romantic charm for her.

Her mother went out shopping, and Lily and I crammed everything I owned into my little Toyota Corolla. She sat in the passenger seat, and I piled all my pants and shirts, still on their hangers, on to her lap. We left a note in a laundry basket in the middle of the living room floor, so her mother would be sure to find it. We asked her to reconsider coming to the wedding.

We left Lily's Wedgewood and Waterford and drove to the farmhouse, which some friends had taken over after I had graduated. For a few days, I slept on the mattress they used as a crash pad underneath an indoor climbing gym someone had built in a walk-in closet. I found an apartment across the road from Cedarville's campus, at the end of a street that dead-ended near the Cedarville public high school football field. On game days, you could hear the announcer's play-by-play.

Why were we in such a rush? It didn't feel that way. Mick, Rachel, Chad, and Kim were all getting married that summer. Josh had graduated early and married his girlfriend the previous spring; they were twenty-two, just like Lily. It was just what you did. The only difference was, we weren't waiting till she graduated, and that was just a financial decision.

Joe had offered us $1,000, and we could use it to elope or have a wedding. Even though we didn't have any money, and neither did my parents, I had insisted that we have a wedding. I couldn't imagine getting married without my family, including Nanny and Poppy and Mom's brother and sisters. We'd always been so close. Lily and I fought about that. Her family wasn't nearly as close, and it wasn't as important to her. Plus, planning a wedding by ourselves with almost no money was stressing us out. We were timing the wedding for the start of her spring break, so we'd have that week for a honeymoon. That meant she'd be taking her final exams just days before the wedding. All I remember about Valentine's Day, a month prior to the big day, is we went out to dinner and she was mad at me.

At my bachelor party the night before the wedding, Ben asked, only half as a joke, if Lily was pregnant. She and I had just met a year earlier, then we'd moved up the wedding date, and it all seemed so fast to him. Mom, Lily's mother, and now Ben. Were they all trying to tell me something, something I wasn't hearing? I'd finally gotten the girl. This was my moment. I wasn't afraid. Should I have been?

Our friends and family helped us get through those stressful days. Ben's sister and brother-in-law cooked our rehearsal dinner for about fifty people the night before the wedding: Irish stew from a Celtic cookbook I'd found online. Friends from our church helped us decorate the fellowship hall. One friend drove out from New Hampshire, and his wife took charge of covering our storebought angel food cakes with whipped cream and berries for our dessert reception. That couple, Reuben and Sheryl, also got us a hotel room for the night so we wouldn't have to go back to our messy apartment where I'd had wedding guests for the weekend.

At the ceremony, Poppy shot video, while Dad, Marco, Katie, and Suzanne played Van Morrison's "Moondance" for the bridesmaids' procession. Dad said he married Mom because of that song. My ten-year-old brother Steven was the ringbearer. Lexie, the four-year-old daughter of Lily's high-school friend, was the flowergirl. Lily only had three close friends she could think to have in the wedding party, one of them being my friend Kim. So I had to choose three of the eleven guys I wanted as groomsmen: my brother Marco, Kim's fiancé Chad, and my high-school friend Mike. I gave out as many important jobs to the others as I could think of. Ben was our photographer. Kevin read Donne's poem "Love's Growth" and Herbert's "Love (III)." Josh played guitar while I sang Lily's wedding march—Duncan Sheik's ballad "Days Go By":

> I know it's not sensible
> To be this passionate, every day
>
> ———
>
> These are the most precious
> Of all my days

Making Love

Lily wore a rebelliously mauve, Medieval-style dress she bought for about $100 at a Yellow Springs boutique. She had nothing but ribbons on her bare feet, scandalizing her grandmother, who had pulled herself out of Appalachian poverty by her bootstraps. Shoes were a sign of success. Arthur, a retired Anglican priest, officiated, played his violin, and served us Communion. If not for a bottle of wine Reuben and Sheryl had left us at the hotel room, Jesus's blood would have been the only alcohol we drank that day. We couldn't afford any for the reception. The crowd threw glitter at us as I carried Lily to my little maroon sedan. With a naughty grin on his face, Mick handed me a package of edible undies just before we got in the car.

We did not consummate our marriage that night, nor the next. We tried, but the chemistry we'd had as unmarried, forbidden lovers trying to stay pure—that was gone. This wasn't just about hormones, though: It was like Lily's body was there, but she was somewhere else. Our wedding night didn't remotely live up to our expectations for it, and maybe that was the problem: Maybe the anticipation was more than two people could bear. My friend and Cedarville classmate Lisa Walker plays in the Cincinnati twang-rock band Wussy. In their song "Waiting Room," a "sad, Midwestern, Baptist girl writes sorry on the mirror, crying in the bathroom on the first night of the honeymoon." Whatever Lily had been feeling those first two nights, I suspect it had something to do with the pressure we all felt to get married and the overwhelming sense that we weren't ready for it. We needed intimacy, and it terrified us. Josh's marriage lasted only a few years. Lisa's lasted months.

My aunt had given Lily and me her condo in San Diego for a honeymoon, and on the second day there, we finally made love. Still, I was scared. This was harder than it was supposed to be. This was not the heaven I expected. Something wasn't right.

We did have a lot of fun on that trip. We walked around Old Town San Diego, drank margaritas and watched a woman make tortillas on a giant griddle. We boiled lobster and grilled filet mignon at the condo. We toured an herb garden and bought handmade soap. We strolled the beach at La Jolla; Lily was a vision in her swimsuit, one of those "tankinis" that were all the rage at the time. We stayed in Malibu one night and saw the Christian rock bands Jars of Clay and Burlap to Cashmere on a grassy plateau at Pepperdine University. The hillside ran so steep down toward the ocean that from where we sat up above, it looked like the grass just dropped off a cliff into the water. We bought a new camera and a frilly pink ballgown that was on sale for $100 at a designer outlet; I couldn't imagine when she'd ever wear it, but I knew I'd have to hold down Lily's spending in our marriage, and I wanted the honeymoon to be special.

By then, I'd been a few weeks on the job at the *Xenia Daily Gazette*, making $1,700 a month and buying groceries at the discount store Aldi. The *Gazette* was low-paying but also low-pressure. I could take Lily with me to city council or school board meetings a couple of nights a week. After one meeting, she napped on the big leather chair in Nick's office while I wrote my story. If I had to cover a livestock contest at the Greene County Fair or a Friday night high school football game, she could tag along. The *Gazette* did not allow overtime, so if I worked at night, I had hours off during the day.

Lily's libido had warmed up in the months after the wedding. One morning in July she called me on my newsroom phone and asked me to come home at lunchtime and make love to her. When I got there, she was afraid she'd be ovulating in a day or two and she wanted me to wear a condom. Most guys hate the way condoms dull the sensation, and I wasn't any different.

I wasn't afraid of pregnancy as a concept. My parents had had me in their early twenties, and four kids after me. I'd spent my whole life helping with babies. Sure, I knew parenthood wasn't easy. But we loved each other, and I figured that was enough. I figured that when and if that time came, we would be safe, because we were together, forever, and if we had a baby to take care of, that would only bring us closer.

Let me be clear: I didn't *want* to become a father in my early twenties. In fact, from as far back as I could remember, twenty-eight, not twenty-three, was the age when I'd intended to marry. By then I thought I'd be established in a career and maybe even own a house and be ready to take care of a family. So I was way ahead of schedule.

I just wasn't afraid. My family had never had much money, so I knew you could have a good life without a lot of it. "Before Selden left college, he had learned that there are as many ways of going without money as of spending it." When my Corolla had broken down, preventing a trip to see Lily's grandparents in Kentucky that summer, it conjured memories of Mom's Ford Taurus station wagon overheating in Midtown Manhattan. We were already blocking the southbound traffic when a kind-hearted deliveryman swung his big box truck around nose-to-nose with the car to try to jumpstart it, thereby blocking the northbound traffic. Horns blared from both directions, and the truck driver finally gave up and drove away.

"Anything else we can do for you today?" one New Yorker screamed as he drove past us. I'm sure he was a Yankees fan.

Making Love

I remember Mom receiving WIC vouchers during the bankruptcy, to make sure my baby sister and brother had the food they needed. My family had survived on a lot of pasta, not just because we were Italian and it was something Dad could handle cooking, but because it was cheap. I didn't have dreams of fancy cars or homes or clothes or vacations. I was happy with friends and books and music and, of course, love.

I wasn't trying to get Lily pregnant. I really didn't think it would happen. But I felt an inarticulate freedom to risk it, especially if that meant I wouldn't have to wear a condom. The shame and fear about sex that had haunted me for fifteen years were gone. No more inhibition, no more repression. We were married now. There was nothing to worry about. A baby, whenever she came, would be a gift from above.

"I think we'll be OK," I said.

6

Cub Reporter

In the fall before the wedding, I had gone to New Haven to visit Mick. Also studying at Yale was Mark Totten, who had been Cedarville's student-body chaplain when I was a freshman. That year, Mark had inspired my first-ever article for the *Xenia Daily Gazette*, an essay about Joan Osborne's theologically curious song "One of Us." It had been my first attempt to try and bring gospel truth to a secular audience, an inauguration, I thought, for my career. I didn't get paid anything for it, though.

Mark was studying for a PhD in ethics. In my mind, that was *the* theological discipline for our time. George Lindbeck, one of the granddaddies of narrative theology at Yale, had convinced me that Christian truth concerns how we live more than what we say or believe: ethics, in other words. Mark asked me if I was looking at any other schools besides Yale. Maybe Duke, I told him. Big-name Duke faculty like Stanley Hauerwas, Richard Hays, and Will Willimon had studied at Yale in the seventies, and you could argue that Duke had since become the center of narrative theology. What was at stake here was not just a question of geography or the institutional name on a degree; this was a question of what sort of Christian I wanted to be and how I would develop my particular gifts and calling.

On that trip to New Haven, I read Mick's copy of *Evangelicals on the Canterbury Trail*, a collection of essays edited by Wheaton College professor Robert Webber about evangelicals' attraction to the mystery, liturgy, and social conscience of the Anglican tradition. These writers knew they didn't have all the right doctrinal answers, but they found a sense of belonging in Christ by sharing the Eucharist with other Christians and serving alongside them to meet the world's needs. I started to think maybe the Episcopal church—one of the most liberal of those mainline churches I'd heard so much bad stuff about—was for me. And maybe the faculty at a big university divinity school wouldn't turn my brain to mush but would instead lead me to deeper knowledge of God.

Hauerwas and Willimon, in particular, had already begun to influence me with books like *Lord, Teach Us: The Lord's Prayer and the Christian Life* and *Resident Aliens: Life in the Christian Colony*. I'd started practicing prayer in the pattern of the Lord's Prayer, using it as a fill-in-the-blank outline with specifics from my life: for example, asking for the capacity to forgive people like the cheating pastor of my childhood or the faith to share my daily bread with neighbors in need. On one of my first days in the newsroom at the *Gazette*, I read a column by Hauerwas in *Prism*, a magazine published by Evangelicals for Social Action:

> The fundamental issue of journalistic ethics is what larger story we are a part of that helps us determine what we will report as news stories. Christians know and name that story: it is the story of God known in Israel and the church. It is no trivial thing that our most prominent news sources report on the world as if God does not exist.

I had no idea how to write about a new real estate development proposal before the Xenia City Council as if God exists, but it sure sounded like a noble calling. The big theme of the honors program at Cedarville had been the "integration of faith and learning," and that stuck with me. I was working as a writer, and I wanted to know how to be a faithful *Christian* writer. Maybe I would figure it out in seminary. I realized not everyone had the luxury of formal theological training to show them how to do their jobs faithfully, but it was what I wanted, and I thought theological reflection would be part of my eventual vocation, whatever that turned out to be. I was still leaning toward Yale because my friends were there and it was closer to home. I didn't know for sure whether I could get into either school, but Mick had made it into Yale, so I thought I had a shot. I compiled my application to Yale and requested information from Duke at the same time I had been looking for a job and planning the wedding.

I'd already found a PCA church to join if we moved to New Haven, but on my first Sunday back in Ohio, one of the elders at South Dayton Presbyterian Church had preached a sermon focused exclusively on hell. He said it was a reality that nobody wanted to talk about, but we needed to talk about it because we had neighbors and loved ones who were going there. The reality of that punishment told us something about God's holiness that we had to understand, he said. I couldn't take it. How could I desire intimacy with a god like that? I never went back. Lily and I soon found the Episcopal church in Xenia where we ended up getting married.

Christ Church gave us an immediate sense of community, as the churchpeople frequently hosted one another for meals, I sang in the choir, and we volunteered with the youth group. Before I got hired at the *Gazette*, I had applied for a job coordinating youth programs for the Episcopal Diocese of Southern Ohio I'd heard about at church. I was distinctly unqualified, but the pull of the pulpit was still strong in me, and I thought the job might help prepare me. Lily and I were still struggling to keep up with the Book of Common Prayer in worship. The Reverend Arthur Ransome, the elderly vicar from Cornwall who'd retired to Xenia to be near his daughter's family, often had us over for English tea in perhaps Xenia's only Tudor cottage, right across the street from the church.

When my application materials arrived from Duke Divinity School, they included contact information for an alumna, a Methodist pastor in Ohio who could answer questions about her seminary experience. We traded emails, and I shared my story of denominational wandering.

"If you feel drawn to Duke, maybe you should consider becoming a Methodist," she said.

That decision felt a long way off, I was happy at Christ Church, and I still felt Yale was the place for me, so I didn't think much of that comment. I would just submit these applications and see what happened.

Meanwhile, on my second day on the job, the *Gazette* publisher had delivered to my desk a package of Reese's Peanut Butter Cups stapled to a tearsheet of the front page containing my first news story, a feature about three Xenia High School seniors who were named National Merit Finalists.

"Didn't take you long to win the Reese's," the publisher wrote. "Good work! Will be watching for many more like this."`

My successor as class chaplain had devalued my storytelling, but here it was prized. Maybe I would be good at this job?

I tried to do what Hauerwas had said, to write a story as if God exists. I only felt like I did it one time at the *Gazette*, writing a feature about a Quaker preschool that had moved *inside* a local nursing home so that little kids and the elderly could keep one another company all day. It looked a lot like the Jews' *shalom*, the "peaceable kingdom" that Hauerwas was always talking about, the weakest among us taking care of one another, the elders sharing their wisdom and the children their energy. The publisher, who was a Christian himself, took note.

Cub Reporter

"You really enjoyed that story," he told me.

By the summer, I'd gotten a raise. Now it was $1,800 a month! Lily wasn't going to be able to graduate in June as planned. Some of her transfer credits from Marshall had fallen through, and she needed another term. But she was tired of Cedarville: tired of the Ohio pollen, tired of the strict dress code (no spaghetti straps, skirts below the knee, for example), tired of the narrow-minded trustees, one of whom had bristled at the news of a beloved English professor's Methodist sprinkle baptism (not immersion) with a lunge toward a board-room table, throwing his arms in the air, and crying out, "He's not even saved!" Whether we were going to New Haven (to Yale), or Durham, North Carolina (to Duke), or back to New Hampshire to save money before seminary, Lily wanted out of Ohio. I waited to hear from Yale and looked for jobs in New Haven and Durham. Almost nobody stayed at his first newspaper job more than a year, so looking for the next one after only a few months was normal. Nick told me North Carolina was beautiful. Then I got a letter from Yale. I'd been wait-listed.

In August, Lily and I drove to Fairfax County, Virginia, just outside Washington D.C., for Mick and Rachel's wedding. I had to read scripture in the ceremony. Some of Mick's parents' friends let me, Lily, Chad, and Kim stay in their giant northern Virginia home. On the drive from Ohio, Lily said she needed to go to a drugstore, but once we arrived, there was too much catching up to do before the rehearsal dinner. Some other friends were also living nearby and teaching at a Christian school. In the morning, before the wedding, we drove to visit them. Finally, when we got back to our hosts' house, Lily got Kim to go with her to the pharmacy. Before I understood what was happening, Lily was in and out of the bathroom, asking me to look at the pregnancy test. It was positive.

"This is all your fault," Lily said to me. She'd known we weren't safe for that nooner in July, but I hadn't listened.

She was right, of course. It was my fault, if there was blame to be assigned. But I didn't think there was. I thought this came with being married—maybe even that this was *why* you married: You can't always control when a pregnancy happens—even condoms can break—but if you were married, and she got pregnant, at least you knew your baby would be born into an intact family. I embraced fatherhood fully, from day one. I was too naïve even to be afraid of a miscarriage. During the wedding reception later that same day, we called both sets of parents with the news. If any of them was scared for us, I don't remember it. I remember only excitement.

This pregnancy changed everything. By the time I found out I wasn't coming off the wait-list at Yale, we'd already decided to move back to New

Hampshire. I flew there for a weekend, to interview at the Lowell *Sun* and Lawrence *Eagle-Tribune* in Massachusetts, the Lewiston *Sun-Journal* in Maine, the Manchester, New Hampshire, *Union Leader*, and my first choice, all things being equal, *The Portsmouth Herald* on the New Hampshire coast. (I couldn't get the interview I wanted at the *Portland Press-Herald* in Maine). Portsmouth had the smallest circulation of the bunch, 15,000 daily, about twice as much as Xenia, and it seemed like I had the best shot of getting hired there. It was a historic seaside town with beautiful architecture and great restaurants, close to the beaches. Plus, it was within an hour from my parents and half an hour from Mike and Reuben, two good high school friends.

Arriving for my interview, I parked across the street from the *Herald* building, which lay between the high-rise North Church steeple downtown and the Maplewood Avenue bridge over South Mill Pond. Getting out of my car, looking over the pond, I could see tall pines reflecting on the water's surface. Natural beauty would be a part of my everyday life there in Portsmouth. I'd never spent much time in the city until the previous summer, when Lily and I would come with Reuben and Sheryl to eat out and stroll the lively streets. When I was growing up back in the eighties, we'd lived for a while in North Beach not far down the coast. Mom would go shopping at the malls in Portsmouth but never downtown. Now I could be a writer in an old New England town, like Hawthorne in Salem or Thoreau in Concord. It felt like home.

Managing editor Lars Trodson and I covered the essentials: what I'd been doing for the *Gazette*, the expectations for the education reporter at the *Herald*, the work schedule, that sort of thing. He commented on a copy of the *Gazette* where I had written four stories the weekend after a tornado wrecked 100 homes and killed a man a few weeks earlier. "You wrote the whole front page!" he said. Sometimes, that's the way it was at a tiny newspaper. Telling the stories of families and churches trying to recover from the loss of their homes and buildings felt like a huge privilege; I was bearing witness to epic experiences of suffering and resilience. It felt important.

Then Lars asked about Cedarville. I braced for him to warn me against bringing religion into the newsroom. Instead, he said he wanted more spirituality in the paper, and would I be interested in writing stories about faith from time to time? Lars said he wasn't sure what he believed, but he knew that some readers had faith, and he wanted to serve them. At the very least, I thought, I'll be able to write as though God exists. It

Cub Reporter

seemed too good to be true. Wasn't the newsroom, especially in New England, supposed to be full of hard-nosed materialists, skeptical of any claim to the supernatural? Lars defied my expectations.

A couple of weeks later, Lars' boss, the executive editor, called the Xenia newsroom to offer me the job. The pay was less than $2,100 a month, before any withholdings, only about $600 a month above the federal poverty line that year. That editor was incredulous when I told him we were going to try to live just on my income; almost nobody did that in New England. I knew rents were well over twice as high as in Ohio and the fifteen percent pay increase wouldn't make up for that, but I hoped we could make it work. I told Nick I was leaving for the Northeast. It was October 2000, and he asked if I would stay through the presidential election in November. If I stayed, I asked him, could the *Gazette* cover my COBRA payments so Lily would have maternity coverage for the three months before my new benefits kicked in? The publisher said he would try, and my new employers said they would wait for me.

On the weekend before Election Day, we packed our Penske moving truck for our eastbound trek. By then we'd inherited a couch and a bed from friends and a separate bedroom suite from Lily's grandparents. That Tuesday, we towed my Corolla behind the fully packed truck to my coworker Frank's apartment complex, where he let Lily sleep while we wrote about local and state-level races and the editors waited for those much-contested results from the Bush-Gore presidential race. I wasn't crazy about either candidate, but I thought Bush had done a good job improving schools in Texas, so I voted for him. Gore had two strikes against him: He seemed both less capable than Clinton and also soiled by his predecessor's lies.

I wasn't sure about the alleged "big issues"—abortion and gay marriage—but the Republicans still seemed to have the moral high ground. I wasn't thinking about Texas's death row or universal healthcare, and I didn't imagine the tax cuts and torture to come. I had some book learnin' and no life experience. Capitalism ran in my veins. *Charity begins at home.* I was glad the government provided a safety net for hurting people, but I still thought individuals ought to take care of their neighbors, even though I hadn't seen many great examples of that, outside of my own Mom.

I'm not sure I can convey the power of what happened to me on my last day at the *Gazette*. I still didn't know if the paper would pick up my COBRA payments, and I was prepared to pay them myself or have Lily skip a few early doctor visits. Instead, Nick dropped an envelope on my desk.

"Your co-workers pitched in for your healthcare," he said.

Nick had chronic back pain, and we all walked on eggshells trying not to stress him out, which is some feat in a newsroom. Every now and then, his dark sense of humor would let loose with big grin and wild cackle. But he was usually in survival mode. Nick's envelope contained a personal check for $200.

Then there was Frank. He was my best friend at the paper. He had a Christian background and we were able to talk about things that mattered to me. Frank also had a dark past, with consequences he couldn't escape: He had spent time in prison for manslaughter after a drunk driving accident in college. He had no driver's license. He covered the Greene County government in downtown Xenia on foot. Frank gave me $400.

Terry was Nick's deputy managing editor. He was not much more than five feet tall, a head shorter even than me. He was in his fifties, lived with his mother, and drove fancy cars. Whenever he said the word "Christian," contempt dripped from his lips. He wasn't sure about me, but as a rule we were bigoted, hateful, repressive people, a stain on the planet. Terry gave me $500.

The rest of the gang gave some smaller checks, and it all added up to $1,300—almost a month's pay and enough to make my COBRA payments till February. I hadn't received gifts like that since my high school graduation, and those were mostly from my family. This generosity, especially Terry's, struck at the foundation of the us-and-them anthropology the Christian Right had taught me. We Christians were supposed to be the light of the world, not this unbeliever. Could God speak love and grace through an atheist newspaper editor? What happened to original sin, which only Jesus could wipe clean? The divine image, stamped on the human heart way back with Adam and Eve: was it still alive in people like Terry, faith or no faith?

Here was Nanny's theology of creation again. It turned out my Irish grandmother had been articulating a Celtic anthropology banished by the Catholic church at the Synod of Whitby in 664. The doctrines of divine image and human depravity had been in tension throughout the history of the church. Whitby emphasized sin over human goodness, defining the church's theology forevermore. But what if God's image was there all along, in people like Nanny and Terry? What if Jesus is already there, kindling love in all of us, and just needs to be uncovered, recognized for whom he is? What if Paul was right when he wrote,

> The Son is the image of the invisible God, the firstborn over all creation. For in him all things were created: things in heaven and on earth, visible and invisible, whether thrones or powers or rulers or authorities; all things have been created through him and for him. He is before all things, and in him all things hold together. (Col 1:15–17)

It was a hard winter. My benefits in Portsmouth kicked-in earlier than promised, but Lily and I still needed all the help we could get. For two months I commuted an hour from my parents' house in Manchester, at first dropping Lily off at a temporary job in Dover and then driving another twenty minutes to Portsmouth. Living in Mom and Dad's basement wasn't easy. Little space, little privacy, and their own marriage falling apart. The same intense personality that led Mom to the fundamentalists could explode into rage because of her seething frustration with Dad's drugs, gambling, and scatter-brained business management that always left her picking up the pieces. Dad had spent many evenings of my childhood lying on the couch, watching TV, defeated by his own demons. Mom's helping hands could either soothe or threaten him, depending on his immediate capacity to receive love.

One evening, my fourteen-year-old sister had been pushing Mom's buttons, and Dad made one of his typical jokes about Mom being crazy. Lily laughed knowingly, and Mom came flying out of their bedroom with a crazed look in her eyes, yelling about how her anger was all his fault and no one could see it. And she was right. My boyhood experience, mediated to Lily, was of Mom coming home to a messy house and screaming at us kids for twenty minutes as we quickly cleaned up to appease her. I knew she didn't like to rage at us, but I didn't know how little control she had over it. I didn't know about her seventeen-hour workdays cleaning up Dad's bookkeeping messes or his "protecting" us from chores because he'd been afraid of his own father. Lily didn't know either. I would learn later that she was rebuffing Mom's requests for help around the house, saying, "I'm making a baby." In the kitchen that night, she grabbed my shaking mother in a big bear hug and screamed for her to calm down. Mom said later she yelled for someone to pull Lily away because she was afraid to push her off and hurt the baby. Their relationship was never the same after that. Mom felt misunderstood, judged, and also guilty for exposing Lily to her anger. Lily was afraid of Mom, afraid of all our family drama, and saw enough of it in my own personality not to want anymore.

This Littler Light

Joe and Bootsie bought us tickets to see *Phantom of the Opera* in Boston. Mom was kicking Dad out of the house to go live in an apartment above his office down the street. In a fancy hotel room my in-laws had paid for, I wept for my family in Lily's arms.

We bought Lily a used Nissan to get to work, but within a couple of weeks, she slid on an icy bridge going home from Dover and smashed into the guardrail, totaling the car. An ambulance took her to the hospital for the baby's sake. I spent the day at her side in the emergency room, but they were both fine. Then Lily got sick with Bell's Palsy and lost muscle control in her face; we didn't know how serious it was and spent another day in the hospital to monitor the baby. Again, they were both fine, but these were days spent in fear. Soon, a big SUV T-boned my Corolla, and the dented metal scraped and squealed anytime you opened and closed the front-passenger door for the next few months.

This was the winter of 2000-2001. The effects of the dot-com crash weren't yet being felt in the wider economy. The housing bubble was still inflating, especially within an hour's commute of a major city like Boston. My salary gave us about $600 a month for housing, but we couldn't find anything cheaper than $800 within a thirty-minute drive of Portsmouth. Fortunately for us, my parents were in real estate. Mom found us an old Victorian on a hillside street in Somersworth, looking over the Piscataqua River and Berwick, Maine, on the opposite shore.

The bubble hadn't quite reached that far north yet. We paid less than $90,000 for the house. It had been converted to an up-and-down duplex, so the rent from the downstairs would come close to covering the entire mortgage. The house had ornate carvings around two front bay windows, but it needed a paint job and a new porch at the main entrance, and the inside screamed rental property. The plaster was cracked and pock-marked. The paint on the staircase was worn to the bare, splintering wood. Cheap, low-pile carpet was bubbling up in places. Linoleum floors in the downstairs kitchen and bath were curling up at the edges, while the heavy-duty speckled floor tiles upstairs belonged in a butcher shop, not an apartment. The weirdest part was that we shared a driveway with the duplex next door, so the people in the back apartment had to come on to our property to get in and out of their house. One of their relatives worked for a company that sprayed grass seed in a liquid solution out of big tanker trucks. One afternoon, he backed his truck into our driveway and emptied his excess grass solution, leaving a weird green hue all over the sandy soil. I'm sure he thought he was doing us a favor, but he hadn't even asked us. People in neighboring towns called our city "Scummersworth." It wasn't ideal, but it was what we had to do.

It was January when we moved in, and we trudged through the snow and ice as we carried furniture and boxes up the steep and slippery front stoop. Lily and I had worshiped with the Presbyterians in Manchester, and I thought we had built some sense of community, some Trinitarian bonds. But when it came time to move out of the basement, I had called the pastor's wife to ask if she could recruit some church people to help us load our moving truck as they had recently done for another couple. For no reason I can conjure—despite my propensity for self-blame—she said no. That hurt, deeply. I concluded, with the finality and self-assurance of a twenty-four-year-old theologian, that the image of the Trinity was not to be found among the Calvinists, who were content to leave young expectant couples to fend for themselves. I hadn't yet learned that you have to pay attention to your pain, but not let it control you. Thankfully, I had met an aspiring Ukrainian Orthodox priest in Portsmouth, and he helped with the move.

After the first snowstorm that January, I was a few hours late for work from shoveling out the seventy-foot long driveway enough to pull the car from behind the house where we had to park. Some days that winter, I had to take an out-of-the-way path home because the direct route up our hill was too slick for the Toyota. With the baby on the way, Joe and Bootsie bought us a 1998 Subaru with all-wheel drive. We lost that for a few weeks after a guy pulled out in front of me on the way to work and I accordioned my front end, our third accident in as many months. I hit my head on the windshield and have had off-and-on back pain ever since.

Lily and I drove to a few Episcopal churches, but eventually settled on Berwick United Methodist Church, just across the river in Maine. It was one of the closest churches to our house, and that Methodist pastor's email had stuck with me since Ohio. If I was ever going to seminary, I did want to study with Hauerwas at Duke, so maybe I should be a Methodist. On Maundy Thursday, we stood in line for the footwashing ceremony to commemorate Jesus's washing his disciples feet before the Last Supper. Lily and I arranged ourselves in line to avoid the crusty feet of the elderly parishioners and washed each others' feet instead. With the move and my parents' troubles, we had to take care of each other—a spiritual communion of two.

Aurora was due on Easter Sunday, April 15, 2001. She was a week late. Lily went into painful back labor on Saturday night, April 21. We lay in bed, and I applied counterpressure to her lower back like they'd taught us in birthing class. Finally, the pain became too much. We drove through freezing rain and slushy roads. Reuben's wife Sheryl had recommended her obstetrician at Exeter Hospital. Once a month, I had taken time off work to drive Lily back and forth the forty minutes from Somersworth, passing two hospitals along the way. This time the weather and the circumstances filled us with fear. I hadn't anticipated having to drive on icy roads in the middle of the night. I was still a kid myself, after all.

Lily was in labor through the night, all the next day, and into Sunday evening. An epidural took the edge off the pain. When it came time to push, I stood by the head of the bed so she could squeeze my hand. The umbilical cord got wrapped around Aurora's neck in the birth canal. She was gray and lifeless when she came out, but the nurses revived her, no worse for the wear. She had a full head of blazing auburn hair and almond-shaped Mangiapane eyes, from Mom's side of the family.

Lily had already forbid anyone from coming to the maternity ward to see us. She didn't want my messed-up family anywhere near our little nativity scene. I didn't see it that way, but what could I do? She was the one who had gone through childbirth. I had called Dad to tell them we were in the hospital, so sometime on Monday, Mom called to say they were down in the parking lot of the hospital, and could they please come up to see us? Lily didn't like it, but I pleaded with her. This was my family! This was their granddaughter and niece! How could we just send them away? Finally, she compromised and let Mom come up alone, just to see the baby for a couple minutes.

We spent the better part of three days in the hospital, and when we drove home, the sun was shining and green had sprouted all over the Yankee landscape. Aurora had missed Easter, but her birth was still a rite of spring, christening Earth Day 2001 as a living sign of the Creator.

I took the week off work to help Lily adjust; she knew nothing about babies! One of my co-workers complained to the executive editor that I couldn't possibly have this much vacation time with only a few months on the job. He assured her that I was taking unpaid leave. I was 900 miles from Frank, Terry, Nick, and their generous gifts, and I felt every inch of it.

Still only twenty-four years old, I had to prove myself in the newsroom, especially since I would rush home at the five o'clock bell to help Lily with the baby. Before the birth, I had spent a couple of evenings staking out a drivers ed teacher suspected of riding with his students to a liquor store to pick up his booze. That sort of off-hours "shoe-leather" reporting could make a young journalist's career, but it wasn't an option for me anymore. As it was, I had mandatory school board meetings one night a week. I tried to cram as many stories into my eight-hour workday as I could.

It didn't help that I was Lily's husband, chef, housekeeper, accountant, and lactation consultant all rolled into one. We'd been arguing about housework since back in Cedarville, when I'd work all day and she was taking only a couple of classes but would expect me to come home and make dinner, do laundry, and clean the bathroom. Now that the baby was here, there was even more to do.

The downstairs tenants had moved out just before the birth. I had put an ad in the paper, so when we got home from the hospital there were a dozen messages on our answering machine. One happened to be from a mother looking for a place for her twenty-three-year-old son. By complete coincidence, he was a friend from Cedarville. He liked the apartment but asked if we could get rid of the nasty carpet. I told him I wanted to refinish the wide-pine floors underneath, so that project commenced almost right away. He and his brother stripped the paint that covered the wood, but I had to shop for their materials and look up contractors who could sand the floor. Then I had to help apply multiple coats of polyurethane, leaving a day to dry between each one.

Meanwhile, Lily would call me several times a day at work, where my phone was my lifeline to sources and my desk was surrounded by reporters and editors who could hear every word I said. Lily was completely lost. The baby's diapers are leaking, what do I do? The baby's fussy, is my milk making her sick? The baby's still fussy, I think she's allergic to the milk formula. Now she's allergic to the soy formula. Is she supposed to sleep this much? Is she getting enough food? My nipples are really sore. I think they're getting infected. The baby rolled off the couch! Is she going to be OK? What are we going to have for dinner? There's a mistake on the phone bill. Customer service people don't respect women. Can you call them?

These were reasonable questions for a first-time mother, but she was pouring all of her worries onto me. She'd run away from her parents in Kentucky and was keeping my Mom at arm's length. She had no mother to teach her how to be a mother. She had only me. When she caught the skin of Aurora's belly in a zipper or the baby got sick, I comforted them both. When I changed Aurora's diaper at a family gathering, my aunt smiled at Lily: "Oh, he does that baby stuff?" When I was there, I did it. When I wasn't, I talked Lily through it. When Lily struggled to put a pair of pants on Aurora, she explained to my mom, "Jesse always does this sort of thing."

By the time her second or third phone call of the day would come to my desk, my voice would turn sharp and my sentences clipped. "You can't call me to fix every little problem," I would tell her. "Ok," she would say. But years later, with our marriage in trouble, she would tell me the truth about how she felt: "You crushed me," she said.

Lily's answer to baby problems was to throw money at them. We couldn't just have a good sturdy car-seat; we had to have the $300 Britax. We couldn't just have the $50 electric breast pump; we had to have the $200 Medela. She shopped online for what I'm sure seemed like necessities to her: A set of mirrors so you could see your rear-facing baby in the backseat of the car; a gadget that could cut your seatbelt and shatter a window in case you drove off a bridge and into a body of water; a special bag to hang off the back of your headrest and hold your first-aid kit and Kleenex. But I was making a little over $2,000 a month, paying a mortgage, and buying supplies to fix up an apartment for a tenant, and these things seemed like a waste of money. Lily was like her namesake in *The House of Mirth*.

> All her life Lily had seen money go out as quickly as it came in, and whatever theories she cultivated as to the prudence of setting aside a part of her gains, she had unhappily no saving vision of the risks of the opposite course.

I was the big brother who'd been taking care of little kids for most of my life. I knew what to do, and she came from a home where she'd never had to do anything. Sometimes, I lost my temper and screamed at her. I couldn't bear all her burdens. She wanted me to take care of her every need, and she tolerated no rival for my love. She resisted spending time with my family, though I craved that time, especially playing music with Dad and Marco. She forbade me from having coffee with a female co-worker who was old enough to be my mother. This woman was a Christian, and we wanted to talk about faith in the newsroom, but Lily insisted that Billy Graham never spent time alone with a woman who was not his wife, and neither should I.

I wanted Lily to reach through her insecurity, to deal with her parents' abandonment, but she refused to talk about it. *Our* problem was *my* problem: the anger I'd inherited from Mom. She wouldn't see it any other way, and it was hard to argue. I wasn't proud of my temper. If I could just be more Christ-like, love her more, control my emotions, maybe we'd be all right. That, after all, was what God had called me to. Pastor, writer, seminary professor: all of that was more or less irrelevant at this point. Now I was a husband. For most of us (the willfully celibate excluded), a loving marriage was the core of faithful Christian life on earth, a picture of Christ and the church, and I wasn't measuring up.

Lily had had enough of New England. The neighbors across the driveway would park carelessly, blocking our exit from behind our house. I left the Corolla unlocked one night, and the neighbor's father-in-law stole a pocketwatch I'd left hanging from my rearview mirror because the dashboard clock didn't work. Reuben had given me the watch as a gift for being a groomsman at his wedding. Lily had to listen to the kids screaming at each other in the driveway. She'd hear the mother verbally abusing them and fear worse. Eventually, social workers came to take the kids away, but not before they had thrown a rock through one of our basement windows.

Lily was now even talking about going back to Appalachia, the place where she'd said most of our peers were on welfare or drugs or both. That generalization had seemed a little far-fetched, but what did I know? Ottaway Newspapers, the company that owned the *Herald*, also owned the Ashland *Daily Independent*, in the town where Lily had gone to high school. I interviewed with a couple of editors by phone. I convinced myself I was willing to go, but I don't think I really wanted to. The *Herald*'s executive editor told me it wouldn't be a great career move, but I thought that might just be his New England bias against the South. I decided to check out the situation very carefully, going so far as to ask the executive editor in Ashland to set me up to talk with the local schools superintendent, who would be one of my key sources as the education reporter. That was a really brazen thing to request, and before I even gave the editor the chance to respond to my email, I booked a flight for the days that we'd tentatively talked about my coming down to interview. The editor emailed me back and told me not to bother. He clearly didn't like the idea of my checking outside the newsroom to see what the job would be like.

I'd subconsciously sabotaged Lily's chance to go back to Kentucky. I didn't want to go there. If I stayed in New England, I could at least take some classes at Gordon-Conwell, where I'd been admitted. I'd already taken a church history course by correspondence from there. If I was going to make another big move, I wanted it to be to North Carolina, where I could go to Duke. Even though seminary was a low priority, I just couldn't give up the dream.

One morning, I had breakfast with our Methodist pastor, a Korean immigrant who had been engaged to another Methodist pastor, an American woman, down in Massachusetts. Lily and I had hosted them for brunch one Saturday, and she had loaned me a book, *The Little Flowers of St. Francis*, because I was thinking about writing on the saint from Assisi for the church history course. At my breakfast with the Reverend Lee, he told me his fiancée had broken off their engagement just before they were supposed to go to Korea to visit his family. He'd had to return to his homeland alone, in the sort of shame that's magnified in Eastern cultures. I asked him if he would see her again, and could he return her book? He said he could.

He seemed a little down about the break-up, but we had a nice breakfast, and we talked about my dilemma. Would I ever get to go to seminary? Would the Methodist church ever ordain someone like me, who had wandered among the Baptists, Presbyterians, and Anglicans? We talked about Hauerwas and Barth. I had just read Richard Hays's book *The Moral Vision of the New Testament* and was captivated by its picture of peacemaking and sacrificial love. It spoke into my home and my heart, where I felt called to make peace and sacrifice the tightwad inside me to Lily's cravings.

"It would be a sin for you not to go and study theology," my pastor announced. He sounded like a fundamentalist, but it was good to hear: My sense of calling wasn't just inside my own head.

Three days later, we arrived at church to a strange scene. People weren't smiling. They shifted uneasily in their seats. A man I didn't recognize, in clerical vestment, stood at the pulpit. He announced to us that Reverend Lee was in jail, accused of raping and beating his ex-girlfriend at gunpoint.

That church had thrown us a lovely baby shower. One white-haired lady called Aurora "the church's baby." But we never went back. We missed the Anglican liturgy, but more importantly, we lacked the strength and courage to walk with those people through the valley of the shadow of death. There I'd learned the lyrics, "Let there be peace on earth, and let it begin with me." What did it mean now, when our pastor was capable of such violence?

And what of his words, anointing my call to seminary? Was that confirmation of a divine vocation, or the ravings of a lunatic? And was this all my fault? Did he go to her under the guise of returning the book I'd borrowed? I half-expected a call from the police. It was too much to bear. We had to go.

Ever since I'd started at the *Herald*, Lars had been encouraging me to write about religion. He'd wanted something meaningful for Martin Luther King Jr.'s birthday in 2001. Just months into my new job, I'd written an essay comparing the lives of King and his namesake, the German Reformer

Martin Luther. Both, I said, had stood against oppression, whether it was poor Catholics paying indulgences or poor blacks denied equality. A copy editor asked me to make some changes because it was "too preachy." I told her Lars wanted an essay, not straight news. A local Catholic priest I had interviewed said this was too ambitious for a daily newspaper and belonged some place like *The Atlantic Monthly:* In other words, I couldn't handle it. After it was published, one of his parishioners, a city councilor I would later need as a source, complained that I was anti-Catholic. I'd used the word "sinister" to describe the medieval Catholic hierarchy. That showed me I would need to be more careful. I'd always thought the Reformation was irrefutably necessary, not because Rome had a false church, but because it had taken some very, very bad turns. Clearly, I couldn't assume my readers had the same perspective. At the time, I hadn't appreciated why the election of JFK had been such a big deal in the sixties—how American Catholics for centuries had learned to defend their faith against Protestant persecution.

With the summer tourism season approaching, Lars had an idea: He asked if I wanted to write "a history of God," to enlighten our customers with some light beach reading. A short, hefty man, Lars wore well-trimmed whiskers on his generous jowls; he had a grounded sort of optimism, a wicked wit, a lust for life, and a belief that covering the news should be fun. Like your favorite uncle, he'd rib us younger reporters and get people together for drinks after work. I wanted to please him, and I actually started to work on that History of God—even plotting out some timelines of God's great acts in history and going so far as to call Will Willimon down at Duke. After a couple of weeks, though, I gave up. My Christian high school diplomas and college Bible minor hardly qualified me for such a monumental task.

In the meantime, I prepared a story for July 4th posing the question, "How do we celebrate the American Revolution without celebrating the violence that came with it?" I quoted a black activist pastor, some Quakers, and a local Roman Catholic communications scholar, Vincent Rocchio, I had found through the pacifist Ekklesia Project, all criticizing the American culture of violence. Vince, who would become my friend, pointed out the editor's note that accompanied my story: "On this July 4, 2001, *Herald* reporter Jesse DeConto decided to ask a provocative question. Here are his results." Always on the lookout for the hegemony of the status quo, Vince was certain my editors were trying to blunt the power of my story, to head off complaints. I was just glad they published the piece.

Persuaded that my first allegiance was to Christ, I had started standing quietly, trying to pray, whenever a roomful of people pledged the American flag at a school board or city council meeting. Assigned to cover the Independence Day fireworks, I asked some revelers if the connection with violence ever made them uncomfortable. What was clear was that my questions made them uncomfortable. I vowed never to cover the Fourth of July again, if I could help it.

Soon, I offered Lars an alternative for his History of God: What if I told readers about God through the story of some living, breathing human beings and their lives with God? Lars let me write about my friends Reuben and Sheryl, who had come to symbolize God's work of creation and redemption for me: Sheryl, because she had been raising her son as a single mom since she was sixteen; and Reuben because he'd embraced both mother and son, despite the shame and judgment that hung over premarital sex in the fundamentalist culture that had raised us. I wrote about Sheryl's desperate prayers for food and shelter, her decision not to abort, and the Christians who came alongside her. It was a three-part series. In the last story, Sheryl talked about how much easier life was in her early twenties, with a new baby, and a husband to care for them all. She also talked about how much harder it was to feel close to God when she wasn't on her knees, pleading for her daily bread.

The series ran just days after the 9/11 attacks because Lars wanted to give readers something positive to take their mind off things. On that morning of infamy, I had sat at my desk, staring at the newsroom TV. "Are you all right?" the Christian lady asked me. I guess it was my vacant stare. Aurora was five months old. Her life would be so different from mine.

By then, Lars had promoted me to be his assistant city editor. It came with about a ten percent raise. I was now making $2,300 a month. I was twenty-four years old. I wasn't sure if they did it because I was fit for the job or because they knew they would lose me if I didn't start making more money. Either way, it felt good. I knew I had to climb somewhere above $2,500 monthly, and fast, if I was going to keep working as a writer and also giving Lily what she wanted. I just had to get her out of "Scummersworth."

On September 11, I felt overmatched for my new job. This was probably the biggest news day I would ever see. I was supposed to be a leader among my peers. What did I have to contribute? I went out looking for reaction from the public. I went to a gas station because I figured people were talking to the clerk. People, of course, were in shock. But no reader would need me to tell them that.

By then Lily and I were going to St. John's Episcopal Church, whose slate-topped brick cupola served as the focal point for the east end of downtown Portsmouth, near the bank of the Piscataqua. Built on a hilly perch in 1732, it trailed only the Puritan Congregationalists' North Church, built in 1712 with a 193-foot spire, as the oldest and highest-steepled church in town. St. John's, with its Tory connections, could never rival the free church on Market Square for the city's affection, but what it lacked in democratic symbolism, it made up for in star appeal. A mahogany chair, rescued from a fire that destroyed the original wooden church in 1806, was said to have borne George Washington, himself an Anglican, when he worshiped there in 1789. The church bell, plundered from the French-Canadians in the Battle of Louisbourg in 1745, was damaged in that 1806 fire and recast by none other than Paul Revere.

St. John's, like so many Episcopal parishes, was a congregation of power and privilege. A new city councilman would soon be elected from among us. But what drew me was the high ceiling painted with square panels like windows to heaven; the Lord's Prayer, Ten Commandments, and Apostle's Creed inscribed almost two centuries earlier on the wall behind the altar, reminders of how ancient we Christians were; the antique mural of a dove, descending to meet us; the Common Table, a weekly community meal in the fellowship hall for hungry people; and the Interfaith Hospitality Network, where we partnered with other churches to use our buildings as rotating shelters for homeless families. It was the liturgy that took us to another place and the community service that kept us grounded in the here and now.

Still struggling to find my story on 9/11, while my colleagues were interviewing family members of actual victims, even the wife of one of the hijacked pilots, I found out St. John's would be hosting an interfaith service that night. I wasn't sure anyone would care, but I told Lars about it and offered to cover it. Lily understood. I had a job to do. Walking through Market Square to the church that night, the cross atop that high cupola beckoned me, as village churches have done for centuries, all over the world, calling people together to walk through important events with God. That night, local clergy, including a Jewish rabbi, offered words of comfort and urged us against vengeance. One of our photographers captured the image of a little girl blotting tears from her mother's eyes. On a day when most newspapers led with the smoky buildings, we put that photo on the front page.

This Littler Light

That December, St. John's hosted an afternoon discussion group on a book called *Courageous Incarnation*, by Episcopal theologian Fredrica Harris Thompsett. I explained to Lars what for a Christian might have been obvious: Reflecting on the Incarnation, the coming of God into human flesh, was a way to celebrate Christmas. "That's what it's all about, really, isn't it?" he said, with dawning appreciation. What if I went to this book group and wrote a story about it each week leading up to Christmas? He agreed. The discussion focused on the spiritual: the meaning of the historical Jesus of Nazareth, and how people experience God's presence in human relationships, birth, child-rearing, and aging. It also turned political: Talking about the Incarnation in the workplace yielded a critique of capitalism. I summed up the conversation like this in the *Herald*: "Americans are a people who don't know when enough is enough, who value themselves on how much money they make, and who don't appreciate work that doesn't produce something they can sell." Our pastor, the Reverend Tim Rich, pointed out the ancient Hebrews set minimum wage at whatever it took for a man to support his family. "How far we have strayed from that standard," said Rich. It was clear that finding God in the American workplace wasn't easy.

But I didn't need anyone to tell me that. I had chosen a job where the corporations that employed me traded intangible values like "making a difference" or "setting the agenda" or "serving my community" in exchange for my accepting low pay, the mentally taxing work of trying to dig up the truth—sometimes when powerful people wanted to hide it—and writing in such a way as not to tick anybody off, at least not if I could avoid it. Journalism, certainly not small-town journalism, didn't come with the cultural cachet of Woodward and Bernstein or Edward R. Murrow. The TV gotcha reporters made people suspicious toward all of us: We just wanted a story and would leave others to deal with the fallout. The local schools superintendent, my primary source as the education reporter, stopped talking to me for awhile after I wrote a story saying the federal government had found one of his schools deficient and given parents the choice to go elsewhere under President Bush's No Child Left Behind legislation. The superintendent's work, just like my work, was out there for people to judge every day. Reporters' low pay-grade made us easy to dismiss: We'd bounce from job to job looking for higher pay and, though our work had higher standards for truth and fairness than many other professions, readers could and did cast doubt on it, usually by speculative suggestion rather than evidence, because we had no real cultural power. The pen may be mightier than the sword, but with the electronic revolution, one reckless blog post or online comment can undermine a well-researched news story, regardless of where the truth lies.

Journalism is a set of skills—writing, of course, but also digging through records, reading people, observing for detail, asking the right questions. These skills grow with experience, but smaller newspapers are built on the backs of young, poorly paid reporters proving their worth so they can go make a decent salary at bigger papers. This is the economic model, and the employers know it. I was profoundly blessed to carry out a Christian vocation and hold on to a job in an environment where a young reporter like me could be replaced like a spare part. Even those with years of institutional knowledge were targets in the early rounds of layoffs and buyouts that scarred the industry in the new millennium. Advertisers generally don't scream for more spirituality in the newspaper, and religion writers were some of the first to go. I knew I had to make myself useful in other ways and also try not to offend people with my writing on faith. I tried to cover my bases: a Greek Orthodox priest on the real St. Nicholas, a Hannukah party at the local synagogue, a Muslim scholar explaining her peaceful religion post-9/11. I don't think I understood the risks Lars and I were taking by putting so much religion in the *Herald*, but it was what I felt called to do.

In the spring of 2002, the Powerball jackpot got really big. I don't remember how big, exactly—tens of millions, one of those numbers that gets co-workers and family members pooling their money to buy reams of tickets. I went to the liquor store to interview people about their winning dreams: paying off mortgages, early retirement, fancy cars. This one woman had a gleam in her eye and told me I should play too. She made me think of 1 Peter 3:15, a Bible verse I had memorized as a kid: "Be ready always to give an answer to every man that asketh you a reason of the hope that is in you." She was an evangelist, with a prosperity gospel stripped of religious pretense but full of religious hope for the pearly gates, the streets of gold, and the diamond sea, courtesy of the New Hampshire Lottery Commission. I just *had* to write a column about it. My essential point: Why was it culturally acceptable to proselytize with that kind of irrational hope, but talking about the sort of religious faith that had sustained people for thousands of years was taboo? Our Sunday editor, a long-haired, laid back hippie sort of guy, put it on the front of the weekend opinion section, with a rainbow descending from heaven into a pot of gold.

A few days later, our new executive editor gruffly asked when I had had time to write that; I told him I had just squeezed it in; I was on salary by then, working ten-hour days, so I didn't usually have to account for my time, just did what needed done. Not long after that, he called me into his office.

"Are you a born-again?" he asked me.

"It depends what you mean by that," I said.

He wasn't asking the reason for the hope that was in me. He was trying to figure out if I was a loose cannon that would make trouble for him. Someone claiming to represent a coalition of readers had written to our publisher complaining that, ever since I had arrived in Portsmouth, I had been trying to push religion on the city. I was a marked man.

Lars backed me up. Here was a man professing no faith, but fostering a developmentally disabled son with his Jewish wife, living the gospel of sacrificial love, and supporting me, just a kid, in my dubious vocation of seeking deep truth as a daily newspaper reporter. I censored myself more carefully, but within a few months, Lars asked if I wanted to start writing a weekly column on religion. Maybe it was a way for both of us to keep God in the paper, but to corral the Creator in a page-two slot that people could easily ignore if they wanted. I wrote mostly about being a young father: how our unplanned pregnancy yielded a precious gift; how to practice nonviolence in a world that threatened my baby girl; how I tried to ride the bus, instead of drive, to lessen the need to make war on oil-rich countries so perhaps Aurora might live in a world of peace one day.

Writing a column can be a very lonely endeavor; you put yourself out there, open to personal criticism, and never get much feedback. You don't really know what people think. Am I just full of hot air? One time I wrote about the military recruitment slogan "An Army of One," and how it preyed on young men's desires to be heroes without educating them on what they were really getting into.

"[That column] was written by an individual too cowardly to serve in the armed forces of the United States military. Someone not man enough to serve his country in defense of all that America stands for, as well as family and friends," a retired Army major wrote to me. "Your picture depicted that image and compounded my initial feelings."

And he was right: I barely looked my age at twenty-six—not man enough for much of anything, yet a father, an editor, a spiritual sage.

"Your article is an insult to our country and to all of our military personnel in general," he wrote. "Were it not for the news media and so many of their distorted articles and juvenile stories, perhaps the military would not have to advertise as heavily as they do."

This was the sort of criticism you just had to let roll off your back, unless it started to pile up. More important was what my superiors thought. Our publisher, who had agreed to promote me but also had his eye on me because of the reader complaints, never said much about my columns. Just one time, he complimented a piece I wrote about a local church working with City Hall to waive a zoning rule so they could build an apartment for their new youth pastor, who otherwise couldn't afford to live in Portsmouth. That column touched on the city's main problem—high housing prices—and took readers inside the nuts and bolts of municipal zoning. Researching for that column, I told the church's pastor that I had once thought about becoming a youth pastor myself.

"If God wants you to serve, he'll never leave you alone until you do it," he warned me.

He was Assemblies of God, a voice from my fundamentalist past. God only called people to the pulpit or the mission field; everyone else was just making a living. The pastor might have been easy to ignore, except I knew he was right. God hadn't left me alone. God kept calling me to write about the moral challenges of today's world: the hypocrisy of American immigration laws, the hubris of pyrotechnics after a deadly Rhode Island nightclub fire, the danger of posting the Ten Commandments in a public courthouse. An old Anglican on the copy desk, retired from the managing editor's chair, often edited the column and told me I'd wind up in the pastor's study one day.

I'd already been accepted to Duke Divinity School and even had a telephone conversation with Hauerwas, a Texas Methodist who without knowing what church I attended had suggested an Episcopal church near Durham if I decided to go down there. That seemed like a sign. Lily, Aurora, and I went down to visit. We liked North Carolina. You had the beach, the mountains, and charming little college towns that offered the education and culture of New England without the cold weather.

I couldn't get an interview with *The News & Observer*, the big, well-respected newspaper in Raleigh. But I did interview with some smaller papers and got an offer from one in Burlington, about half an hour west of Durham and what looked like another opportunity in Wilmington on the coast, about two and a half hours away. Wilmington, North Carolina's historic port city, reminded us of Portsmouth, but commuting to Durham for class even once a week seemed ridiculous after we had actually tried out the drive. And the pay in Burlington wasn't going to leave any money for tuition, so what was the point? We decided to stay in Portsmouth, for the moment.

Soon after I'd gotten promoted, Mom had found us a little condo in Portsmouth. We could afford it with my higher salary and the rental income from the Somersworth duplex. Lily complained about neighbors leaving trash in the hallways and the dim lighting from windows positioned just above the dirt outside our basement unit. She wanted a house. But at least I could get to work in five minutes or sneak home for lunch.

Sometimes late at night, I'd drive downtown to St. John's. The sexton lived across the street. He'd unlock the doors, check the nave and the balcony for homeless guys who'd occasionally try to sleep there, and lock me inside for safety. I'd kneel near the cabinet where the wafers and wine were kept. I'd begun meeting with a priest in Concord, a spiritual director who was helping me discern whether I was called as an Episcopal priest. He'd suggested praying near the consecrated host for guidance.

After a few months, we still weren't sure I was called to the Anglican priesthood. If that had been clear, I might have started thinking about Gordon-Conwell again, or the Episcopal Divinity School in Cambridge, Massachusetts. But where I felt called was Duke—a silly sort of calling, no? Why would God call someone to a particular school? Wasn't it the work *afterward* that mattered?

Maybe not. It might have been that the vocation I was carving out was that of *truth-seeker*. Doubtless, seeking truth is one of the tasks of a pastor, and maybe that's why my sense of call was so confusing. I was a young man earnestly trying to seek out the best way to live and teach it to others. That's what my friends had said about me at my bachelor party. One of them called me a "true philosopher." Heck, my column was called "Cereal Box Philosophy," a nod to that Edie Brickell song—"Philosophy is the talk on a cereal box"—a self-deprecating poke at my ponderous personality. When I showed up at a friend's wedding talking about riding buses and wanting a Toyota Prius to lower my carbon footprint, one of my Cedarville friends said I had gone back to New Hampshire and become a liberal.

I was just trying to figure out what God wanted from me—from all of us. For the moment, I had to figure it out within the context of newspaper writing, which was an uphill battle. As Marxist-turned-Catholic journalist Dorothy Day wrote,

Life on a newspaper, whether radical or conservative, makes one lose all sense of perspective at the time. You are carried along in a world of events, writing, reporting, with no time at all for thought or reflection. . . . It was impossible to suffer long over the tragedies which took place every day. One was too close to them to have perspective. They happened too continuously. They weighed on you, gave you a still and subdued feeling, but the very fact that you were continually busy left you no time to brood.

But brooding was in my nature. Do you know people like that? Maybe if I went to seminary I could begin to understand something about life, maybe eventually share some wisdom through sermons, or magazine articles, or books, or the songs I'd started writing for my family band. I wanted to mine what little experience I had on this planet for whatever eternal truth might be buried in it. Could I discern God's movement in the mundane happenings of human existence?

I knew I had to start writing my own songs after a party at a friend's house where we played folk and rock from the sixties and seventies because that's what Dad knew. I was singing lead vocals on a Led Zeppelin medley, and afterwards I was exhausted. Zep put muscle in their music like no one ever had before, and I had to respect them. But only God knows what Robert Plant was trying to say. I love *Lord of the Rings* as much as the next guy, yet it's hard to get much out of a song about the Land of Mordor. I wanted to sing words I had actually lived, to tell truths I had felt in my bones. I didn't want to write so many newspaper stories I didn't care about—to put in long days of stressful work trying to explain how different tax reform proposals would affect readers' pocketbooks, for example. Newspapers cover the political economy of scarcity, the zero-sum game where everyone has to fight for their share. I wanted to write and sing and maybe preach about the political economy of love, where people share what's theirs. We are so much more than taxpayers. We were put on earth for love, and love's war against this cruel world is the source material for humanity's best stories. Still, I had to think like a taxpayer battling other taxpayers, because that was my job.

Duke faculty wrote compellingly about that other economy, that peaceable kingdom. I didn't know if they'd make me a good Episcopal priest. In fact, I was frustrated to learn that most dioceses required candidates for ministry to study at least one out of three years at an Episcopal seminary, which Duke was not. I worried about having to move my family multiple times, just to get ordained. But there was something special going on at Duke, and I wanted to be part of it. Dr. Mike Lopez, one of my favorite professors at Cedarville, had said he would want to do the same thing if he was starting his career at this moment in time. Men and women were going from all over the U.S. to "get their marching orders from Hauerwas." Even *Time* magazine had named him America's Best Theologian. Duke was speaking peace in a time of great violence. The faculty's books seemed like a trail of breadcrumbs, leading me on a path toward truth, and I wanted to follow it.

My spiritual director and I decided that maybe Duke would help me discern how to be a better Christian journalist—how to tell stories as if God exists. From a practical standpoint, that didn't make much sense. If anything, I probably needed to be less thoughtful about what I was doing, not more—to just tell people what was happening at City Hall and leave it at that. That might have been my job, but it wasn't my calling. To pursue my calling, I had to seek truth, maybe at seminary, but wherever I could find it.

And so I kept at it. When a group of citizens petitioned the City Council to pass a resolution against the war in Iraq, I covered it closely. As weeks passed and the council refused to vote on the issue, I called them out on it. My final story noted the mayor had cut the time for the anti-war protesters to speak at a council meeting and silenced their applause, which she hadn't done with the pro-war speakers. One council member predicted these activists would mistreat returning veterans like they had during the Vietnam war. "Dozens turned out on both sides of the war debate, but the City Council's unanimous vote against a peace resolution Monday night did not reflect that diversity," I wrote. "From the beginning, the odds seemed stacked against those sponsoring an anti-war resolution."

The mayor, typically a good sport and a reliable source for me, wrote a letter to the editor, complaining about my bias. I'd been opining against the war in my column, she said, so how could the council have gotten a fair shake in rejecting the resolution? Without a doubt, she was right. As someone who opposed the war, I was more likely to notice and report facts revealing the sort of attitudes that allowed us to go to war in the first place: anger, vengeance, blind loyalty, or plain old complacency. "Do not defame our president during a time of war," one Republican councilwoman had said. The council revealed its bias against the anti-war crowd and for quiet submission to the war machine. To ignore those facts, as another reporter might have done, would have revealed other biases: toward appeasing readers in a Navy town or appearing patriotic, for example.

There was no use in arguing. When someone accuses you of bias, it generally means only one thing: They disagree with you. What was more important, I thought, was what this meant for my sense of calling. Did it make any sense to publicize my religious and ethical convictions in a regular column and then also expect readers to trust me as a news source in a medium operating on the myth of objectivity? Well, yes, that sort of honesty would be a great thing for the profession. It's how newspapers in America used to work and those in Europe still do. Each publication aligns with a particular ideology or political party. But that's not the social contract American newspapers make. We're supposed to keep our opinions to ourselves. This, of course, is completely unrealistic. We're human. We exercise our biases every day in choosing which stories matter and how to present them. Normally, those biases remain opaque and don't really matter. Most reporters, including me, don't have well-formed opinions on the things we cover every day. The world is just too complex, and we struggle just to figure out what's going on and explain it. Our biases are there everyday, but they rarely come to light.

But every now and then they do, and when they do, because of the myth of objectivity, it puts you on the defensive. That's not a good place to be, and I began to wonder whether I wanted to be columnist. I didn't mind unveiling my own personal search for truth for others to see. I just wasn't sure it was compatible with storytelling as constrained within the bounds of modern American journalism. I thought the facts were more powerful than any meaning I might find in them. I didn't mind hiding behind the myth—removing my photo from page two, letting people ignore my byline—so readers would experience life through the eyes and ears of the people I wrote about, rather than myself. The Bible talks about "entertaining angels unaware" and about the Christ hidden in the "the least of these." I wanted to find and bear witness to the truth and beauty in the world without always naming "God." If writing a column might prevent readers from trusting me to do that, I didn't want to risk it.

A few months earlier, I had written stories about Sam Tombarelli, a Portsmouth High School history teacher who had been leading a team of teenaged volunteers into the local shelter to tutor homeless children after school. Sam had grown up Catholic and now worshiped in a large evangelical church. His Christian faith led him to care for poor kids and to try and teach altruism to his high-school students. In our interview, Sam and I talked a lot about Jesus, and I ended one story like this:

> "If Jesus were in Portsmouth today, he'd go to Crossroads House," Sam said, revealing his deep faith. He's not interested in proselytizing, he said, but in helping kids experience God in giving.
>
> "You lead by serving and by helping other people who are less fortunate," Sam said.

Sam later told me some of his students had questioned him about those quotes, and the direct reference to Jesus had done him more harm than good: He was trying to show love to these kids, and if they thought he was just out to convert them, they wouldn't trust him.

It was something to think about, not only for my sources like Sam, but also for myself.

7

I Will Sing for the Meek

During our last two years in high school, Mike had convinced me that God wouldn't strike me dead for listening to Christian Contemporary Music. Remember that Bible camp sermon against Amy Grant? Well, our Christian high school was more gracious, but we still tended to brand things and people as either good or bad.

There was this kid John Z who came to Calvary just for our senior year. He was chubby and socially awkward and lived in a room at a hotel where his mom was a housekeeper. Kids tended to make fun of him. Anyway, our senior class had to put together a year-end chapel service, and John Z wanted to play his electric bass guitar for Michael W. Smith's "Friends (Are Friends Forever)" or some such song. Coach, our class advisor, told him no because we couldn't have rock instruments in the chapel. Here was an opportunity to show love to an outsider, and our school, though it was named for the hill where Jesus sacrificed his own life for the world, blew its chance in the name of not being "of the world." I guess the teachers thought they were protecting us, but it just made John feel like even more of a weirdo. Jesus made wine and hung out with prostitutes, but we couldn't handle a bass guitar?

So listening to CCM, grooving as it did over the syncopated rhythms of the bass guitar, constituted more of a rebellious act than you can possibly imagine. What made music OK, in the eyes of the more enlightened fundamentalists I found at Cedarville, was that it had words about Jesus. Bono was in his ironically devilish Macphisto phase, so U2 was off-limits. In the early nineties, I went for bands like Third Day (named, of course, for Easter) because they sounded like Hootie and the Blowfish on one album and Pearl Jam on the next; or a singer like Jennifer Knapp, because she sounded like Natalie Merchant. Nobody sounded like The Cranberries, but I browbeat my high-school girlfriend into not listening to them, so she found CCM's Smalltown Poets, who sounded like Gin Blossoms.

Even better were bands like Jars of Clay and Sixpence None the Richer, who were creating original sounds not exactly like anyone else and getting mainstream radio airplay. Jars of Clay had layered folk music atop electronic beats, and you couldn't say they sounded just like anyone else, and at the beginning, before they became some of CCM's elder statesmen, listening to something different was important if you were an evangelical kid who needed to feel superior to other evangelical kids. They were the sort of "Roaring Lambs" that Emmy-winning TV producer Bob Briner wrote about during my senior year of high school: Christians who "infiltrate and make an impact on their workplace and world with their faith."

In his book, Briner provides a list of yes-or-no questions to gauge a reader's roar. One of those asks, do "I consider careers in the arts, journalism, literature, film, and television to be as important for the kingdom as pastoral ministry, or foreign missions?" I'd get revved up hearing Jars' song "Flood" on Boston's WXRV 92.5 The River while I worked my summer job behind the butcher counter at Yankee Food Market in Raymond, New Hampshire. Millions of non-Christians were hearing frontman Dan Haseltine sing of God's "casting down all waves of sin and guilt that overthrow me." This lamb was roaring! God had to be in that, right? My first-ever rock concert was Jars of Clay at Mama Kin Music Hall, a nightclub owned by the members of Aerosmith just outside Fenway Park in Boston. When they played "Flood," the acoustic power chords, thundering bass rhythm, and gang vocals got so loud I had to block my ears, and I felt a cold breeze that built with the volume. I wasn't sure if it was the Holy Spirit or the Devil or the kick drum or just some mysterious force of nature, but it was rock 'n' roll, baby! They even had a secular opener, Duncan Sheik, with his big hit "Barely Breathing." So they were, you know, relevant.

Briner's book came out just months before I enrolled at Cedarville, and "Roaring Lambs" was precisely what my school, like so many evangelical universities, was preparing us to be. Our faculty emphasized themes like "excellence" and "the integration of faith and learning." We aimed to gain cultural power by doing our jobs really well and using our positions of influence to point people to Jesus. We'd have doctors and lawyers and politicians come to the chapel stage and tell us how they were doing just that.

I Will Sing for the Meek

At the end of my junior year, I won the first-annual Cal Thomas Scholarship for my potential to "impact the media for Christ." Thank God, because I needed the $2,500 to pay my senior tuition. But it didn't feel quite right. I wasn't particularly familiar with Thomas's body of work, but I knew he was a "conservative" pundit, and that probably meant he said not very nice things about gays, abortive mothers, divorcees, Muslims, and socialists. Wasn't there another model for a young Christian journalist? To be a roaring lamb, did you have to shout and stomp and wring your hands about the decline of American values?

I didn't find a model in journalism. I found it in Contemporary Christian Music. Yeah, I know. *Eeeek!* But it's true.

> I wonder how this world would be
> if I was never here
> to drive this bus around
> from Ashbury to Main
> I'm just a bus driver,
> And what do I know?
> —"Bus Driver," Caedmon's Call

My friend Chris discovered Caedmon's Call in the spring of my sophomore year at Cedarville. Their self-titled major-label debut with Warner Brothers seemed to fit the "Roaring Lambs" model. Producer Don McCollister had also recorded secular stars like the Indigo Girls, Shawn Mullins, and Sister Hazel. Caedmon's had college radio credibility, and they were making a brand of aggressive folk rock I hadn't heard before, especially not in Christian music. They had three lead singers with majestic harmonies, a three-man rhythm section, and a rootsy, acoustic vibe to balance the slick production expected from CCM. Caedmon was a seventh-century saint who learned to sing through a supernatural vision; we were evangelical Protestants who traced our theology and practice back to the nineteenth or maybe the sixteenth century, so there was something subversive about following a band named for a medieval Catholic saint.

Caedmon's Call had built its audience touring secular college campuses, which seemed like honest dues paying compared to bands who had managed to get a hit song played on the radio. This sort of indie, DIY ethic resonated with my evolving faith. Hadn't the Apostle Paul written something about "power made perfect in weakness"? One of their songwriters, Derek Webb, was tackling topics that wouldn't play very well from the pulpits I'd sat under: suicide, eating disorders, the dignity of bus drivers—could a bus driver be a "roaring lamb" or did you need a stage and radio airplay? Our lives on earth really matter to God, Derek seemed to be saying, even if they're filled with suffering, disappointment, and crummy jobs. "How can I preserve and light the way for a world that I can't admit I'm in?" he wrote on "Standing Up For Nothing," the first openly political song I'd heard from a contemporary Christian artist.

By the time Chris and I got back to Cedarville in September 1997, we still hadn't seen Caedmon's live. That summer, I'd driven nine hours from New Hampshire to the Kingdom Bound Festival near Buffalo, New York, only to find out they'd canceled their set. I knew they'd be playing that fall at Calvin College, about half a day's drive from Cedarville. Neither Chris nor I had a car. Then, on Tuesday, four days before showtime, Chris hit the jackpot. Few people had heard of a listserv in those days, and I was a Luddite who didn't know how to reformat a mini-disk, so I was shocked to hear he'd been reading a daily email compilation and found a girl driving home to western Michigan for the weekend and looking for riders to help with gas money.

She dropped us off in the parking lot of Calvin Theological Seminary at the edge of campus around 7 p.m. on Friday night, twenty-four hours before the show. Where were we going to sleep that night? Chris, with his last name Pittenturf, had grown up north of Detroit and two years earlier had attended this Dutch Reformed school as a freshman. He had stories about the dorm room shrines built of candles and empty beer bottles that never would have got past us RAs at Cedarville. We wandered around the all but deserted campus in search of a student directory, hoping we might find some of Chris's old friends. After an hour, we got into a dorm with a desk clerk on duty. She said we could stay in her room if the rules would have allowed it. She dialed us up a pizza and tried to convince some guys passing through the lounge to take us in. Finally, she found a campus phone book. It was last year's, but Chris called the number listed for his friend Conrad. No one answered. We ate our pizza and played cards with the girl at the desk. Chris tried again. Someone picked up. He asked for Conrad. *He still lived there!* He and his roomies were from Vancouver. They had a Canucks hockey game to watch that night at a bar—*at a bar!* We Cedarvillains weren't allowed at businesses where "the main focus of the activity" was alcohol. Restaurants like Applebee's were OK, but not the places where they sold only booze and you might go just to watch a game, shoot pool, or hear a band.

Conrad couldn't pick us up till 2 a.m., so Chris and I snuck into another dorm to play ping pong. We sprawled out in the middle of a soccer field, talking about girls. We laughed at the couple making out in plain sight through a backlit dormitory window. We debated the ethics of swiping one of the soon-to-be outdated Caedmon's Call posters that littered campus bulletin boards, and eventually I did it.

The next morning, Conrad took us to a dim tavern in an industrial park for a greasy breakfast. It felt good to eat at a place like that without worrying if anyone from Cedarville would see us. I wasn't drinking; what did they care? I was my own man, and I was here to see my favorite band. Conrad drove us back to campus that night, with his and his roommate's student IDs so we could get into the show for $2 instead of $10.

The band did not disappoint. I loved how intense Derek's face looked, his eyebrows climbing toward his shaved head as he reached for the high notes, his upper cheeks rising and expanding to resonate his voice. Garret Buell, the percussionist, didn't smile, not once; he was locked in. Cliff, the other guitar player, was barefoot on the old Persian rugs the band hauled on tour. Derek mumbled and stuttered through his song introductions. They broke into a blues jam on the praise chorus "I Waited," with Derek bellowing out raspy vocals, his seldom seen electric guitar screaming improvised riffs. An embarrassed Danielle, the third singer, glared at her boyfriend, Cliff, when he announced they would soon wed.

The highlight was near the beginning, when they sang one of their favorite cover tunes, Rich Mullins's "I Will Sing." Mullins was a key mentor to Caedmon's Call, and then he died in a car wreck only days before this concert at Calvin. The three vocalists soared in their *a capella* version of the song:

> I will sing for the meek
> For those who pray with their very lives for peace
> Though they're in chains for a higher call
> Their mourning will change into laughter when the nations fall
> In spirit poor, in mercy rich
> They hunger for Your righteousness
> Their hearts refined in the purity
> Lord, let me shine for them
> Lord, let me sing

It was like Mullins had risen from the dead. These were Messianic lyrics, rendered in youthful energy, recalling the Sermon on the Mount or Mary's *Magnificat*. Christ had come to bring good news to the poor, and Mullins was trying to follow him. Rich didn't die because of his faith, so you probably can't call him a martyr. But the word simply means "witness," and in creating songs that shine for the meek, the peacemakers, the prisoners, and poor in spirit, Mullins's witness outlived his body. Isn't that what makes a martyr? Martyr or not, his words reframed for me the text of Romans 10, which I had taken as a specific pastoral call on my life two years earlier: "How beautiful are the feet of those who bring good news!" These words had originally come from chapter 52 in Isaiah, the same prophet who would promise the Messiah nine chapters later, in a passage that Jesus would recite in announcing his ministry in the Jerusalem temple:

> The Spirit of the Sovereign LORD is on me,
> because the LORD has anointed me to preach good news to the poor.
> He has sent me to bind up the brokenhearted,
> to proclaim freedom for the captives,
> and release from darkness for the prisoners,
> to proclaim the year of the LORD's favor
> and the day of vengeance of our God,
> to comfort all who mourn, and provide for those who grieve in Zion—
> to bestow on them a crown of beauty instead of ashes,
> the oil of gladness instead of mourning,
> and a garment of praise instead of a spirit of despair.

This was the good news Jesus delivered. He didn't need "roaring lambs" to gain cultural power so we could complain about the liberals and the welfare queens, the environmentalists and the peaceniks, as I had been taught to do. If Jesus had any use for earthly power, it was to give it away for those who didn't have any. You might argue that Jesus roared a lion's roar when he threw the moneychangers from the temple. But that was the vulnerable cry of the poor, oppressed by the first-century TV preachers getting rich off others' longing for God. Like so many of Jesus's prophetic acts, this one would help to ensure his victimhood. Far from an act of social change, it was more like a suicide mission.

And if I was honest with myself, this was a calling both more faithful and closer at hand than the ambition of the roaring lamb. To preach good news to the poor is to preach good news to myself. It is to stand with my neighbors, not to fight against them in a Culture War. Which of us has not felt poor, like something was lacking in body or spirit? Who has not been

I Will Sing for the Meek

heartbroken by a lover, a parent, a sibling, a boss, a friend? Who has never felt trapped, like every option was a bad one? Living in darkness: sadness, anger, injustice, depression, grief, despair? Didn't that cover everyone, big sinners or small? Who doesn't need rescuing from such things? You mean Jesus brought good news for us? You mean we get freedom, communion, comfort, provision, beauty, "the Lord's favor"? Is this what I was called to announce? What we were all called to announce? As a word guy, I love the King James English:

> How beautiful upon the mountains are the feet of him
> that bringeth good tidings, that publisheth peace;
> that bringeth good tidings of good, that publisheth salvation;
> that saith unto Zion, Thy God reigneth!
> Thy watchmen shall lift up the voice;
> with the voice together shall they sing:
> for they shall see eye to eye, when the LORD shall bring again Zion.
> Break forth into joy, sing together, ye waste places of Jerusalem:
> for the LORD hath comforted his people, he hath redeemed Jerusalem.
> The LORD hath made bare his holy arm in the eyes of all the nations;
> and all the ends of the earth shall see the salvation of our God.
> (Isa 52:7–10)

Isaiah brought new (or is it old?) meaning to the saying, "Publish or perish!" His words themselves offer a kind of salvation: Tell this story, and it shall be so! Better yet, it *is* so, whether you believe it or not! *All the ends of the earth shall see the salvation of our God!* Now tell the world! I had been singing in choirs for years and was learning to play bass, but at this point I heard my main calling as a pastor or writer. No matter: Whatever power my words would one day have, by pulpit or pen or song, this I knew: I should write or preach or sing for the meek, the hungry, those who pray for peace.

> Like all the true believers I am truly
> skeptical of all that I have said.
> —"The World Can Wait," Over the Rhine

If you went to Cedarville, the place to see Over the Rhine was Canal Street Tavern, a little listening room just outside Dayton's Oregon District, a collection of nightclubs along East Fifth Street, the sort of place I'd been taught to avoid. We'd drive thirty miles from the cornfields of Greene

This Littler Light

County into downtown Dayton. We'd park in a nearby lot and join the line that had formed outside the bar by 6 p.m. though the doors wouldn't open for two more hours.

Canal Street wasn't a big place—there wasn't a bad seat in the house—but you wanted to sit up close because there was love on that stage, not just in the songs, but in a subtle banter often missed by those sitting back by the bar, separated from the stage by a roomful of shadowy heads. Husband and wife songwriting team Linford Detweiler and Karin Bergquist had developed a hospitality that gave them the right to talk about things a little more deeply than most people would allow on a Saturday night. When you listened to Over the Rhine, the closer you sat, the more it felt like you were sitting around with friends rather than watching a performance. It was like they'd never played those songs for anyone else, like the music belonged as much to you as it did to them. The musical mastery never overshadowed OTR's ability to connect with an audience, making new friends and gathering with old ones in a tavern that became their living room, if only for two or three nights a year. This wasn't lost on Linford, who once wrote, "We hope anyone who hears these songs will find some fresh language and maybe a soundtrack of sorts for the stories we're all writing everyday with our lives, whether or not we ever pick up a pen."

Karin could take Linford's lyrics, lasso my neck and lift me right out of my seat, hovering on a cloud of relentless passion on "Faithfully Dangerous." When I should crash to the floor under the weight of her sadness in "Poughkeepsie," I'd ride to safety on her angel chorus. The intimate chemistry of the couple always came through on the *Besides* tune "Bothered" as Linford's rhythmic keyboard threatened to take center stage, only to give way to Karin's mesquite melody: "Your fire burns me like a favorite song, a song I should have known all along / I feel you move like smoke in my eyes, and that is why—don't be bothered by the fears." This give-and-take was at its playful best in "Jack's Valentine," as Linford, the occasional beat poet, spoke his lyrics, which never quite matched the CD jacket, while Karin skat-sang in between, showing just what a vocal gymnast she could be.

OTR had a way of phrasing things, forcing me to reconsider what I took for granted. At first I heard "I'm Happy with Myself," the first track on their early album *Eve*, as an arrogant anthem of American individualism, like Karin was asserting her independence from social constraints, prizing her own self-esteem above peace with others. I judged a book by its cover, as though the title signified a self-absorbed sort of subversion, one that flew in the face of the OTR I knew. Eventually, though, I heard the song differently: It invited me to freedom from people-pleasing. Karin reminded me to be humble enough to be whoever I turned out to be. "I'm happy with myself / And I don't have what it takes to please you."

In college, we were still learning how to be ourselves: Christians, unafraid of the world, thinking we might have some good news to offer it and yet still curious about what it might teach us, as though Christ our Incarnate Redeemer and Christ the Creator of this world of beauty and violence were one and the same. Linford and Karin were role models. It was funny to hear people compare Over the Rhine to 10,000 Maniacs, in the way that evangelicals would often link a Christian band to a successful secular band, to show how *relevant* they were. For all we knew, 10,000 Maniacs might as well have been a literal legion of headbangers, smashing guitars, starting riots and orgies, and getting kids hooked on crack. (Someone should really calm that Natalie Merchant down.)

That's how we had learned to imagine bar bands. OTR threw off our categories, by playing in tiny bars instead of churches. They weren't really CCM, but they weren't roaring lambs either. They weren't feeding us simple biblical truth, but they weren't making the gospel palatable for mass media either. They expressed thoughts about God in fear and trembling, inviting believers and nonbelievers into a conversation—one that struck fear into those who thought they already had all the answers. For a band to play at a place like Canal Street, in the fundamentalist imagination, they must be up to no good. But when I listened to OTR's song "All I Need Is Everything," I heard an artful message about grace that wouldn't have been out of place in our daily college chapel services.

> Slow down. Hold still. It's not as if it's a matter of will.
> Someone's circling.
> Someone's moving a little lower than the angels.
> This voice calling me to you:
> It's just barely coming through. Still, I clearly hear my name.
> I've been fingering the flame like tomorrow's martyr.
> It gets harder to believe.
> All I need is everything. Inside, outside, feel new skin.
> All I need is everything. Feel the slip and the grip of grace again.

In a very real sense, we went to Canal Street Tavern to worship, and the repurposed pew seating only magnified the metaphor. We could transcend our terrestrial toil through the gift of music, a music whose beauty pointed the way to something beyond ourselves and beyond even the musicians who created it.

Years later, I would discover there are churches who do use Over the Rhine's music in worship. But the Cedarville deans were never able to see beyond the "appearance of evil" to the beautiful treasures that lay within. They didn't associate a place like Canal Street with anything but tobacco, drugs, and alcohol. Needless to say, we didn't publicize the OTR concerts on campus any more than the band did, telling only the right people at the right time. Our shroud of secrecy couldn't last forever, though.

In the spring of my junior year, 1998, I got back to my dorm room to find a surprising message on my answering machine. It was Long-Haired Lover Boy, the guy who had tried to seduce my crush Heloise a few months earlier, and he needed my help. His alcohol consumption was the stuff of legend. The deans knew about his partying, but could never quite catch him in the act and follow through with the mandatory expulsion. Finally, his drinking had caught up with him, but in an unexpected way.

He explained to my answering machine that he and a group of friends had gone to a local bar, W. O. Wright's, named for the flying brothers Wilber and Orville, to see a band of Cedarville grads, called One Tree Hill for the U2 song. Lover Boy's story was that he had not been drinking, but one of his companions had gotten drunk, gotten caught, and gotten expelled, and not before she'd ratted out everyone else who had been at the bar. Lover Boy was also on his way out, unless an appeals board made up of faculty and students could convince the deans otherwise. He couldn't expect much mercy, since he had made a college career of defying authority, but he was asking for my help, so I had to think about it.

Of course, the defendant did not fail to point out that I, an RA and junior class chaplain, as well as other student leaders like the student body vice president, was a big OTR fan and didn't miss a show at Canal Street. I was just busy enough with studies and other responsibilities not to feel too bad about ignoring Lover Boy's recorded message. Two weeks later, he left me another one saying this was Judgment Day.

I tag-teamed with a couple of my favorite trouble-making professors in telling the board that the rulebook was very unclear on the matter and that I myself had gone to bars to see bands play, arguing that music was "the main focus of the activity." Carl Ruby, the dean responsible for off-campus students, had been pulling for Lover Boy throughout the process. Whenever Dean Ruby and I would pass each other on campus after my appearance at the disciplinary hearing, he'd smile and call me "the renegade RA." Relations with my boss were less friendly, as the Dean of Men told me that I could not serve as resident director in charge of my whole dorm

I Will Sing for the Meek

the next year because he couldn't have an employee who would ambush him in a disciplinary hearing. This stung, because I had put in two years as an RA in Bethel Hall, and I had lived there longer than the current RD, a carpetbagger who was one of the few to transfer from another dorm and take charge of Bethel, which had a long history of internal promotion. Lover Boy got a three-day suspension, and I got labeled a subversive—all in a day's work.

Should I have been proud of what I'd done? Was this singing for the meek? The truth is, I had no idea what I was doing. I had stalled in agreeing to help because I wasn't so sure Lover Boy shouldn't have been expelled. Let's face it: They weren't kicking him out for going to a bar to see his friends play music. Years of trespasses were coming home to roost. A few months later he got his girlfriend pregnant, and neither one could return to school the following year. I blamed myself for this, thinking that maybe if he had gone home, she wouldn't have had to drop out of school to care for a baby, and he might have straightened up, which, to be fair, was the deans' goal all along. But in time they would end up with their degrees and married with a flock of children. What could Cedarville have given them that they didn't have? The truth is, I had no idea what would happen to me or to Lover Boy if I spoke up. All I knew was I couldn't let him pay the price for a crime I'd also committed. I had to help the rule-makers see that life was messier than they wanted it to be, and they shouldn't punish him for the mess they had made worse with their vague rules. That might have been an arrogant validation for my choice that made trouble for so many different people. I'd heard rumors, but I didn't know Lover Boy's history like my bosses did. I didn't know what was best for him. I didn't even know what was best for me. I didn't have any answers, but I had to speak, nonetheless.

A couple of years later, after I had graduated and left Ohio, Over the Rhine put out *Films for Radio*. The album opened with Karin's desperate wail, "The World Can Wait." The lyrics are full of fear: What if we've got this all wrong? What if we're selling the world a false gospel?

> Tomorrow, I can't imagine.
> How am I supposed to know what's yet to go down?
> Is there any one religion,
> the kind that whispers when nobody comes around?
>
> ———
>
> Haven't I said enough, haven't I said far too much?
> Haven't I done enough, haven't I done far too much?

This Littler Light

Linford and Karin had Methodist and Presbyterian and Quaker roots. They were Christian college kids, and these were dangerous questions. And, yet, looking back on my adolescence, the judgments I'd made on other people, my theological wonderings on the pages of the student newspaper, deemed heresy by a member of the Bible faculty, my ignorance of what Lover Boy really needed, hadn't I said far too much? Maybe I should just admit I don't know anything and shut the hell up!

But Over the Rhine didn't do that. For them, these doubts were part of being true believers. Holding up those lyrics were a marching drum beat, soaring harmonies, staccato strings, and Linford's plodding, persistent piano: a courageous battle song about storming God's throneroom in prayer:

> I want to drink the water from your well
> I want to tell you things I'll never tell
> The world can wait, the world can wait
> I'm wide awake, and the world can wait

Later on the disc, ripping a page straight from a Southern Baptist hymnal, the eight-minute epic "Little Blue River" suddenly turns into the old hymn sing favorite, "In the Garden," urging the listener never to separate a simple faith from honest doubt. "I seldom think of my faith in terms of statements," Linford wrote in an "Over the Rhine Statement of Faith" distributed at the Cornerstone Music Festival in Illinois. "I speak a faltering language that at best consists primarily of questions, asides, and whispered midnight prayers."

It's not as though Over the Rhine had nothing to say. Like Caedmon's Call's bus driver, Over the Rhine's next record, *Ohio*, would come to honor Appalachian coal miners and a woman in a tattered coat in a New Orleans saloon. That's saying something about who's important in the kingdom of God. Linford himself wrote that his music "speaks of a desire to know the Man of Sorrows, the Friend of Sinners." They recognized how little they knew this man, Jesus, and chose to spend their songwriting energy searching for more instead of rehashing what had already been said. "This music was my way of trying to find new ways of expressing gratitude for the sometimes frightening freedom to discover what I believed to be true," Linford continued. "As often as not, a journey of faith is a special state in which we struggle to ask the right questions, and not just a question of stating special right answers." They couldn't concoct a spiritual panacea or peddle it through the medium of music. They weren't out to change the world with some gnostic vision that rendered all previous thoughts

I Will Sing for the Meek

meaningless. Instead, they had a ravenous hunger to learn, to grow, to seek out truth in the cracks and crevices of a complicated world.

Like Over the Rhine, I didn't always know what was worth saying, but by the time I got to the newsroom, I had a career where I had to say *something*. Better to say something useful than not. There were school board or city council meetings to cover, political campaigns to decipher, and development proposals to explain, but there was also time to find stories I thought were important and pursue them. Don't we all have opportunities to stand up for the poor, the weak and the peacemakers, no matter what job we do? Lawyers and doctors can provide pro bono service. Merchants can give necessities to the needy. Craftsmen and women can fix pipes or stitching for people who can't afford a plumber or seamstress. Police officers can investigate thefts from victims who lack the voices to influence city budgets. Skilled accountants, cooks, fundraisers, and plain old go-getters can mean the difference between a nonprofit social service agency succeeding or failing. Any worker, anywhere, can befriend a friendless colleague.

One day a young dad like me telephoned the *Herald* newsroom. He'd gone to a local supermarket to buy milk and baby food for his daughter. Times were tough, and he'd dug through his seat cushions for change: three dollars and thirteen cents, to be exact. He'd even gone to the trouble to roll 150 pennies into three of those little paper sleeves, to make it easier on the store employees. But a cashier refused his coins and sent him away without his groceries.

I interviewed the young father, learning about the three jobs he worked to support his family. I confronted the store manager, who reiterated his dubious claim that 9/11 had given merchants fear about anthrax in rolled coins.

"I saw no reason to take it just because he was going to open it up in front of me," the manager told me. "I don't want to put a bunch of pennies in the drawer."

Readers from as far away as the Midwest reacted to my story, sending me donations for the young family and criticizing the supermarket's decision. The company made a public apology and reassigned the manager for retraining. I saw that my words could level the playing field and maybe beat back just a bit of the injustice that the poor suffer. I won a newswriting award from the New England Press Association. Here was worldly affirmation for a story that seemed to fulfill my Christian calling. Maybe this is what it meant to bring good news to the poor.

This Littler Light

My main reporting beat was education, and I covered the planning for a major renovation project at Portsmouth High School. Ned Raynolds, a local green building consultant, kept lobbying the school board to make the renovated building as energy efficient as possible. The board resisted because Ned's suggestions seemed too expensive and the technologies untested. Ned, who went to my church, would one day win election to the City Council, but his voice was falling on deaf ears. I covered the issue closely because it seemed like environmental stewardship was something the Creator must care about. Ned bought one of the first Honda Insights, and I started writing about opportunities to lower pollution and dependence on foreign oil by driving hybrids or riding buses. One auto dealer even let me drive one of the first Toyota Priuses. The environment was another voiceless victim I might help to protect, so I wrote stories about how bad land management and other human activity hurt ecosystems and how different agencies were working to preserve them.

A World War II POW and former Air Force pilot, school board member Charlie Vaughn wanted to open a Junior ROTC program at Portsmouth High School, and local Quakers rallied against it. I wrote a three-part series about the potential that JROTC could build students' character and the fears that it would feed the war machine. I even managed to work Jesus's admonition to "turn the other cheek" into one of my stories. The school board rejected ROTC. I won an education-writing award from the state press association because I had taken a minor school board agenda item and magnified its social, moral, and political implications.

You have to understand: These were piddly awards. I was competing against other papers below 50,000 circulation. I was a long, long way from a Pulitzer. But, you know, most baseball players don't make the majors, most doctors don't become surgeons, most musicians don't get played on commercial radio, and most journalists don't work for *The New York Times*. In short, most of us are not going to be Roaring Lambs, and God doesn't ask that from us. Still, we all have the voices to say something, and even we "bleating" lambs need to know we're hitting the right notes every now and then.

A couple of months earlier, an email in my inbox had threatened to upset the delicate balance of my work. Two girls at a local high school had been voted "Class Sweethearts" by the senior class, but the principal had banned their photo from the yearbook, saying the honor had to go to a boy and a girl. I had a sense this was a big story, and no one else knew about it. Plus, the school was in a town that we didn't normally cover, so it was a chance to swoop in and scoop our chief rivals. On the other hand, I wasn't really sure where I stood on the issue of homosexuality, which is to say, I didn't really know what I thought God thought about it. The Apostle Paul seemed to think intercourse between the same sexes was grave sin, and I generally tried to listen to Paul. But Jesus loved everyone, regardless of their sin. And I knew my immediate supervisor Lars and especially our lesbian photo editor would see it as a huge story; if anyone found out I had sat on it, I would lose credibility.

I broke the news and became a reluctant gay rights advocate. The national media soon followed, and within a day the district superintendent had overturned the principal's decision.

"We did that," Lars said.

The Phelps family from Westboro Baptist Church in Kansas came to picket the high school, holding up signs with messages such as, "God Hates Fags." If there were only two sides in this debate, I most surely wasn't on theirs. Is this what it meant to "sing for the meek, for those who pray with their very lives for peace"? Standing up for gays and lesbians? Or was that just doing my job, what was expected of me as a newspaperman in the new millennium? Whose power was I bowing to? Could I serve both God and the corporate media?

I don't know if I had ever said it out loud, but I had a lingering inerrantist thought: Wouldn't tolerance of homosexuality undermine the authority of the Bible? If I couldn't trust Paul on that, how could I trust him on anything? And didn't I need to trust him when he said God was in Christ reconciling the world to himself? Wasn't *that* pretty important? In a column a year later, I would lament how the election of Gene Robinson in our New Hampshire diocese as the first openly gay bishop in the Episcopal church was fracturing the global Anglican Communion because our African and Asian brothers and sisters couldn't stomach it. But, then, wouldn't Christ have stood up for that bishop and those girls, like he did for the adulteress who faced a stoning by the Pharisees? Even if they were "living in unrepentant sin"—and I wasn't sure of that—but even if: Shouldn't a follower of Christ try to protect their dignity and equal rights?

Like all the true believers, I was truly skeptical of all that I had said.

8

No One Said It Was Easy

One afternoon our executive editor called a staff meeting. He was the one who had asked if I was "a born again." At this meeting, he announced that an editor from our weekly sister papers was moving into the Portsmouth newsroom to become "assistant managing editor." That sounded an awful lot like my job.

I had no idea what was going on. The boss didn't bother to explain how this would affect me. I don't think Lars was at that meeting because I didn't get a chance to talk to him about it for at least another day or two. I went home that night and started to look hard for a new job. Aurora was a little over a year old, and Lily was pregnant again, another surprise.

Job hunting had been more or less constant since we'd come to New Hampshire, and that wasn't unusual. Some of my co-workers openly searched journalismjobs.com on their newsroom computers. Looking for the next job is a way of life for young, small-time journalists. In my case, if I wasn't trying to move Lily back to Kentucky or get us closer to Duke Divinity School, I was just trying to make more money so I could buy Lily the quaint, restored New England house she wanted.

There they were, tempting us everyday, with their proud peaked roofs, jutting and turning, all window dormers, gables, and tall turrets. The leaded glass in their ancient windows crinkled in the sunlight. At our tiny condo, we had to stow our gas grill out the back door, under our upstairs neighbor's balcony. We shared a picnic table in the grass with a dozen other apartments. Downtown, residents had summer parties on their wide front porches, with carved columns and bistro tables. Some of the homes had little signs telling you they dated as far back as the 1600s, not that far removed from the Pilgrims and Plymouth Rock and the First

No One Said It Was Easy

Thanksgiving. The cheapest house you could find in Portsmouth would go for $200,000, and that was a beat-up, one-story ranch from the 1960s smelling like cat pee. The houses we liked would have taken more than my whole paycheck every month, never mind the down payment—more than my entire annual salary.

I loved those old houses almost as much as Lily did, but what I really loved was walking: to City Hall to interview the police chief or look through files; to St. John's for a meeting with Father Tim; to Market Square for "man-on-the-street" interviews. I could take these walks from the *Herald* building, but not from our condo, located as it was a couple of miles down Route 1, in a commercial strip with shopping plazas, car dealers, a water fun park, busy traffic, and no sidewalks. I worked in a dense urban area, but I lived in suburbia. I had city lust. There were "ethical" reasons for it: I wanted to run into my neighbors on the street; I wanted to "reduce my carbon footprint." But I also just liked the *feel* of urban life, the energy, the people-watching, the *idea* of strolling to the Press Room Tavern for an evening drink, and doing it often enough that the bartenders knew my name. In a Thanksgiving Day column, I thanked God for our little "hobbit hole" of a basement condo, but I sure would have liked a place downtown.

When I was in junior high, Mom had gotten her dream house. All my life, we had been living in houses while Dad fixed them up, only to sell them once they were nice. Back in Brentwood, just down Highway 101 from this dream house in Candia, we had lived in a tiny two-bedroom house on a couple of acres along a busy two-lane road, with a storefront building we rented to a pizza shop and a racquetball court we rented by the hour. One time I answered a phone call from a guy wanting to schedule some court time, but he sounded just like my Uncle David, and I playfully argued about his identity until I realized this stranger did just want to book some racquetball. Cars were always pulling into the parking lot where we played, or racing by at sixty 60 miles per hour. That house backed up to a dense forest with an old logging trail where we'd go cross-country skiing in the winter or where Marco and I and friends would build forts or play war with plastic guns. "I shot you!" "No you didn't!" "Yes I did!" Before that, we'd lived at Hampton Beach, where we moved from one of four tiny cottages to the next, to the next, to the next, arranged in a ring on the same little plot of land, so Dad could rent out or sell each one as it was finished. In one cabin, Marco and I shared a loft above my parents' bedroom, not even tall enough for us to stand up. We were a block from the beach and two blocks from a general store that sold baseball cards and submarine sandwiches. By the end of the first summer, they'd learned to make my ham-and-cheese hoagies with no mayo.

Mom's farmhouse in Candia was better, though. It had four bedrooms with a family room *and* a living room with a giant, black, coal-burning stove; in winter, I'd lie next to it on the new teal carpet, reading Tolkien. We had a barn with a second floor where I could climb up and hide out. We lived two doors down from a country store that sold not only baseball cards but Swedish fish and Sour Patch Kids for a penny! Our friend from church, Joey, lived on our same road. We could walk to his house and play Baseball Stars or Super Tecmo Bowl on his Nintendo. And right next door was a horse farm with a big sand track where we played football. We had a basketball hoop in our driveway, and the backyard was the perfect size for a wiffleball field—a real home run fence, not too close and not too far. There, Dad also built our first swing set, which I used as a goal to practice my soccer shot, and a back deck with a gas grill. He and Mom had tiled their bathroom floor with these tiny, meticulous, one-inch turquoise squares. Dad also built a future "master bedroom" out in part of the attached barn, where his brother Eddie was staying so Mom and Dad could try to keep him sober.

A couple of years later, though, the bank foreclosed. My parents, my little brothers and sisters, and I stood in the yard as they auctioned it off. Dad wrote a song addressed to President George H. W. Bush: "I Can't Afford a Good Night's Sleep." Like a lot of people in the early nineties, Mom and Dad went bankrupt. Life felt out of control. They'd been taking us to Disneyworld and the Grand Canyon and Fenway Park in the previous few years. What was happening now? My youngest brother Steven was just a baby, and all eight of us crammed into that tiny house with the racquetball court back in Brentwood. That was when I'd had to go to public school for the first time. Maybe this was more of the Lord's chastening of those he loved. But I didn't want to be chastened, or have to beg God every day for food to feed my children, like George Mueller. When I grew up, I wanted something calmer.

> If people are fighting and hit a pregnant woman and . . . if there is serious injury, you are to take life for life, eye for eye, tooth for tooth, hand for hand, foot for foot, burn for burn, wound for wound, bruise for bruise.
>
> —Exodus 21:22–25

I was twenty-five years old, the sole breadwinner for our little family, and buying a single-family house seemed like a distant dream even with my promotion and a little extra pay for my column. I couldn't imagine Lars or the Sunday editor going anywhere, nor did I want that. Yet I needed to advance, not regress. Less than $2,500 a month wasn't going to cut it. Where would we put the new baby? I thought I could handle four of us in a two-bedroom condo, but I didn't think Lily could. With this new threat of another person competing for any chance at promotion, I searched hard for work, in North Carolina and all over New England.

Meanwhile, the weekend after our top boss made this earth-shaking announcement, we were to drive to Philadelphia for Ben's wedding to Leslie, a girl he had met through Kevin, who was living there in the city. Lily, Aurora, and I were to stay with Chad's parents about an hour north of Philly. Feeling stressed about my job and the baby inside her, Lily resisted the seven-hour drive. But I couldn't miss this time with my best friends, especially since we hadn't built many relationships in Portsmouth. I felt burdened, trying to care for Lily and Aurora, and I needed my friends. I insisted we go.

By the time we got there, the guys were already planning on a bachelors night in the city and staying over at Kevin's apartment. I asked Lily if she'd stay with Aurora at Chad's house that night; she again resisted. Couldn't we just go to a bar in the suburbs? I asked, they said no, I pressed. "Mick's hellbent on going into the city," I grumbled. "I'm not *hellbent*," he said, annoyed. This was a once-a-year reunion for me; I couldn't miss it. I went.

The power went out at Chad's house that night. It was ninety-five degrees, and they had no air conditioning. Aurora kept Lily up, crying all night.

A week later, Lily and Aurora flew to Kentucky to visit Lily's parents. I was to join them a few days later. It was less than a year after September 11, 2001. I couldn't follow them to the airline gate. I'd never been away from them for more than a night before. I teared up, watching them walk right past me on the other side of a giant window past the security lines.

Lily started bleeding on the flight. She called from the hospital in Kentucky. She'd miscarried.

I got there a couple of days later. We held each other and wept in the guest bed at her parents' house. Lily believed the baby was a boy, and we named him David Angelis. David was my beloved uncle. "Angelis" gave the baby life after death, at least in our hearts. Back in Portsmouth, I wrote a song. Here's part:

This Littler Light

> Tears in an airport for the ones I care for
> Three darlings departed, one life barely started
> All three ascend, but one never lands
> Why did you fly away?
>
> ---
>
> I need to forget because I can't protect you
> This poem has told you that someday I'll hold you
> My song will remind you that someday I'll find you
> When I fly away
> There's a time to stay
> And a time to fly away

I would stay up late on nights that fall. Sometimes I would write songs, but usually I was on the computer, searching for jobs. It was my compline, a moonlit prayer seeking answers from a digital divinity: How could I continue to write and still make Lily happy? She was alone in bed. I sometimes thought that's where I belonged too. But couldn't I do her more good out here with this nightly liturgy, every click a petition for a better life? What could I do for her in there? I knew she blamed me for the miscarriage, for making her go to Philadelphia. Maybe I thought I could somehow make it up to her by earning more money? I didn't know.

I didn't know.

I just didn't know.

That winter, I happened upon a credit card bill. Lily typically paid them, and I rarely looked at them. We were $2,100 in debt. What? This was not how I lived my life; I didn't spend money I didn't have. Weren't we pinching pennies, shopping for discount groceries, wearing Goodwill clothes, waiting for our property values to go up and for me to get a better job so we might be able to afford that historic house she wanted? I was devastated. I threw a fit. I screamed and yelled at her. How could she do this? How could she sabotage her own dreams? Aurora's future?

Lily had been drowning her sorrow over the baby's death with online shopping. New clothes, clothes I never saw, hung in her closet. She had been web-chatting with a filmmaker she'd met from Sweden and wanted us to meet up with him when he visited the U.S. I wasn't interested. My life was here, now. That's when she wrote a short story, a "fiction" about that leather-clad biker dude back at Cedarville who was courting her at the same time I was. I hadn't thought much about it back at Cedarville when she told me a poem she had written about me for her English class had sparked him to say, "I wish someone had written that about me." Too bad for him, right? But now her affection seemed anywhere but here. She was searching for something she didn't have.

No One Said It Was Easy

I'd ask to take her out to dinner, or a movie, or to see Over the Rhine when they came through the Northeast. She used to like these things, but she never wanted to go anymore, always saying she didn't want to leave Aurora. This was no romance. It was just survival. Coldplay's song "The Scientist" expressed it best: No one said it'd be easy. They just didn't say it'd be so hard.

I got a job offer from the Lowell *Sun*, a Massachusetts paper in my preschool hometown with a circulation three times as big as Portsmouth's, about an hour to the southwest. A monthly salary of almost $2,700 to cover a small town near where my grandparents lived. It wasn't much of a raise, but it was something, with many more chances for promotion. I wasn't sure what to do.

Lars was surprised when I asked his advice. He didn't know I'd been job hunting. I explained I had started in earnest when it looked like I was being replaced. "Ohhh," he said, clearly grieved about how the whole thing went down. The new "assistant managing editor" had only lasted a few weeks before the executive editor made her editor of another weekly paper, instead of the three she'd been managing before. What had happened was that she'd burned out, and he'd called her to the mothership for some nurturing. I wish I had known that at the staff meeting. My job was safe. Still, Lars said going to Lowell might be the best thing. "You can't stay here forever," he said.

I wasn't ready to go. I loved Portsmouth, and an extra $250 a month didn't seem worth a big move. The *Herald* agreed to match Lowell's offer and moved me from schools to the more prominent City Hall beat, while keeping my managerial duties. I helped Lars keep track of what all the reporters were working on and pinch hit for him in the daily "budget" meeting where the editors discussed the stories for the next day's paper and how to play them.

Within a year, though, both Lars and the Sunday editor would leave the paper. They were tired of acting as human shields between the executive editor—whom we called Con-Man—and the rest of us. My "born-again" Inquisition was the tip of the iceberg. Everyone seemed to have a con to complain about.

My "replacement's" replacement wasn't faring much better editing three weeklies, so they promoted me to manage one of them that had two versions each week for two distinct readership geographies. I also spent part of my week writing long features and in-depth stories for the *Sunday Herald*. These were the tales of pathos I loved to tell: a church treasurer whose embezzlement forced the congregation out of its building and left his friends, family, and other investors with big losses as his business failed; the fallout from the Episcopal church's new gay bishop; an Iranian political refugee returning home for the first time in twenty years.

They had bumped my pay to $2,900 a month. We lived under less pressure and paid off our debt, but it still wasn't enough for a house. The Sunday writing felt close to my sense of calling, but well over half my time went toward orchestrating photographers and freelance reporters to fill twenty or thirty pages of local content every week. We had one staff writer in my satellite office in Stratham, so I lived by email, rarely venturing out into the 250-square-mile area our scattered writers covered from their homes. Lars told me once that editing felt like clerical work, and now I understood. I remember telling one of my co-workers that Lily dreamed of us living in an English village one day, but I couldn't imagine why a European publication would ever take a chance on a Yank like me. "I haven't accomplished anything yet," I said. It wasn't a very sensitive thing to say to a woman in her fifties who had been there for decades, but it's how I felt. If I were going to be able to write, *really write*, and give Lily the lifestyle she wanted, it wouldn't be here at these tiny papers. There had to be more.

I reapplied to Duke. At the same time, I applied for a journalism fellowship that would pay $3,300 in monthly salary plus $10,000 in expenses for a year-long reporting project of my choice. The money and the flexible schedule would allow me to take some classes at Duke, so I proposed the best story I could find in North Carolina: Latino immigration. California and Texas, OK. But North Carolina? When I'd visited Durham a couple of years earlier, I'd been shocked to see so many Hispanic grocers and Mexican restaurants and to learn that North Carolina had the United States' fastest-growing immigrant population in the nineties.

Immigration had been on my mind that spring. John and Esther were the closest friends we had at St. John's. They had two young kids, not much older than Aurora. They made good money, but chose to live in a humble apartment complex. Unlike so many at our church, we didn't have to pretend to be keeping up with them. John sang with me in a small choir. Esther, a food scientist by training, introduced us to kimchi and pork dumplings.

She was from Korea, he from Malaysia. They'd met at college in the Philippines and had lived in Singapore and Canada before moving to New England. When John lost his job as a software engineer, I got a crash course in immigration law: They had to go back to Canada because they were in the U.S. on John's work visa, which expired six weeks after his layoff. I wrote a column, quoting Leviticus on welcoming foreigners and the Indigo Girls on immigration checkpoints: "You know, it's funny I think we were on the same boat back in 1694." But if I were going to rescue my image of Lady Liberty, her torch beckoning all people to America's shores, I would have to do more than write a column. A year showing both the promise and the exclusion of America's biggest immigrant class seemed like it would be time well spent.

At the same time, though, I had applied for a writing job at a paper in Florida. Lily's and my grandparents had all moved there permanently, and my parents were riding one of the Sunshine State's cyclical real estate booms. My three youngest siblings were in school down there. Lily was pregnant again, this time because Aurora had started asking for a little brother or sister. Raising our kids near family seemed more important than chasing any academic dream or writing project in North Carolina.

I had already accepted the job in Florida when I got a call from the Phillips Foundation saying I was a finalist for the fellowship and could I come to Washington, D.C. for an interview? I called the Florida editor and put off my start date by a week to buy some time. I was going to start my job and live with Mom so Lily could take her time packing and follow me a couple of weeks later. I packed some clothes for Florida and drove south to D.C. Lily wasn't getting along with either her family or mine. We put off the final decision until we knew if I'd be offered the fellowship.

Ten of us gathered in a conference room in a D.C. office building. The Phillips trustees, which included right-wing luminaries from the Reagan administration, the Heritage Foundation, and the Claremont Institute, called us into another room, interviewed us, and sent us back, one by one. I had discovered the foundation on journalismjobs.com and had only a vague idea that it was politically conservative. I didn't think I would have any trouble supporting "American culture," "democratic society," "constitutional principles," or "free enterprise." I didn't know, for example, that "free market" philosophy might mean tax cuts for the rich or that President Bush would start to justify the "War on Terror" on the grounds that Iraq needed democracy. Publishing mogul Tom Phillips, whose Regnery Publishing would be responsible for inserting the term "swift-boating" into American politics that year, noted that I had taken some "courageous" stands at the *Herald*. I suspected he meant my story about a woman whose mother had almost aborted her and who as an adult was touring the country speaking against abortion; or maybe my post-9/11 series on Reuben and Sheryl and their walk with God. I learned later that columnist Robert Novak had liked my shoe-leather reporting experience. Most of my competition was aspiring pundits working for conservative magazines or editorial pages. I suspected my Cedarville pedigree must have helped too.

The interviews were complete. One by one, the trustees called the applicants back in and quickly sent them out. The first few people returned, quietly collected their things, and left the building. Once the interviewees started returning and saying the board had told them to stay, we guessed that the rest of us would be offered fellowships. We were right.

The foundation gave me some time to accept, but I had to decide immediately whether to continue on to Florida or return to New England to pack for a different move. I called Lily from a gas station parking lot. She still wanted North Carolina. I called the editor in Florida and told her I wasn't coming. She was mad. I felt bad. But the fellowhip was hard to pass up, and it was what Lily wanted. We were moving to Chapel Hill.

I turned around and drove north.

9

Dirty Sheets and Purple Horses

> Therefore I tell you, do not worry about your
> life, what you will eat or drink; or about your
> body, what you will wear. Is not life more
> than food, and the body more than clothes?
> Look at the birds of the air; they do not sow
> or reap or store away in barns, and yet your
> heavenly Father feeds them. Are you not
> much more valuable than they? Can any one
> of you by worrying add a single
> hour to your life?
>
> —Matthew 6:25–27

For seeing Myrtle Beach on the cheap, they picked the worst possible time. It was mid-July 2005, and my friend Buca and his brother-in-law Lucio wanted me—the one who'd been speaking English all his life—to find lodging for us, our wives, and two kids apiece. I found nothing on the for-rent-by-owner sites. The weekend was two days away, and they were all booked. Two years earlier, in the off-season, my friends, immigrants from Las Choapas in southern Mexico, had rented a studio at the beachfront Bermuda Sands Hotel, with a full kitchen, two queen beds, and a pull-out couch for the eight of them. It cost them $75 a night. By the time I called

This Littler Light

Friday evening, that type of room had no vacancy. I phoned Buca and told him we could reserve a room like it, minus the pull-out couch, for $133 a night, plus two single rooms at $60 each, and that only if we waited till Sunday. We could stay together in one room, I said, if some of us slept on the floor.

Buca said he didn't mind. I knew I did.

Myrtle Beach may have been the last place on earth Lily and I would ever have chosen to take a vacation, much less at the height of the tourist season, with ferris wheels spinning, bombs bursting in air, and a dirty carpet for a bed. We liked to have the beach to ourselves, even if that meant it was thirty degrees outside with sand blowing in our faces. This weekend, we'd have to share. But Buca's daughter Darby had just about begged us to come, and when she looked up at you from that squishy four-foot frame, with her mother's brown eyes that sparkled like cola, and her father's chubby cheeks that rose high on her face and hid her eyes when she smiled, it was hard to say no.

I'd met eleven-year-old Darby, her little sister Daisy, age five, and their parents, Buca and Amanda, the previous November at a Hispanic Baptist mission in Ashe County, North Carolina, the Christmas-tree capital of the East Coast. About two months after arriving in North Carolina for the Phillips Journalism Fellowship, I had decided to focus my research on Christmas-tree workers in the Blue Ridge Mountains. In an environment of brutally hard work, crowded quarters, and fragmented families, Buca was among the few immigrant farmworkers growing his own trees for the wholesale market. His boss had co-signed on a loan so Buca, one of the farm's crew leaders, could buy a mobile home on about an acre of steep mountain land. There he grew his Fraser firs among the luxury cabins that rose up around them.

The boss offered me shelter, too, as I looked into the lives of his workers for the Phillips fellowship. It was January by then, and his crew had gone back to Mexico for the winter, leaving dirty sheets on their bunkhouse beds, whiskers in the bathroom sink, and a fridge full of meat so rotten I couldn't open the door for the smell. I had the place to myself, but I only lasted one night. I had brought my own sheets but still spent a sleepless night, itching all over, meditating on how farmworkers bring pesticides into their homes on their clothes, and trying to convince myself I had a good reason for being three hours from my wife and young daughters, alone in a dirty shack with only the vaguest idea that this year-long project would advance my journalism career.

Dirty Sheets and Purple Horses

Amanda offered me their couch the next night and as often as I liked. I'd been going just about every Sunday since then—to church with the family, playing soccer with Lucio and the rest of their work crew, breakfasting on Darby and Daisy's Animalitos crackers floating in milky, sugary coffee like cereal, and working with the men on the farm each Monday. Darby often told me I'd become like part of her family.

Darby's vacation almost didn't happen that year, and she knew it. Always conscious of her parents' finances, she'd constantly compare my car to her mom's car, ask how big and nice my new apartment was, or apologize for the large ants that marched along the wood trim in their living room. Her broad smile hid her low self-esteem about the two things that may matter most to a pre-teen girl: family wealth and her own body. Darby smelled trouble back in the spring, when Amanda was sending almost $100 a month to help pay for her father's chemotherapy in Las Choapas. Already Disneyworld had dropped from the short list.

"If we keep sending money to them, we're not going to be able to go on vacation," Darby had blurted out one Sunday evening back in May. Amanda quickly shushed her, as when Darby would ask questions about how much people weigh, how old they are, how much money they make, or how much their cars cost.

Not long after that, Buca's boss handed me a wad of cash for several days I had spent applying pesticides, digging landscape trees, planting, and trimming Fraser firs over the previous couple of months. I had asked him to let me work for free, so I could experience Buca's life firsthand. "I feel like I'm taking advantage of you," the boss said as he gave me the money. I figured it was a day's pay that would help me with gas ($25 round trip).

When I unfurled the roll and added up $220, I immediately knew Buca and Amanda should have the money, even though they'd refused any payment before. I felt like I was taking advantage of them: a free place to sleep or shower whenever I needed it, a hot lunch packed carefully into my cooler Monday mornings, dinner before my trip back to Chapel Hill. They wanted a friend, not a tenant, but I knew they were living paycheck to paycheck, even with WIC supplements and Medicaid.

I left a check with a note inside their screen door a few weeks later. When Buca confronted me about it, I suggested saving it for Darby's college fund. Buca had another idea: Now they knew for sure they could go on vacation, back to Myrtle Beach. They'd gone there three years in a row before skipping the previous summer because Amanda couldn't get time off work in a North Carolina barbecue house. This vacation had been two years coming.

This Littler Light

We rolled up to a stop light around 5:30 Sunday evening. Looming above the line of minivans ahead of us, a rickety wooden roller coaster rattled and swerved behind a tall chain-link fence. Lily and I hadn't ridden one since high school. It wasn't our thing. Our little Toyota Corolla was stuffed with seldom-used shovels and pails, coolers full of smoked turkey breast and organic fruit, and three suitcases of shorts, t-shirts, and bathing suits, Lily's new Anne Cole one-piece still smelling that chemical smell of unworn merchandise. We were always arguing about money, but I'd gone to the mall with her to help pick this one out. Our girls, ten months and four years old, peeked out from their car seats buried among the rubble. It was late July in Myrtle Beach, South Carolina, playground for the coal miners of Appalachia, where Lily grew up, a place she had permanently left behind in the spring when her parents sold her childhood home and moved to Florida. I was giving it my best shot—trying, as best I knew how, to sing for the meek, to tell stories of families like this one, living on the margins of the wealthiest nation in the world, and simultaneously to give Lily the middle-class lifestyle she wanted.

It was our first family vacation, more than five years into our marriage. The four of us had been living on my income alone. We'd made weekend trips before, but always to visit people, not destinations, and opening my wallet for no more than one night's lodging. We'd rather have paid $150 for a night in a quaint bed and breakfast than for three nights in a Best Western off the freeway. We wanted nothing more than to see the world, but we had an unspoken rule: If we couldn't do it right, why bother? We couldn't very well tramp across New Zealand, sleeping in hostels with a travel crib and high chair in tow. Paris? London? Buenos Aires? Forget it. We settled for free-range chicken and Doc Martens from Overstock.com. "It only takes a little more to go first class," Joe, my father-in-law, liked to say. Buca and Amanda lived on less than two-thirds of what we did, yet our vacation was a special occasion; theirs was a tradition.

We pulled into the parking lot at the Bermuda Sands. The chlorinated Lazy River, which Darby had regaled, swirled around the center of the five-story complex. Children rode on their parents' shoulders, or floated on yellow inner tubes with blue handles, their gleeful squeals echoing off the stacks of rooms that surrounded the river like a U-shaped canyon. Teenagers raced in slow motion around the 150-foot loop, flirting, splashing each other, and yelling insults. It was all on display on what at that moment may have been the busiest street in the Carolinas. On the exterior hallways at the edge of each upper floor, older folks sat on beach chairs outside their rooms, watching the flow of the Lazy River.

Dirty Sheets and Purple Horses

When I had told Buca three rooms would cost us about $250, with two for $190, I had asked him to call and book them. I didn't want to be the one to decide we should all spend more money to sleep in beds with mattresses. But he had misunderstood and thought I was going to book them, so I had called back the Bermuda Sands and deposited $130 to hold all three rooms. I wasn't about to let my brown-skinned friends sleep on the floor while Lily and I took a bed. A little too Jim Crow, even among friends. I'd rather have paid for the rooms myself.

At the front desk, Dustin, a teenager with surfer's indifference to match his long, tousled hair, said no one else had checked into any of our rooms yet. I paid the balance of $120 plus $28 in taxes and key deposits. Room 103 was on the first floor: no defense against the bass blasters cruising Ocean Boulevard or the beach junkies looking for drug money. When you've worked as a reporter, you know too much—you know what to be afraid of. Back in New Hampshire, we'd see crime multiply four-fold in summertime along the beaches. I stopped at the car to grab some luggage, then visited our room, a few feet from the boulevard with a "pool view": no defense against the screaming banshees who would haunt the Lazy River well past midnight. The Bermuda Sands was not for peace and solitude.

From inside the room, a metal fence shrouded the view of the pool, but not the shrill young voices. Room 103 was smaller than your average bedroom, just enough space for a full-sized bed and a nightstand. There was no closet and no place to hang any clothes. There was a mini-fridge, microwave, and a small dresser. I wasn't sure where I'd put the portable crib. Which reminded me: How was the baby going to sleep with all that racket going on outside? Maybe this was what you got for $60 a night during the peak season in the most popular beach resort destination on the East Coast outside Florida. I went back to the front desk. Dustin was surprised. Didn't I want a pool view room? He had one other room at the $60 rate. In the lingo of beachfront living, it was a "side view" room, as opposed to ocean view, on the fourth floor.

We collected the girls and as much stuff as we could, and began to snake through the labyrinthine hotel. A staircase climbed the tower to the right of the pool, next to the front office and our discarded room. Any of the long balconies on that side could take us into the beachfront stack, which formed the bottom of the U, where an interior hallway, steaming with exhaust from the wall-mounted air conditioners, stretched to the right and left edges of the building. This hallway smelled like a moist, dingy basement. The Bermuda Sands was sort of an indoor/outdoor hotel.

This Littler Light

Every hallway was covered by the one above, but also open to the elements. The stucco walls were painted yellow, to mimic Bermuda's traditional architecture, I suppose. Flip-flops tracked sand and parking lot grime onto the short-pile carpet. It was worn and dirty, in perpetuity. The metal stair rails were detached in places, sharp edges just the right height to scar a four-year-old's face.

Sucking wind (we didn't notice the elevator) we reached the fourth floor. Outside our room, a five-gallon bucket sat half-full of yellowish water, with a dirty article of white cotton clothing soaking in it—maybe a t-shirt, maybe men's briefs. I didn't inspect it too closely. Cigarette butts floated on top. Inside, the bed remained unmade. The sheets smelled of sweaty flesh. A pile of dirty towels, not just wet, but stained brown, sat behind the bathroom door. A bubbly, travel-sized bar of Beach Winds brand facial soap rested among the remnants of its torn wrapper at the edge of the sink. Obviously, the room had not been cleaned. Back at the front desk, this did not surprise Dustin. No, it probably hasn't, he said. He'd send someone right up.

The Bermuda Sands was beginning to remind me of the motels Dad used to take us to when I was growing up. Mom tells me it started in the summer of 1978 when I was eighteen months old and it was so hot that maggots were squirming around our trash can inside the kitchen of our hundred-year-old New Englander in Lawrence, Massachusetts, the first of my parents' handyman specials. Mom begged Dad to take us to an air-conditioned motel. He chose one where the room next door had a new pair of occupants every hour. Then there was Daytona Beach. Our neighbor there was a snake skinner who lived in the motel year-round. Of course, we were the ones who showed up with a dead rattlesnake in a yellow plastic cassette tray we'd driven across the peninsula from Clearwater Beach, where a couple of drunks had dropped a concrete block on its head to protect us kids. Snake-dude was happy to take the rattler off our hands. I guess it was a match made in paradise.

When I was fifteen, we landed at LAX around midnight and had to find lodging before we drove to San Diego to see my aunt the next day. Dad passed by all the usual suspects, Hampton, Comfort, Days, Holiday. He didn't want to pay that kind of money. So he drove and drove and just kept driving, all over Los Angeles. He had no idea where he was going. We started seeing concrete walls around entire neighborhoods, bars on doors and windows. He pulled up alongside a young couple who instinctively cringed in fear at the sight of a slowing vehicle. Dad asked them about

Dirty Sheets and Purple Horses

a motel. They pointed us down a residential street, where we found an Indian man in a home office. He opened the gate to his backyard to reveal some small cottages he rented nightly. He locked us inside the complex for the night.

Three years later Dad drove me to Ohio for my freshman year of college. He found the President's Inn, in the midst of abandoned warehouses and boarded-up shops in downtown Springfield. The President's Inn became a tradition. Several months later, when he and Mom came to see me perform in a spring play, I stayed with them Saturday night. I had two shows the next day and needed my sleep. I woke around 3 a.m. to the sound of beer bottles smashing against a dumpster outside our window.

In South Carolina with Lily and the girls, at least the beach was right there. Looking south by southeast, we could see para-sailors and crashing waves, more beachfront hotels, nicer than ours, and amusement park rides a block from the sand. We left our things in the room and crossed the parking lot. Four-year-old Aurora, oblivious to her parents' plight, played tag with the waves as they caught the hem of her purple cotton dress from the Gap.

In half an hour, we went back to the hotel. From the parking lot below, I spied a kid coming out of our room with a pile of sheets in his arms. This seemed like good news. We climbed to the room and found the bed had been made, but the bathroom was untouched. Maybe it was a different crew that cleaned the bathroom, I reasoned. They just hadn't come yet. I called Buca's cell phone. They were still half an hour away. We were hungry and tired of deli turkey and peanut butter and jelly, which we'd been snacking on since lunchtime.

We found Big Daddy's a few doors up from the Bermuda Sands. It was perched on stilts jutting from the sand and served as the entrance to a 900-foot fishing pier. To get to the restaurant, you had to go through a gift and tackle shop and a small video-game arcade. Forty-five minutes after we ordered, the waitress, an Irish student on summer break, came to apologize and brought the girls each a slice of plain white bread on Mickey Mouse-shaped paper plates, with single-serve packs of butter and jam stuck in his ears. Lily's flounder sandwich came out riddled with bones and smelling funny. Big Daddy, the immense cashier, didn't charge us for it.

Back at the hotel, we climbed to our room. The used soap was still in the bathroom. The dirty towels were still on the floor. Who knew what manner of germs still infected the sink, the toilet, the bathtub, the gray tile floor? I went downstairs and again told Dustin the bathroom hadn't been cleaned. He and another teenager immediately grabbed their towels and spray bottles and raced upstairs. Apparently, this surfer was sick of seeing me in his lobby. Meanwhile, I learned that our friends were there, in room 236, overlooking the pool. They never checked into Room 103 on the first floor.

I headed upstairs to find Lily and the girls huddled on the balcony, waiting while the boys cleaned our room. We twisted our way down two flights of stairs and through the guts of the hotel, passing sacks of garbage some guests had left outside their room. The next day, it would be chicken bones swimming in a hollowed-out watermelon rind, and it would sit there overnight.

I knocked on the door of Room 236. I couldn't hear anyone approaching over the hustle and bustle of the Lazy River. Buca's sister Laura answered. "Pása le," she said with a smile. The eight of them were crowded inside the hotel room. At least this one had the kitchen and two double beds. The kids were watching TV, waiting for their parents to unpack. They had taken a wrong turn, and their trip had lasted more than seven hours. They'd already eaten, and they were ready to play. They didn't realize I'd booked a third room, and they were fine with sharing this one. Buca was immediately concerned about my $60 deposit on the other room. If I couldn't get it back, he and Lucio would pay me for it, he said. I told him we could split it three ways.

The three of us went down to the front desk. Dustin said I'd have to talk to the manager in the morning. Outside, Buca and Lucio each handed me $68 cash to cover the deposit on their room. They didn't want to be in my debt any longer than they had to. They again promised to pay me if the manager wouldn't release the rest of the deposit on the empty room.

It was almost 10 o'clock, and our friends were ready to walk ten or twelve blocks into the Myrtle Beach they'd come to see, the video games, the virtual reality shows, the carnival rides, and seashell vendors. After a month of anticipation, the cousins were finally there, anxious to get out of the hotel room. It was too late for our girls. Lily took the baby upstairs for bed. I would take Aurora to the Lazy River to wait for our friends to come back.

Poolside, Aurora aimed straight for the bridge that crossed the river to a concrete island with its own kiddie pool, a foot deep with colorful pipes rising up to spray showers of cool water on hot skin. More water cascaded off the rounded edges of two tall plastic mushrooms, creating quiet

Dirty Sheets and Purple Horses

hideaways, like caves behind a waterfall, where the only sound was eternal splash. At one end of the wading pool, two large buckets hung slightly askew, so that as water filled them from a pipe above, they'd suddenly tip over, dumping three or four gallons onto the boys waiting below.

Aurora was in heaven. She lunged from sprinkler to sprinkler, getting as close as she could without actually getting her face splashed. She was drunk with freedom, Daddy all to herself, playing just like the big kids, well past her bedtime. This was not her real life, where I had to leave for work every morning or lock myself in my bedroom to write, against her protests. She ran in zig-zagging patterns, tripping where the water hit her shins, falling face-first, laughing, and coughing diluted chlorine as I picked her up, over and over again. Once, she lost her balance and hit her head gently on the edge of the pool. The euphoria was too much for her.

It was after midnight. We wiped our skin dry with white hotel towels, and Aurora shimmied into her pink beach dress. We were putting on our sandals when Buca stepped onto the pool deck with Darby, Daisy, and their cousin Melissa. They'd come to ride the Lazy River, but I was tired. We wished them goodnight and went upstairs, where Lily and the baby lay sleeping in bed. I helped Aurora rinse off in the shower, brush her teeth, and put on dry clothes. I lifted her into her old portable playpen with the inch-thick mattress, since there wasn't room for all four of us in this little bed and the baby wouldn't sleep apart from Lily or me. I showered and fell under the covers. Lily had already warned me the sheets still smelled dirty. I was afraid to sniff them myself.

We woke to a knock on the door around 10 a.m. It was Buca and Amanda. After a night on the floor of their hotel room, they'd been up for hours. They'd already gone to the Food Lion for a few days' worth of groceries. They liked the Bermuda Sands because they could make their own meals in the kitchen. A couple of vacations worth of tourist food was enough for them: "Jumbo" shrimp the size of popcorn shrimp, cheesesteak subs for $10 apiece. This time, they stocked the refrigerator with hot dogs, bologna, deli ham, and watermelon. We had an organic version of Cheerios, but no milk. They invited us down for breakfast.

Aurora sat at one of two chairs flanking the dining table, its leaves folded down so it was the size of a desk, cluttered with cereal boxes, paper plates, and napkins still in their packaging. She couldn't sit still, what with her friends bouncing on the beds, throwing balls around the room, and watching cartoons. Breakfast took us nearly to lunchtime. We made plans to hit the beach, but Lily wanted some plastic sandals to keep her

Berkenstocks from the saltwater, and we needed a beach towel or something to sit on. Buca agreed to meet us on the beach.

We walked a couple of blocks inland, to where we'd seen a row of big-box beach supply stores selling everything from mesh trucker-hats that said "PIMP" to dried starfish and live hermit crabs. We found Lily some beach shoes, a bead necklace for Aurora, and a large towel with a picture of a white palmetto tree and crescent moon on a dark blue background, the South Carolina emblem. We were getting into this tourist thing.

Back at the hotel, Lily took the baby upstairs to nurse. We were to meet Buca and the girls on the beach directly in front of the hotel. Aurora and I walked slowly to the left, across the sand. Among the hundreds of bodies bobbing in the water and packed densely on the beach, we couldn't spot them. They'd already proved willing to sleep on the floor of a dive hotel and eat bologna sandwiches to give their kids a vacation. I was really curious how they'd choose to spend the next couple of days, but I'd barely had an hour with them since we got here.

Aurora and I would just have to play by ourselves. The sun was blazing, the water refreshing, but just barely. I lathered her in sunblock and tied a dark green bandana around her head to protect her fair skin. The little blonde beauty in the doo-rag drew smiles and laughter. We found a vacant spot where she could fill buckets with sand and water, and dump them out. She wasn't building a sand castle, exactly. Just filling and emptying her buckets. In New England, we lived a few minutes from the beach. Once she got over her fear of the sand moving beneath her feet, she loved it. We told ourselves moving to Chapel Hill would be good for her—good schools, lots of young families and kid-friendly fun—but at this moment I wasn't so sure. What is better for a kid than playing at the beach, the sculptable sand inviting her creativity, the violent ocean setting limits?

> Some went out on the sea in ships.
> They were merchants on the mighty waters.
> They saw the works of the LORD,
> his wonderful deeds in the deep.
> For he spoke and stirred up a tempest
> that lifted high the waves.
> (Ps 107:23–25)

My castle-building skills don't go far beyond the molds of plastic pails. I dripped wet sand from my hand like wax from a candle, making irregular spires that somehow mimicked a fairytale palace, just like my aunt Peg taught me one summer back in New Hampshire. Nanny and Poppy used

Dirty Sheets and Purple Horses

to rent the same green beach cottage, one block off Ocean Boulevard in Hampton every summer. We'd walk to Blink's fried-dough stand, bumper cars, waterslide, or the arcade, where I'd win reams of tickets playing ski-ball. I don't remember trading those tickets for anything in particular, just the joy of pulling them out of the little slot and of banking those little wooden balls off the end of the rail and into the tiny fifty-point target. A kids area at the Hampton Beach Casino had a spin-art machine where I could drip different colors of paint onto white paperboard as it whirled like a kaleidoscope. I couldn't mess it up because it was meant to look messy. I loved just being at the cottage: I could eat food that didn't pass Mom's nutritional standards, like Frosted Flakes or Ritz crackers with cheddar cheese and pepperoni, or eavesdrop on my aunts and uncles watching scary movies when I was supposed to be asleep.

Aurora and I walked up and down the beach but never did see Buca until we went back up to the room for lunch and he came knocking on the door. He pointed to where they'd been. We'd passed them three times. Down in their room, we found shelter from the afternoon heat. After sunset, we'd walk a mile-plus to Ripley's Pavilion, the amusement park we'd seen when we first rolled into town. Lucio offered me a taste of salpicon. It's ground beef with jalapeño, onion and lemon, spread on a crispy yellow corn tostada. I wasn't crazy about it. The beef was brown, like it should be, but soft and smooth, not at all crumbly like scrambled hamburger. I was pretty sure salpicon was raw meat. Later, Lucio would explain the meat is cold-cooked with the juice of fifteen lemons. It was probably safe to eat, but I couldn't stomach the mushiness. We snacked on watermelon, the kids watched cartoons. The clock showed 5 p.m., and we were ready for the carnival.

Lily decided to stay behind with the baby. Neither my sense of calling to understand these immigrants nor the friendship we had were ever hers. The rest of us walked to the Pavilion. We adults were anxious because no one knew how much it was going to cost. I was hoping it wasn't $25 or $30 a person. Fortunately, there was no admission charge. You could buy individual ride tickets or pay a flat fee for unlimited rides. Children were only $15 a piece, and adults could chaperone on the kiddie rides for free. Not a bad deal.

Inside, the girls went straight for the merry-go-round. Aurora and Daisy chose the same purple horse festooned with pink rosebuds. I redirected Aurora to a boring beige mare. She rode the purple one the next time around. Darby, Aurora, and I spun inside a teacup. I took Aurora on her first roller coaster. Darby took Aurora and Daisy on a whale that leapt up and down as it swam around in circles. Aurora and Daisy steered a green boat around a circular canal. They rode a little train that crawled along a winding track.

As we walked from ride to ride, it occurred to me that Aurora had never been to a carnival before. It dawned on me that our high standards could actually deprive her of the fun that marked my childhood. On the other hand, I fretted about saving money for really big experiences. What, exactly? I didn't know. Maybe my prudence wasn't any better than Lily's extravagance.

Dad's dad, Grumpy, had died the year before. I was 750 miles away and missed the funeral. Grumpy and I were never close, but I'll never forget when I was eleven years old and we visited him after a trip to Disneyworld. He told Dad he was proud of him for taking us on vacation. Grumpy was not much of a father, and Dad struggled to escape his legacy. At least the old man knew when his son got it right.

Dad used to take us to Fenway Park for Red Sox games every summer. Speeding south on I-93, we'd pass by the Somerville housing projects, where Dad grew up flipping baseball cards down the hallway with his friends. Whoever card landed closest to the wall won the whole lot. That's how he lost Mickey Mantle's rookie card. Eventually, it was worth $50,000. Goodbye Buenos Aires.

Grumpy retired as an elementary school janitor at Hanscomb Air Force Base in Bedford, Massachusetts. I never thought he and Nana were poor, maybe because most of Dad's brothers and sisters were successful, third-generation Italian immigrants who got rich as third-generation immigrants are supposed to do. By the time I was born, Nana and Grumpy lived in a humble multi-level house in Burlington, a wealthy suburb far from HUD housing in Somerville. Nana hung the laundry out to dry in the fenced backyard. She is a frugal woman, reusing Christmas wrap and buying cheese ends from the supermarket deli. For the big fun, we went to Dad's sisters' houses—in-ground swimming pools, billiards tables, pinball machine. Over the years, aunts and uncles bought my brother and me an electric go-cart, a Nintendo, and a seven-foot long, plastic G. I. Joe aircraft carrier.

Grumpy shared Darby's inferiority complex, as though it mattered to us that our other grandparents, Nanny and Poppy, had a bigger house or more electronic gadgets. Whenever he saw me, which wasn't often, Grumpy always puzzled over the question of how I was going to make

Dirty Sheets and Purple Horses

the family rich when I grew up, not just solidly middle class like my aunts and uncles, but really rich. He didn't have any answers, but the question occupied his mind, like Newton pondering gravity. Maybe that's why Dad always told us to do what would make us happy. He eked out a living in real estate, but at heart, he's a musician. Dad admires people who can work mundane jobs, go home, forget about work, and just enjoy their paychecks. But money was never enough for him.

Still, there was something satisfying about having enough money to take a family vacation. Buca and Amanda didn't fret about "having enough money" like I did. They worked hard for their money, but what was it worth if they couldn't spend it making their kids happy? They had to hop trains and dodge sex-traffickers near the border. Once they got to North Carolina, they lived in rotting, rat-infested trailers and once had to eat moldy tomatoes because that's all they had. They'd survived with much less so why not enjoy it while they could? Lily and I struggled just to maintain something close to the lifestyle she grew up with, more extravagant than these friends' but what we expected. If you can work with your back, the saying goes, you'll always have work. Maybe Buca had a sense of security that I'd never know. So far I'd been able to make a living doing something I more or less enjoyed. Eventually, that had to catch up with me, no? How many people can be that lucky? Or maybe Buca and Amanda simply had a level of mutual trust and cooperation that Lily and I didn't. Maybe I was prudishly prudent because one of us had to be.

Myrtle Beach was not for such worries. What happens in Myrtle Beach stays in Myrtle Beach, at least until the credit card statement arrives. Tuesday morning, our friends were going back to the beach, but Lily didn't want Aurora in the sun for a second day in a row. We took our girls to Broadway at the Beach, a 350-acre outdoor mall with a man-made lake, an IMAX theater, a sixteen-screen cineplex, a fire-breathing dragon, and just about every major chain restaurant and clothing store you can imagine. I plunked down $40 at Ripley's Aquarium, packed to the gills because every mother and her children were trying to beat the heat just like we were. We rode a conveyor belt through the "Dangerous Reef," a glass tunnel surrounded by swarming sharks and graceful stingrays.

"I like kitschy family vacation stuff," said Lily. "It's fun."

I was a hero.

After outmaneuvering the other necrophiles to escape the crowded *Titanic* exhibit, I valiantly led my family through the gift shop, which doubled as the aquarium exit. Oh, Aurora was tempted by the pirate swords and cuddly Great White Sharks, but her father was one sailor they weren't going to pillage. I wasn't so vigilant at the Key West Grille. I had already surrendered $3 to a sidewalk vendor for a lemon-lime shaved ice so Aurora wouldn't melt as we hurried through tropical bazaar to the restaurant. Drenched in sweat, Lily and I ordered $9 economy plates from the lunch menu. As usual, we asked for water to drink, because it's free. At least, in New Hampshire, North Carolina, and everywhere else I'd been in the world, it was free. At the Key West Grille, it was $2 a glass. I could have had sweet tea for the same price. Of course, I didn't discover this until we saw the check. You can't win 'em all, not when your adversaries are ruthless and ravenous tourist-hawks.

Meanwhile, back at the Bermuda Sands, our friends were outsmarting them, dining on hot dogs and leftover salpicon between dips in the ocean and the Lazy River. They were Myrtle Beach veterans, ready for anything. Rip them off at your restaurant, they'd go to the Food Lion. Double your fees for the peak season, they'd sleep on the floor. Dad would be proud. So would Grumpy.

In one of those weird coincidences, Dad was driving south through the Carolinas while we were driving home on Wednesday morning. Unwittingly, we passed him on I-95. He had tried to call us several times so that he and my little brother, Steven, could stay with us on their way from New Hampshire to Florida. By the time we got home to Chapel Hill, they were somewhere west of Myrtle Beach. I called his cell phone. After a few minutes commiserating on our bad timing, Dad told me how he'd grudgingly paid $100 for a hotel room near D.C. the night before. I told him about our hotel experience and our friends' sleeping on the floor.

"And they probably had a good time, right?" Dad said.

"Yeah, they did."

"God love 'em."

10

The Image of the Trinity

> Unless the LORD builds the house,
> its builders labor in vain.
>
> —Psalm 127:1

For reasons I can only attribute to divine intervention, a Duke Energy customer-service representative asked me to go to the house and shut off the main breaker before they turned on the power. I'd moved many times, and no one had ever asked me that before. We'd been living in North Carolina for two years, first in a rented townhouse during the Phillips Fellowship, and then on campus at UNC-Chapel Hill in my first year as a graduate student at the journalism school. Lily and I had contracted to buy a duplex at the end of a quiet street in Carrboro—the "Paris of the Piedmont"—a little town next to Chapel Hill, where the hippies and artists fled as the university town exploded in growth in the eighties and nineties. Legend had it you could smoke pot and sleep on the sidewalks in Chapel Hill back in the seventies, before mall stores like the Gap or Gamestop had replaced the independent Intimate Bookshop or Fowler's Grocery and "Big Bertha," its walk-in beer cooler. Carrboro had the sense of community I'd been seeking since Portsmouth: On Thursday nights and Sunday mornings, if you lived close enough to town, you could stroll to the local food co-op, Weaver Street Market, and listen to a live band on the lawn, share a meal from the organic salad bar, and watch Hula-Hoopers dance for hours. You could walk to a playground or the farmer's market or any number of restaurants, bars, music venues, or do-gooding thrift stores.

By the time we got there, all of this had made Carrboro at least as popular as Chapel Hill, with commensurate housing prices—about $300,000 on average. I didn't have a job lined up, but we did have $80,000 in the bank from selling our condo and duplex in New Hampshire. With a big down-payment and renting out one side of this two-family fixer-upper in Carrboro at $220,000, we could live pretty cheaply. The kitchens and bathrooms needed updating, the rooms smelled musty, and the units were each only about 725 square feet. We had visions of building an addition or knocking down walls and building new ones to make our side bigger and the rental side smaller. We were charmed by the wood floors, the backyard where the kids could play, and the walkable Carrboro lifestyle that had eluded us in the student apartments, segregated from the rest of the world along a highway at a remote end of the UNC campus. Those apartments had just been built when we moved in, and Lily wanted the newness. She'd never been happy with the condo Kevin had helped me pick out when we'd first moved to Chapel Hill: the kitchen was as old as we were, the carpets were worn, management left fallen leaves all over the woodsy grounds, and there were too many mosquitoes outside. That condo held memories for me: Rowan's first months, lying on my chest, asleep, while I read the *Oxford American*; the 2004 World Series on TV; Aurora finally getting potty-trained by my Mom at almost four years old. For Lily, it was just another shitty apartment. Then when we'd moved on campus, we had only one parking spot and had to give up one of our cars, and she never embraced the free Chapel Hill buses like I did. She wanted her freedom.

We'd bought two properties before, and I'd watched my parents do it all my life, but this smelly duplex was one of the hardest purchases I'd ever seen. First, we'd had to hire an engineer to check out the foundation where tree roots had cracked the bricks. That made me nervous, but the expert had signed off on it. Then our lender hired an out-of-town appraiser who didn't understand the Carrboro market and undervalued the home, meaning the bank wouldn't loan the asking price. We could have walked away at that point, but Lily really wanted to move, so we pushed through, paying for a second appraisal—another $500, bringing our inspection costs to $1,500 in total. Add in $2,500 in earnest money, and we were risking some serious cash.

The Image of the Trinity

The day before closing, a neighbor saw us drive up to the duplex, just because Duke Energy had asked me to shut off the power. She came rushing over.

"You didn't close yet, did you?" she asked.

"No," I said. "Why?"

She told us a previous tenant had an incurable chronic illness in her lungs because of mold growing all through the walls; a water main had burst beneath the house, and the seller hadn't adequately dealt with results. Our home inspector hadn't noticed any of this.

That was the last straw. There was no way I was bringing my two daughters into that house, but we'd already given our notice on campus. All our worldly possessions sat in piles of boxes covering the floors of our two-bedroom apartment. By this time, between heavy semester loads and summer classes at UNC, I'd almost finished a two-year master's degree in about twelve months, and I was up for a job at *The N&O*. We were trying to make a permanent home, and there it went.

> The foolish man built his house upon the sand
> The foolish man built his house upon the sand
> The foolish man built his house upon the sand
> And the house on the sand went SPLAT!

At the same time, the Florida real estate market was tanking, and my parents were looking for stabler investments. Mom found a property in Carrboro, a few blocks from our house upon the sand. From the front, it looked like any other 1960s brick ranch, except for the brick-and-iron gates leading to the backyard on either end of the house, like a suburban estate. It had an addition, making five bedrooms and three bathrooms. The seller had rented it to students—$400-500 a month for each bedroom. He'd even lived in a van in the driveway to make room for more renters. Plus, he'd built a two-story carriage house in the back, where the faux garage door hid a studio apartment on the ground level to match the one upstairs. This place had a potential income of almost $3,000 a month, but Mom's tenants had been moving out, and she needed to find some new ones just as Lily and I had no place to go.

Dad offered us cheap rent—$850 a month, including utilities, for the original three-bedroom, two-bath house. Mom wasn't happy with the schools in Florida and wanted to move my fifteen-year-old brother Steven to Chapel Hill High School, one of the best in the country. She and Dad would live back and forth between Carrboro and Florida, sharing the two-bedroom, one-bath addition with Steven while two tenants remained in the garage apartments. Everyone would share our kitchen until Dad could build a new one out back.

I wasn't sure it was a good idea, Lily this close to my family, even part-time. My dear friends at Nazareth House had invited us to move in there, live cheaply, and help them serve the homeless and death-row families. They had plenty of spare bedrooms, lots of space. I wasn't sure I had the strength to live in community that way, and I doubted Lily did, but what if?

But Lily chose my parents' house. Waiting for a job offer from *The News & Observer*, I was working a part-time internship at the *Carolina Alumni Review* and taking a Spanish class. In between, Steven and I renovated the house that summer. Lily and Mom picked out new paint, appliances, cabinets, countertop, sinks, faucets, doorknobs, and light fixtures. Steven and I tore out the old kitchen cabinets, the bathroom sinks, and vanities. Mom found an antique end-table cabinet for the master bathroom, and we installed one of those pretty basin sinks on top and waited for Dad to put in a fancy wall-mounted faucet to feed it.

It was in many ways a wonderful place for us. The fenced backyard was ringed with thirty-foot tall bamboo, like our own secret garden. On the Fourth of July, Aurora and I took a long walk through town looking for fireworks. We didn't find any, but we did spot a deer loping across a neighborhood street. One of our first nights there, Lily and I walked a few blocks to a party at one of my grad school classmates' homes, the sort of adult socializing we never did. I could ride my bike to play Ultimate Frisbee.

But Lily could not abide the comings and goings of the grad student biologist from the first-floor garage apartment. She complained for a couple of weeks until Mom put another refrigerator in the addition so he wouldn't have to use our kitchen. We still had to share the laundry room, though. I had to urge Lily's patience while demanding that Mom get him out! Mom needed the money, Lily couldn't adjust, and I was stuck in the middle.

Meanwhile, I was trying to get our $4,000 back from the failed real-estate transaction. We figured the seller owed us our deposit, plus the $1,500 we had blown on inspections and appraisals after he failed to tell us the house was full of mold. The neighbor had gotten hold of a mold inspection report detailing the problem, dated months before the house went on the market. We showed a copy to the selling agent and demanded recompense. But the seller denied responsibility, and Lily wanted to take

The Image of the Trinity

him to small claims court. I wanted to just let it go. That's what our realtor advised. I was trying to finish school, work part-time, find a full-time job, renovate the house, mediate between Lily and the rest of the world, and take care of two little girls. I didn't need to play lawyer. Lily insisted.

So I studied the mold inspection report, learned about the different kinds of organisms listed on it, looked up arcane real estate laws and pored over our contract-to-purchase. There was no question in my mind that the seller had known the house had a problem and should have disclosed it. But the magistrate-judge wouldn't admit the mold inspection report as evidence because I hadn't hired the environmental expert who wrote it to come and testify in court. Our key proof was useless. We lost, just like my realtor told me we would.

One evening soon after that, I came home from work hungry and started boiling water for pasta. Lily had been home all day, but, as was often the case, making dinner fell to me.

"Here, why don't you put some salt in the water," she said, pushing past me at the stove.

I blew up.

"You think I don't know how to boil water??!!! I've been cooking since I was twelve years old! I taught you how to cook!! Just get out. Just go! Why don't you just go??!!! Just leave us alone!! Just leave!!!!!"

I hadn't meant it. I told her I was sorry later. I hadn't meant it! I didn't really want her to go.

> Unhappy marriages so resemble one another that we do not need to know too much about the course of this one.
>
> —Joan Didion,
> "Some Dreamers of the Golden Dream"

One of my favorite photographs shows us kneeling at the altar at Christ Church, Xenia, Ohio. My face is turned to Lily's with a big smile. Sunlight shining down from a high window reflects off her carefully curled hair and the flowered crown that held her veil, like Maid Marian. In the background, you can see the hand and clerical robe of the Reverend Arthur Ransome, the white-bearded, bespectacled Church of England vicar from Cornwall who had retired to Xenia to live near his daughter and grandkids. Lily had decided on the first day we stepped foot inside this little stone church that Arthur would marry us.

In the months leading up to our wedding, I had been reading the Croatian theologian Miroslav Volf, who imagined human relationships as sacraments—earthly pictures of heavenly realities, especially the divine relationships among the three Persons of the Trinity, Father, Son, and Holy Spirit. "God came into the world so as to make human beings, created in the image of God, live with one another and with God in the kind of communion in which divine persons live with one another," Volf wrote. I had expected to see the image of the Trinity stamped on our marriage and on the Episcopal church, with its sacramental worship and social conscience, two elements I was sure would sink their teeth into our very flesh, make us walk and talk more like Jesus.

Our friends Chad and Kim gave us a leatherbound journal as a wedding gift that day. "To Jesse + Lily on your sweet wedding day," reads a handwritten inscription. "With love from Chad + Kim prior to their sweet wedding day." The leather is carved with Celtic scrollwork, and three-pointed, Trinitarian knots adorn the pewter clasp for the rawhide closure. The Celtic knotwork of Lily's wedding band held a triangular garnet. I'd given it to her at Christmas a few months earlier, along with a cross necklace with another garnet, our common birthstone, and molded with triquetra, ancient, three-sided Celtic knots that symbolized the Trinity.

I wrote text for our wedding invitation, a shape poem in the form of a cross, ending with a holy mission: "To enact God's image on life's stage, where dialogues portray what soliloquies never will: Holy Trinity, Self-giving Community, Divine love." Our wedding hymn was the Trinitarian "Holy, Holy, Holy," as though divinity would emerge from our spiritual union like the Holy Spirit emerges from the love between the Father and the Son in Catholic doctrine. "In the image of God he created them. Male and female he created them." Our wedding programs were printed in an Old English font on mottled beige parchment paper with edges I burnt by hand with a candle. The program began with the words "Marriage is the Greatest Image of the Trinity" followed by a poem I wrote:

We
Worship,
Come together,
Share the Divine love,
Thank the source of our love

That's what I'd seen for our lives: shape poetry in the flesh, the Truth Incarnate.

On the second page of our leather journal, just after Chad and Kim's inscription, I wrote this, on Valentine's Day 2002, about a month before our second wedding anniversary, with Aurora about ten months old and my parents' marriage in shambles:

> When my tears could have drowned us both,
> She wholeheartedly held me, and here we float
> Clinging to each other, lovers unclothed

I showed Lily that poem and asked her to write notes or poetry back and forth with me in the journal, but the next entry is mine, five years later, lyrics for a song written by lamplight on the night she told me she thought our marriage was over:

> I want to be the one to make you smile
> To wipe away the tears that you cried
> When I hurt you, for what? I still wonder why

I find some comfort in Didion's words. Maybe the question isn't why lovers stop loving but why they keep loving—or why we don't all cheat on each other or kill each other like Didion's characters did. There are as many reasons why marriages fail as there are words in a language, expressions on a face, tones in a voice, and nerves beneath the human skin.

I didn't know what Lily expected out of our marriage. For years, I would tell her I loved her—not nearly often enough, but once or twice a week, maybe. Her response was usually the same: "Where did that come from?" I know she despaired that she would never live in the English village of her dreams, write a novel, shoot a movie, or make friends with globe-trotting actors or artists. None of these fantasies seemed to have very much to do with the life she had, the life with me and our precious daughters, and maybe that was the point. Whatever she wanted, it wasn't what she had, never had been. She told me she had tried to leave me at the altar and Joe had talked her out of it. She told me she had never loved me.

> "She said, 'I will go after my lovers, who give me my bread and my water, my wool and my linen, my olive oil and my drink.'"
>
> —Hosea 2:5

This Littler Light

Lily had taken the girls to visit her parents in Florida when the bank statement came. I'd been dragging her to counseling sessions and to look at houses so we could get away from my family and try to rebuild. We were supposed to be trying to make our marriage work. I'd offered to spend thousands on the Lasik surgery she'd been hinting at for years, and I didn't understand why she'd now decided against it. We shopped for a second car, for her freedom, but she hadn't liked any of them. She couldn't afford her own place yet, so I'd even contemplated moving into a homeless shelter to give her some space, but that just seemed like going too far. When I opened the envelope from the bank, I saw them: a $10,000 payment to our credit card company, the last of several I would soon discover, plus a $20,000 transfer to a separate account at another bank. I hadn't looked at credit card bills or bank statements for years, just taking Lily's word for it because I'd thought it was my job to trust her after the post-miscarriage depression spending. In less than a year's time, the $80,000 we'd had for our future home had been cut in half, and she'd moved half of what was left to her own personal account. I was $60,000 poorer in one fell swoop.

There were the charges, totaling tens of thousands of dollars, to on-line retailers like Urban Outfitters and Nordstrom.com. But where was all the merchandise? I opened Lily's closet. It was packed like a sardine can. Dresses and jackets on hangers jammed so tightly onto the rod you couldn't remove them. It was a mass of expensive fashion, wrapped in plastic, as dense as a heavy bag at a boxing gym. The antique wooden trunk I had yelled at her for buying at $300 when we were supposed to be saving for a house? Here was a second one hiding at the bottom of her closet, stuffed, no doubt, with more clothing, surrounded by shoe boxes, above on the shelf, below on the floor, two deep and three or four high, stacked flush against the closet door like drawers in a morgue.

Four-figure debits and credits had been coming in and out of our bank account like wins and losses at a blackjack table. I learned later that Lily had become the butt of jokes down at the post office, where dozens of packages would arrive every week without my knowing. She'd kept enough of them to destroy our savings, but she'd also returned most of them, a revolving door of e-commerce.

I drove to my bank and moved what was left of my money into a new account under my name only. My heart raced as I realized Lily would soon come back into my home. Did I have to let her in? I called the police. How could I protect myself? I felt like I had nothing left, and now I was going to have to expose what little I had to more thievery. How could I keep my money safe with a criminal living in my house? The officer said I couldn't keep my wife out of her own home. The marital assets were hers to do with as she pleased.

I waited till Lily got home to confront her. Her parents had given her their almost-new Corolla to drive back from Florida.

"I saw the bank statements," I said. "What are you doing? I thought we were trying to make this work. How are we ever going to move out of here if you spend all our money?"

"I'm sorry," she said. "I was sad."

Years earlier, before we conceived Rowan, I had confided to Father Tim in New Hampshire about the depression and anger that made me an irritable and verbally abusive husband. We'd been slipping into the back row at St. John's every Sunday. Lily made little effort to be on time, I think because she didn't want to go to church but didn't have the guts to say so. Our priest then had offered, twice, to counsel me and Lily, to try and bridge the gap. I never took him up on it. Lily had also pushed me, every now and then, to get counseling, though she wasn't interested in it for herself. I always told myself it was my problem to handle, that I just had to be stronger, to love her more, to sacrifice my own impulses. I needed to tolerate a little more frivolous spending and caution her more gently when she was going too far. I needed to be the one to confront every neighbor who made too much noise or left trash in the hallway. I needed to pick up and move whenever she tired of a house or a town, six times in six years. I tried to jump through every hoop, but it was never enough.

In North Carolina, when I was finally ready to ask for help, it wasn't there. We had attended an Episcopal church nearby for nearly three years, our marriage falling apart. In an upper-middle-class congregation of doctors, professors, and unattached graduate students, everyone else's lives looked perfect, so I tried to pretend mine was too. My Baptist mother-in-law phoned and told me our priest had given my wife $250 to help with getting a place of her own.

"If we'd have known she was gonna try and move out, we never would have given her that car," Bootsie said. "We were trying to help you guys."

I called our priest and told him my side of the story. He'd had almost no contact with us for three years. A gifted and studied preacher, he'd always seemed too busy. I hadn't wanted to bother him. He had no idea that she'd spent most of our savings—real estate equity we'd agreed would pay for a house and eventually our girls' college education. I told him I took responsibility for my anger at her repeated financial betrayals, but she needed to take responsibility for her own actions. I needed someone to intervene, not enable her in breaking up our family. He simply suggested we should go to a counselor. I told him we had tried two counselors and Lily lasted just until they started asking for changes from her: two sessions each. My priest had nothing to offer.

> I pray also for those who will believe in me ... that all of them may be one, Father, just as you are in me and I am in you. May they also be in us so that the world may believe that you have sent me. I have given them the glory that you gave me, that they may be one as we are one—I in them and you in me—so that they may be brought to complete unity. Then the world will know that you sent me and have loved them even as you have loved me.
>
> —Jesus in John 17:20–23

On Trinity Sunday in June 2007, I went to Emmaus Way. Off and on that spring, I'd been coming to this little church that met in a photographer's studio above a coffee shop in a historic business district near Duke University in Durham. They met at 5 p.m., so I could go whether I'd gone to the Episcopal church that morning or not. We'd sit around a circle, on couches or big cushy chairs, and a pro musician, Wade Baynham, who had built a regional following on the West Coast with his band The Basics before moving to Durham, would lead us in singing music from bands like Over the Rhine or U2, songs seeking spiritual meaning in everyday human experiences.

I'd met Wade while working on a freelance story for *The N&O* about Dale Baker, the drummer who had played on Letterman and Leno and toured Europe with Sixpence None the Richer before an angry split in Nashville and his redirection toward teaching drum lessons and preschool in Durham. Emmaus Way had committed to patronage for local musicians, so helping Wade with worship provided one of Dale's regular paying gigs. I'd hung out with the two of them while Dale recorded drums for a client's record in Wade's home studio. Between Wade and Dale and Emmaus Way's tiny size, I'd hoped this church might provide the real friendship I hadn't found at the Episcopal church.

The Image of the Trinity

"Emergent" or postmodern churches like Emmaus Way tend to attract worshippers in their twenties and thirties who think they hear a divine call to love each other and the world around them but at the same time doubt the human ability to understand anything God might have to say. There is no magisterium or dogmatic priest to interpret and explain the world or the Bible with any absolute authority. The people, with all their strengths and shortcomings, success and suffering, idiosyncrasies and expertise, together in conversation with sacred texts and Christian tradition, try to figure how to follow Jesus in the twenty-first century.

The name Emmaus Way comes from a story in the Gospel of Luke where two of Jesus's followers meet him on the road to a Jewish town called Emmaus and don't recognize him until after they offer him hospitality as a lonely traveler. "As he sat at meat with them, he took bread, and blessed it, and brake, and gave to them. And their eyes were opened, and they knew him." Emergent churches are built on the idea that spiritual truth depends upon experience in community, that God is known in relationship, especially sharing meals together, an idea that had motivated so much idealism back on my wedding day.

But there was something more than just the transparency of sitting in a small room, looking at one another across an intimate circle. Wade had gone through a divorce—with his songwriting partner of twenty years no less—and had just remarried that spring. Dale had absorbed betrayal in the Christian music industry that was supposed to be telling a story of love. They had watched hope disintegrate before their eyes, yet they were still here, helping us worship, not denying the pain, but looking for God in it, as though God hadn't been the one to let them down but was, instead, the Comforter who knew suffering on the cross and could walk through it with them. On this Trinity Sunday, Wade led us in a song, a prayer he'd written after his mother's suicide when he was seventeen years old:

> Will you listen and not judge me when I pray?
> Will you hear my voice and listen to my song?
> Will you help me tell what's not and what is real?
> Will you hear my cry and cry with me?
> Will you stay to see the turning of the sky?
> Will you stay with me and be there when I die?
> Will you hold my hand and walk with me and talk with me?
> Will you stay with me today?
> Will you be the one to save me from my fear?
> Will you save, will you save me?

For me, at this point, salvation wasn't just finding hope or making the best of bad circumstances. I thought our marriage could be redeemed. In our counseling sessions, I had seen how Lily's need to be taken care of and my need to take care had whisked us into a toxic soup. She couldn't help but whine, nag, and sigh about all the disappointments of her life. I couldn't help but try to fix them. She couldn't help but be disappointed in my fixes, because what was broken was inside of her: I could never replace her deadbeat parents. I couldn't help but sink into depression, a failure. She couldn't help but pile on more complaints. I couldn't help but explode in rage, once every couple of months or so, screaming about her humble suggestion that salt would help the water boil faster.

The answer, of course, was for her to deal with her shit and for me to deal with mine. So what if she believed in the death penalty? So what if she didn't want to live in a Christian commune? Maybe we just spent money differently. Maybe we just thought differently about what God wanted from us. Maybe I'd become just another liberal fundamentalist, and she had every right to feel judged, as she said she did, by what I left unsaid.

"God's very being is a being that's in relationship with himself, you know, Father, Son, Holy Spirit, eternally in relationship with himself," said Trigger, a skater-theologian, bald-headed and baggy-pantsed, one of several Duke Divinity students at Emmaus Way.

Pastor Tim had prompted us to reflect on the Trinity.

"It's just interesting that there's this otherness, in a sense, within God, and it's kind of like the way that we relate to each other in a body," Trigger went on. "It's engaging with the other, it's like the Trinity itself can be a model for church relationships, human sexual relationships. All sorts of other types of relationships can be understood in a trinitarian way of thinking."

Eternally in relationship, yes. But how had I missed that "otherness" aspect of the Trinity and how it served as a model for marriage?

Pastor Tim quoted the German theologian Jürgen Moltmann, who had mentored Miroslav Volf in his trinitarian thinking.

"'The Trinity is difference and intimate unity,'" Tim said. "The best way to get some really bad theology is to grab one of those two but not the other. Unity often means, 'We'll do it my way, and we'll feel good about it.'"

"Preach it, brother."

I didn't really say that. Episcopalians and Emergents don't say that sort of thing. But I could have. Tim hit me square between the eyes.

The Image of the Trinity

"Unity and difference radically changes a whole philosophy of partnership," Tim said. "Our whole philosophy of ministry should be that of embracing difference, letting different be different, and in some way fashioning intimacies in that difference."

Yes. Yes. How had I missed that back on my wedding day? Yes, Tim said, paraphrasing C. S. Lewis, God does invite us into the triune life, but we have limits.

"We can't do that as human beings," he said. "I can't say that my life is intimately in Andy's life. I can't say that, because I'm not divine. We are not a Trinity. We don't relate in the way God does."

We sang the Irish hymn, "Be Thou My Vision," just like on my wedding day.

> Heart of my own heart, whatever befall,
> Still be my Vision, O Ruler of all.

We celebrated Communion, giving and receiving the bread and wine like friends at a party, talking and eating and drinking together, no priest imparting truth and grace to the rest of us, but all givers and receivers together. Wade called us back to our seats, inviting us to reflect on where we'd seen God's presence in human relationships and where we still hoped to see it.

"I just want to give thanks for Moltmann tonight," I said. Nerd. "I read some of his writing a few years back. . . . When you live a half-truth, you figure it out, it doesn't quite work, and you have conflicts with other people, and I realized that's what I've been doing. I've been really holding on to this idea of unity and minimizing the importance of difference. You really can't have unity without acknowledging the differences that we all have and embracing them, rather than looking for all those differences to disappear into the unity."

Wade could respond out of the wisdom gleaned from his own failed marriage. "I was certainly taught to be the person who was right in an argument or to be the person who won something," he said. "Understanding and appreciating other people in conflict was certainly not something I was taught."

I had hope. Maybe I could accept the differences between Lily and me, not try to change them. Maybe I could sacrifice my own ideals more often, try harder to give her what she wanted. Maybe we could get that newly built house Lily liked, twenty minutes out into the country, away from my family. Maybe I couldn't bike to work or walk to the farmer's market. But whatever. My girls needed their parents to stay together. Difference and intimate unity.

> Little girl there's far too many choices
> for you to ever really get your head clean
> and it's so easy taking cues from California
> soap operas and checkout line magazines
>
> —Bill Mallonee, "Pour Kid"

After so many failed attempts, after so many years, I finally got Lily to go out to dinner with me, just the two of us, without the kids, one Friday night in July, six months after she'd first threatened to leave. After we ate, we sat outside on a brick retaining wall at Southern Village at the edge of Chapel Hill. A band played on the village green across the street. I put my arm around Lily, leaned into her, felt a rush of adrenaline at the feel of her warmth.

"What is it?" she asked me.

"I'm just euphoric to be here with you," I said.

She moved away. "I can't," she said. "I just can't."

"You can't what?"

"I can't be the person I'm supposed to be if I'm with you."

I started to cry. We moved to the car. That was it. She'd already rented an apartment. She was moving out in a week. I'd had a gawd-damn, fucking epiphany, and it was too late.

"Shit," I said. I pounded the steering wheel with my palm in a fist. "Shit."

The next morning we woke up six-year-old Aurora and two-year-old Rowan, whom the priest had baptized, and told them we weren't going to live together anymore. We wept and held one another in our king-sized bed. Rowan had no idea what was going on. Tears came to Aurora's eyes. She understood it all too well. She'd been hearing us fight for far too long. It was the worst moment of my life, watching my little girl cry because her parents couldn't get their acts together.

For months I mourned. I screamed at God until my throat hurt when there was no one else to hear. Why hadn't I asked for help years ago? I was an upside down orphan, my dear children living half the week outside my home. I thought I had done things right. I had remained chaste until marriage. I had wed a Christian woman. I had cooked suppers, cleaned bathrooms, offered my body as an armrest to make breastfeeding more comfortable, woken up in the dark of night to warm bottles and feed the babies. And the person who had promised to love me had abandoned me. In an age of throwaway marriages, maybe this sounds like melodrama. But I didn't believe in divorce. I believed it was wrong. Jesus said that, didn't he? But it didn't matter what Jesus said. It was happening, and it was real. Everyone who was supposed to represent God on earth had let me down. Most painfully, I had let my girls and their mother down. And I had let myself down.

It wasn't a good marriage. From our wedding night onward there was an unbridgeable chasm between us. But I'd accepted that. I knew a lot of people who had it worse. At least I wasn't calling her ugly names behind her back or cheating on her like so many married men did. In the marriage counseling, a therapist told me to stop chasing her and her to stop running. That pretty well summed up seven years of marriage. I didn't lose my soulmate. I lost hope, the religious kind of hope, the hope that some day, somehow, life would be better, that we would be saved, live happily ever after in a promised land, participate in the life and love of God.

My aspiration had been nothing short of embodying the presence of God on earth, and I had failed beyond anything I had ever imagined. It wasn't just another mediocre marriage, or even another bad marriage: I couldn't even hold it together. The image of God was shattered. Light of the world? Please. I couldn't even see for myself, much less show anyone else the way. What credibility did I have, as a moral example? Hide it under a bushel. Satan blew it out. It wasn't my marriage that died. Hope died. My god died.

Christmas came five months later. I fell to my knees on my hardwood floor, sobbing aloud, alone, as Over the Rhine's Karin Bergquist sang:

> Snow angel, snow angel
> Someday I'm gonna fly
> This cold and broken heart of mine
> Will one day wave goodbye
> Goodbye to this cruel wicked world
> And all the tears I've cried
> Snow angel, snow angel
> I'll meet you in the sky

This Littler Light

The prophet Isaiah told me healing might come, here on earth, and I wanted to believe: "Drop down, ye heavens, from above, and let the skies pour down righteousness." I wrote more lyrics in my wedding journal:

> Send a righteous rain
> Wash away the shame
> Soak me, soothe my pain
> Send a righteous rain

I found these words because the Anglican lectionary had told me what to read. But I left the Episcopal church. I knew I needed a smaller place where, if a miracle rained down from heaven, I could build a sense of community quickly, tell my story and hear from people who shared my experiences or could at least relate to them well enough to help me make sense of them. The hospitality I thought I might taste because Emmaus Way was a small church turned out to be the church's "most critical spiritual discipline," according to Pastor Tim. They wanted to hear my story, right in the middle of worship, as though God was present in weakness at least as much as in strength.

I had major questions: How was I going to raise my girls as a single dad? Would I ever love again? Would God bless a second marriage? Post-marital sex? What if a new wife wanted children?

"You're sterile," the urologist had announced to me a few months after my surgery. It was supposed to be good news, but it broke my heart.

Peter Abelard's passionate trysts with Heloise got him castrated. Like Abelard, I blamed myself for my handicap: "How just . . . was the judgment of God that had struck in those parts of my body with which I had sinned." For years quenching my libido had felt beastly, no union of loving souls but a favor from Lily to me, and only on those rare occasions when she felt charitable, or just got tired of pushing me away. My desire was her burden. I had wished I could make it go away, to free her from the duty and myself from the rejection. But I had no more control over my testosterone than a tomcat did. Most of the time, I had pretended I didn't need it, and some of the time she had pretended she did. Vasectomy had solved neither of these problems, but at least it protected us from the babies I both hoped for and feared.

Sensible friends had asked, "Why doesn't Lily just go on the pill?" And, of course, in a sane home that might have happened. But we did not live in a sane home. If I could somehow have escaped the codependence, my need for acceptance, my need to understand the inner life she couldn't articulate, my need to make her happy, I might have chosen a maddening

The Image of the Trinity

abstinence or divorce—the lesser of two evils?—to remedy Lily's fear of motherhood, her fear of the life we had.

Instead, I had made myself sterile. I had watched friends weep and beg God to heal their infertility, and yet I had chosen it. I had no interest in easy answers or pretense. No one was going to convince me that everything would be OK. I thought this might be my last stop on my way out of the church forever.

Wade helped to heal me. Instead of the saccharine worship choruses or doctrinal hymns of my past, we would sing songs of gospel hope in the midst of the worst human experiences, like Julie Miller's "Ride the Wind to Me":

> I've seen a faithless lover
> Take you down to deep water
> And I have watched a fragile wing
> Tangled up in longings
> get broken in the struggle
> In my heart I see you run free
> Like a river down to the sea
> All the chains that held you down
> Will be in pieces on the ground
> You'll drink the rain and ride the wind to me

Emmaus Way was a place where people lingered after worship, and many of my new friends took my daughters into their laps, helping them with art projects and watching over their safety so I could enjoy some adult company. I finally felt like I had partners in raising my daughters, people who affirmed my gifts and filled in what I was lacking, rather than constantly demanding more from me. When large groups of us would go out to dinner after worship, it was nice just to have women around thoughtful enough to take my girls to the ladies room so I wouldn't have to wait for the urinal brigade to clear.

Another musician, Mark Williams, who'd had enough success in the late nineties to open for Caedmon's Call, shared his own story of divorce, the threat of excommunication from a conservative church where he'd been an elder, judgment from his family, and acceptance at Emmaus Way. Wade, Mark, and Tim started meeting with me frequently to hear my experience and share their own. As time wore on, I watched congregants organize weeks upon weeks of meals for families in times of illness or childbirth. A lesbian seminary student visited the pulpit to share her story of finding her sexual identity, suffering rejection from other Christians, and finally finding this church where she could be herself. She soon met a girlfriend and they started worshiping together. Discussions of sexual ethics—a suddenly complex issue for me as a single man in his thirties—brought together diverse voices and left room for faithful sex in loving, committed relationships without the formality of a wedding ceremony.

Emmaus Way provided space where we could explore our deepest vulnerabilities—same-sex attractions, stalled careers, mental illness. In marriage, Lily had made me beg for intimacy in all its forms, and that made for a certain sort of loneliness. Now my bed was literally empty of anyone but me. And into this sexual solitude, the Lord spoke through the Psalmist: "Stand in awe and sin not. Commune with thyself upon thy bed and be still."

My trinitarian theology had surely construed the marriage bed as a place of communion, the love between man and wife as a throne for the Spirit, a sacrament enfleshing God's interdependent, triune love in human bodies. But in what sense could I commune with myself? After a bit of reflection, I decided the writer was not urging me toward masturbation.

Still, I didn't want to run from the sexual analogy. I'd read St. Teresa of Avila and seen photos of Bernini's sculpture of her, in ecstasy, ravished by an angel of God. Teresa wrote of her "ecstatic raptures" in orgasmic language: "She finds herself slipping into a kind of swoon. With a rush of gentle joy, she feels everything begin to fade away. The breath and bodily powers progressively dwindle. . . . The eyes close of their own accord." If Teresa could experience God as a sexual partner, why couldn't I, as a man, do the same? The image of the angel penetrating her with a spear didn't help me. As a straight man, in fact, I found it troubling. But what if I could imagine God as my Beloved, beckoning, waiting to envelop me in her love? What if the Celtic Christians were right, and God's Spirit is a "wild goose"? What if I'm to hunt her like I pursue a woman?

I wrote song lyrics; they come as close as I can to describing the feminine Spirit, the image of God, male and especially female, beloved by men:

> I reach out to touch her, my fingers clutch the air
> Apparition, holy ghost, she's never far, like when she's close
> I look deep inside, to the depths of my own heart
> And there my lover lies, singing, "Never shall we part"
> I look deep inside, in the stillness of the night
> And there my lover lies, singing, "Lie with me tonight"

Sex means different things to different people. To some, it's power: conquest, seduction, worldly success. To others, it's procreation: the unconditional love of a child, a biological imperative, immortality. There might be some pure lovers out there somewhere who do it for the simple joy of the other, but most of us use sex to get particular psychological needs met. For me, sex meant acceptance. It meant my wife trusted and loved me enough to open herself to me. It meant I was worthy of a beautiful woman that other men lusted for. It meant, despite evidence to the contrary, that she wanted me. The more I felt she was hiding her soul from me, the more I wanted her body to tell me she was mine.

Now she was gone, and I had to find my acceptance elsewhere. I knew that sexual substitutes like masturbation or casual intercourse could give me a momentary feeling of acceptance, but I also knew these disappointed in their mere physicality and their brevity. My physical needs were real, but I couldn't try to fulfill them to the neglect of my spiritual need to be loved. "Be still," God's word said to me. With this, I heard an implicit promise: "I am with you."

I tried to believe God remained with me in my suffering, like with Adam outside the garden, Samson at the grain wheel, or Peter as the rooster crowed. I wish I could say with St. Paul that God's grace was sufficient for me. But I still flailed around for human connection.

Even before Lily moved out, something inside me had believed her when she said our marriage was over. There were six months where she remained in our bed (or on the couch) but we didn't live as lovers. I had tried not to give up hope, dragging her to counselors' offices and to look at houses. Still, I tried to brace myself for what was coming, and I couldn't help noticing potential replacements.

And I really mean just noticing. Not dating, though Lily would disappear many nights until 4 a.m., chasing a local rock band around town, leaving me at home with the girls. She would be out with her new friend, the Sexual Revolutionary, who was breaking up with her live-in boyfriend of seven years because she just didn't love him any more. She and Lily had read an article in *Cosmo* or some such magazine about women feeling empowered by leaving their long-term relationships. I tried to believe we could stay together. I tried to trust that she would soon settle down and start to act like a thirty-one-year-old mother of two. I wasn't flirting or barhopping or browsing match.com. Just trying to make new friendships, and wondering.

A couple of months after Lily moved out, I went out with a girl who used to come to my band's shows. There was nothing romantic about it except maybe a smidge of mutual curiosity. A family friend—let's call her Prudence—saw us there. She knew more about me by rumor than relationship.

"What are you doing?" she asked me later. "You're still married."

And that was true. According to North Carolina law, Lily had to wait a year before she could divorce me. In this waiting period, I had to figure out how to interact with people, including women, outside the toxicity of our marriage. As I saw it, I had tried to reconcile, I had failed, and now I was free. People who really knew me were supportive, but I realized I was going to have to live under others' judgment, and be OK with that, something I never anticipated. I was supposed to guide people toward Jesus, not be a stumbling block. Yet my life was my life, and there was nothing I could do about it, unless I took a vow of celibacy, and I didn't feel called to that. My wife had left, and I was going to date again. My friends could either support me, try to help me date in a faithful way, or mind their own business. Was I right? Was I wrong? Who knows? To be human is to be judged, both by God and by other people. I was a broken creature in a broken, beautiful world. My life was pleasing neither to God nor to myself, and my only option was to keep on living it. None of this was what God intended. But it was still no fun when someone pointed that out. God was with me in my mess, and I needed others to be with me too.

I'm calling "Prudence" by that name because of the Beatles song. It seems to me a miracle of twentieth-century pop music—a real divine intervention—that it happened to be Prudence Farrow, the actress Mia's sister, who was taking her human religious practices a bit too seriously when John Lennon and the band went to India in 1968 to study transcendental meditation. "She'd be locked in (our hut) for three weeks and was trying to reach God quicker than anyone else," Lennon told rock journalist David Sheff. Maybe I'm just calling it a miracle because the song has one of my favorite Paul McCartney bass lines. But, really, isn't "prudence" just a double-edged sword of a character trait? Do you know anybody like that, always trying to reach God quicker than anyone else? This little light of MINE!!!! MINE!!! I sure can relate. You have to love the prudent, because they're trying to do the right thing, and yet they (we!) have a hard time admitting that we're incapable of *always* doing the right thing. We praise the prudent, and yet they (we!) are not that fun to be around. In the Gospels, the Pharisees were the prudent ones. Jesus was the imprudent one, healing the lame on the Sabbath, knocking over tables in the Temple, dining with hookers and small-time crooks. The prudent always have something to prove, and it can make us, well, prudes. Lennon's lyrics evoke a sense of

The Image of the Trinity

our place in creation, calling us to embrace what beauty is already within our reach, rather than always striving for the unattainable. I can almost hear Nanny speaking to me in Lennon's song. I wished John could come back and sing it to Prudence. Dear Prudence, notice the bright sky, feel the breeze, hear the birds, try to understand the real world I'm living in, not some ideal world we both wish we had. Dear Prudence, open your eyes.

Worshiping around the circle at Emmaus Way, we were able to look at one another through open eyes. Mine locked with Joy's one Sunday soon after Lily left, and I wondered. To have wound up here, together, in a tiny church, where the pastor doesn't preach but leads dialogue, where we question traditional interpretations of scripture, sing radio hits and obscure singer-songwriter music, and chat boisterously while exchanging the bread and wine with each other—well, we must have had something in common.

We talked briefly one Sunday that summer, discovering a shared interest in Latino immigrant culture. I soon got a phone call from Joy's roommate Tracie, offering for the two of them to bring dinner and babysit my girls once a week so I could do whatever I might need to do for myself—go out with friends, play a sport, whatever. The thing is, I didn't really have many friends nearby at that time. I'd been so consumed trying to make Lily happy that I hadn't put much effort into making friends. For a couple of years, I'd been playing Ultimate Frisbee at a local park but always turned down the invitations to go out for a beer afterward, saying I had to get back to my family. So I told Tracie it'd be great if they brought dinner, but I might just like to hang out with them at the house after I put the girls to bed. Of course, I was curious about Joy, and I thought she was curious about me, but we didn't talk about those ulterior motives until much later.

Over the next six months, we found reasons to spend time together, almost never just the two of us. She helped me plan my girls' birthday parties in September and April. We hung out in groups at my house or hers. We talked about the possibility of dating and started planning for July, when my divorce would be final. We never kissed, held hands, or even hugged, but in some ways got more intimate than that. We talked by phone and a couple of times in person about intense things: our sexual histories (or lack thereof), our desire for each other, my vasectomy and her hope for children, how maybe we could get married, and even how she could come to Mexico and interpret for me so I could finish a potential book on immigrant farmworkers. I wrote in my journal:

This Littler Light

> You were in my dreams in the days when I still dreamed
> Sowing peace together on the battlefield
> But I lost my way, thought alone I could redeem the one I love
> Now I'm crawling back, could you help me to believe?

Back in college, I had chased girls I thought might make good co-pastors with me at some nice progressive church. Lily had needed more from me than any of them, which might be why I ended up with her and not any of them. Struggling to survive in our marriage, I had given up on having a partnership in service to the world. Joy, I thought, was redemption.

But I had a nagging suspicion that this was all too easy, moving from one "lifelong" partner to another in the span of a year. I told Joy we would need to start from scratch that summer, dating without long-term expectations until we got to know each other better. But I met her mom and heard they were talking about shopping for wedding dresses, and I freaked out. I wasn't ready for this. Joy was thirty years old and had never had a boyfriend. I crushed her. If there were civil torts for such things, a judge would have found me negligent. I led her on because it made me feel better. In the midst of it, I believed we had a future, but I didn't do a good job of scrutinizing my motives for believing such a thing.

Looking back, I think I invested much of the gratitude I had toward Emmaus Way into Joy, a lone symbol of my rescue from a failed marriage and its aftermath, a rebirth of hope in a loving God, one with a plan for a flourishing existence in earthly life. But a single human relationship, no matter how romantic or intimate or cooperative, was never going to enact the Trinity here on earth. Like Moses leaning on Aaron and Hur to raise his staff toward God as Israel battled Amalek, I needed an entire community to hold me up. God did create Adam and Eve in God's image, but God soon called a people, Israel, to carry his presence on the earth. Like each ancient Hebrew and every Christian today, I needed to hear God's voice in the quiet of my own bed, to reflect faith, hope, and love into my own community, just as I needed these reflected to me. No one person could do it all. Difference and intimate unity.

11

Intentional Community

For the first time in my life, at thirty-three years old, I'm an honest-to-goodness slob of a bachelor—a grown man who can't get too worked up about a few ants in the kitchen, who lets the beer bottles overflow the recycling bin and might, on occasion, serve friends and family their beverages in stackable, fifty-cent-refill-at-the-gas-station plastic tumblers because it's just too hard to carry all those nice drinking glasses out to the dining room. This sort of indifference annoys my girlfriend, Julie. She's already plotting to redecorate my house if and when we marry. A neon-colored neo-impressionist print of a pirate ship from the seventies and a framed poster of Tolkien's wizard Gandalf hang prominently in my living room. They top her hit list.

Shit, it's her house, after all. She talked me into buying it.

As you know, I'd been trying to move near Duke for nigh on a decade, but now that's an afterthought. I've been a single dad for three years now, working at *The News & Observer* for almost four, covering local government and crime in Chapel Hill. At this point Durham itself, not Duke, is the big draw: Julie's here, Emmaus Way, our favorite nightspots. This house is in the middle of it all: a mile and a half from her work and the church, around the corner from a pool hall, coffee shop, locavore bistro, and a music venue. It's five blocks from Ninth Street—the historic campus-area business district where Emmaus Way used to meet in that second-story studio. And, of course, it's three blocks from the edge of Duke's original East Campus.

Julie and I are walking down Ninth Street from the quaint bungalow she rents with some roommates. I helped her move there a couple of months ago, on the same day I helped Lily move for the second time in less than a year. Hey, if you've got to move your ex-wife and your girlfriend, you might as well use the same U-Haul. It's been almost three years since she left, and it's clear I'll never extricate myself from Lily's needs, not as long as I've got the girls to worry about.

Passing E. K. Powe Elementary School and its brick neo-classical façade, Julie and I chat about my new house on Clarendon Street.

"Do you think you're going to paint any of the rooms?" she asks me.

"I only paint because a woman tells me to," I say with a smirk.

What a jerk, you might say. And you might be right. And I might dodge by saying I was trying to be funny. And I was.

But the more I think about it, the more I believe it. Assuming there's no bare wood that needs a weather seal and no ugly cracks or repair work that needs touching up, and the only reason to paint a wall is for the cause of pure chromatics, I have no internal motivation to pick up a paintbrush.

Lily made me paint most of the rooms in the Portsmouth condo at least twice in the three years we lived there. In between I stood on a ladder a couple of days a week for months on end, painting the trim of the three-story Somersworth duplex to get it ready to sell. My joints hurt from that ladder, making it hard to jog or play Ultimate Frisbee. There, I also painted inside, fixed pipes, ran wires, and installed flooring and insulation. I was working full-time and being a dad through all of this. Five years later, she made me repaint nearly every room in our portion of my parents' house in Carrboro. I was already remodeling two bathrooms and a kitchen, so why not? I understand these are the tasks of a good husband and father. These are the responsible, manly things to do. All I'm saying is, in this brief window of bachelorhood, I'm not gonna do 'em.

This is not what I thought I wanted. I don't see it as the ideal sort of life, this laissez faire domesticity, this selfish, stubborn apathy. It's nothing more than a way to cope. I thought I wanted intentional community. I thought I wanted more connection to others, more of the inconvenience of being close to people, more of the mirroring effect of seeing my flaws in how they hurt those around me, more working together for a common purpose. But after my marriage failed, I needed to regain some hope in the sanctifying power of community.

> There is neither Jew nor Greek, there is neither bond nor free, there is neither male nor female; for ye are all one in Christ Jesus.
>
> —Galatians 3:28 (KJV)

Intentional Community

After church one night a couple of years ago, as we usually did at Emmaus Way, a dozen or so people went out to dinner in Brightleaf, an urban commercial district of renovated tobacco warehouses turned into shops, restaurants, and bars near East Campus. Just a few blocks away was 610 North Buchanan Boulevard, the Duke lacrosse house, where a national media spotlight had shone on the conflicts Durham can't escape: white and black, rich and poor, mansions and crackhouses, country club communities and crime-ridden streets, a world class university and some failing public schools, depending on your particular neighborhood.

An African-American stripper named Crystal Mangum had accused the lacrosse players of race-tinged verbal abuse and gang rape at a team party. Liberals like my own colleagues at *The N&O* had ripped the "upper-crust" players for "Animal House" behavior, reminiscent of "a time when white men raped black women with neither social sanction nor legal penalty." It turned out District Attorney Mike Nifong had likewise gotten caught up in righting history's wrongs in a single, heroic court case, hiding exculpatory evidence and eventually losing his law license because he tried to prosecute the boys for a crime they hadn't committed. The case symbolized everything we knew about Durham and didn't know how to make right. If only it were as easy as sending three privileged white kids to prison. If only Crystal Mangum had been a credible witness.

At Emmaus Way, we at least talked about a more sustained effort. By the time of this post-worship dinner in Brightleaf, the church had moved from that studio on Ninth Street to a storefront downtown, farther from Duke and all the wealth it symbolized, closer to East Durham, where cocaine flowed, prostitutes sauntered, and bullets flew. We weren't meeting in the criminal epicenter, "The Bullseye," but just trying to get closer to where the Two Durhams collided: government halls, the hipster bar and the hip-hop club right next door to each other, the historic Black Wall Street hailed by Booker T. Washington and W. E. B. Du Bois a century ago and now a sleepy side street. We wanted to be fully present in Durham, not just visit for mission projects, but to wade into the poverty, the crime, the needs we would sometimes be able to meet and the needs we would consistently fail to meet.

The girls and I were still living at the DeConto Estate in Carrboro. I felt both beckoned and repelled by Durham. I'd absorbed the fear that led local realtors to steer newcomers to safer areas like Chapel Hill or Cary. Yet Carrboro had started to feel like Celebration, Florida, an entire little town, master-planned by the Walt Disney Company. I wanted my girls to be safe, but I also wanted someplace grittier, more connected to the suffering of the world, honest. These twin desires spun me in circles as I pondered whether a little danger might actually be good for my girls if it meant they would gain a greater understanding of this broken world.

On this particular Sunday night after dinner, I caught a glimpse of what our urban education project might look like. Most of my friends were already gone by the time I strapped my girls into their carseats and Trigger the trinitarian-skater walked toward us. He and I stood chatting about the topic of the Sunday dialogue—the ethics of homosexuality—and Dexter approached us in the darkened parking lot.

Dexter was a middle-aged man with silver caps marring his teeth, an uneasy gait, and the odor of alcohol wafting from his body. He pulled a slip of paper from his wallet and asked Trigger to dial a phone number written there.

"Don't be nervous," Dexter said. "I know I'm a black man."

"Oh! No," Trigger said, taking the number. "Uh, sure."

I had been watching Dexter closely in case I might need to come to Trigger's aid. But Dexter really did just need him to contact the man's brother to pick him up a few blocks away. Trigger left a voicemail, and Dexter was on his way.

In the car as we traveled back to the safe confines of Carrboro, Aurora asked me why Dexter told us not to be nervous. For the first time in my seven-year-old's life, I explained to her the legacies of slavery—the poverty, the crime, the perceptions of crime.

"Daddy," she asked me. "Would you be proud of me when I grow up, if I build a neighborhood where black people and white people could live together? Maybe I could charge less so people who don't have as much money could live there."

"Yes," I said. "I'd be very proud." Difference and intimate unity.

> All the believers were together and had everything in common. They sold property and possessions to give to anyone who had need. Every day they continued to meet together in the temple courts. They broke bread in their homes and ate together with glad and sincere hearts, praising God and enjoying the favor of all the people. And the Lord added to their number daily those who were being saved.
>
> —Acts 2:44–47

Intentional Community

What Aurora didn't know, though, was that something like this neighborhood already existed. Walltown, founded by black Duke University worker George Wall around the turn of the 20th century, lay just at the northern edge of East Campus, a stone's thrown from the lacrosse house and the Queen Anne styles homes of Trinity Park to the east and the neo-colonial and Tudor Revival homes of Watts-Hillandale to the west. Walltown still offered cheap rents in one-story shotgun houses and duplexes, with its traditional African-American population, new Hispanic immigrants, and young white professionals and students craving the walkable distance to Duke, Ninth Street, and Brightleaf, as well as the potential for rising property values. Not only that, but Duke Divinity students and alumni had already been developing a ministry of presence in this pocket of poverty amid the riches of west Durham. I'd first started looking at Walltown years ago, before Lily left, after I'd met New Monastic reformer Jonathan Wilson-Hartgrove when he kept getting arrested with Langley and the others for sitting down in the middle of the Central Prison driveway in Raleigh.

"We come mourning, Lord, the idolatry of this act [of execution]," Jonathan had prayed on St. Patrick's Day, encircled by a dozen other activists in the dark, under a railroad trestle near a corner of the prison grounds. "We come grieving the ways that we as a people have become addicted to death, and we pray, God, that the power of your life that was made manifest in your resurrection would be real here tonight, that it would move in the hearts of all who are gathered here, those whose job it is to carry out this execution, and those of us who have come to resist it. We pray that, by your Spirit, you would make a way for this execution to be stopped. We offer ourselves, Lord, to your service. We pray that you would give us the courage and strength to believe in the power of your nonviolent, self-giving love, whatever we face this evening."

It was two weeks into Lent, and Jonathan applied ashes to the faces gathered around, including my friends from Nazareth House. Jonathan had helped to found another intentional community, Rutba House in Walltown, not focused on death row ministry like Nazareth House, but trying to prevent crime by mentoring young men in the neighborhood toward lives of purpose.

"We pray as we carry the mark of your cross in ashes on our forehead that you would help us to remember you as our Creator and you as the one who has brought an end to sacrifice by giving yourself on the cross," he went on. Jonathan liked to talk about capital punishment as ritual sacrifice for the sins of a whole society, like it was a terrifying scene from an Indiana

Jones movie or the Salem witch trials, not the hidden, sterilized procedure it has become.

"Remember you were dust, and to the dust you will return," he told his comrades.

They crossed over the busy Western Boulevard so they could avoid the bike-rack corral and glaring spotlights the police had set up to contain them. I went back there with Scott to join the throng of peaceful protesters.

"I'm not going to risk arrest yet," Scott had said. "I want to make sure that wouldn't jeopardize my ability to visit somebody and be a spiritual director to somebody on death row."

"I think that's my reason," he said, self-critically. "The thing that was pulling me to do it was kind of wanting the approval of some of the folks that had done it before, you know, like Langley and Sheila and some of the Rutba House folks. And I didn't think that was a good reason."

Difference and intimate unity.

The protestors had soon thereafter crossed on foot back over the busy road directly into the prison entrance. As I watched Jonathan, Langley, and the others sit peacefully, disobeying officers' orders to disband, I talked with Teresa Hurst, whose son Jason, at age twenty-three, had killed his victim for money and a car to go visit his pregnant girlfriend. Here was a youth—barely a man—who had thrown his whole life away and taken another's. The state had decided his life was worthless after what he'd done, but his mother couldn't accept that.

"Just sending him letters is not enough for me," she said. "I want to do something different. I want to do something to help. I want to get this abolished, this death penalty."

Just then, we were interrupted by the sounds of cheering and scores of clapping hands as the protesters left in a paddywagon.

"There they go," I said.

"Is that part of us?" Teresa asked me.

"Yeah, it's all the people that just got arrested."

"I love 'em. I love 'em," she said. "They're wonderful."

A month earlier, I had sat in the living room at Rutba House in Durham, nibbling homemade cookies while the MLK Affinity Group strategized about their day in court for protesting another execution. I'd gotten lost, first knocking on doors a couple of blocks south of Rutba House, in the block nearest to Duke. These same five north-south streets make up Walltown, but the first blocks just to the north of Duke are known collectively as Trinity Heights. This little sliver of a neighborhood has the grand, two-story Victorian and Spanish Mission homes of Trinity Park and Watts-Hillandale, though its streets flow uninterrupted into Walltown. These homes seemed awfully nice for a New Monastic community.

I finally found Rutba House farther from campus, in a cute bungalow across from a little one-story apartment complex with cars parked every which way, signage in Spanish, and squat, brick architecture that dated it some sixty years after George Wall's time. Jonathan and his wife Leah had settled in this neighborhood in pursuit of the racial reconciliation I'd always talked about more than acted on; as more than a dozen white activists sat debating whether to plead guilty to their trespassing charges, a black homeless man, their long-term guest, passed through on the way to his bedroom. These New Monastics offered hospitality to one another and to others as a sign of God's love, taking risks on the margins of society, dumpster diving, and living off donations, embracing those I tend to fear. Even facing potential jail time, their legal strategy session ignored how they might dodge their criminal charges and focused instead on how to communicate their opposition to the death penalty from the courtroom floor.

"I think if we can all agree, then it's clear to the court and the media that we're all doing the same thing," said Jonathan, the de facto leader of the group.

"As far as trespassing, yeah, I am guilty," said Jackie, a mother of young children. "I don't know why I would say I'm not guilty."

"If you put in a guilty plea, then basically it ends there," said Beth, another mother. "There's no opportunity to give any statements in court."

"I don't want anyone to feel like that they can't make an individual decision," said Dan, another member of Rutba House. "It's a very legitimate stance to say, 'I'm guilty of breaking a law that's upholding an unjust act.' And if that's what you're going to say that I'm guilty of, then following the tradition of Gandhi, saying, 'Then it's your job to prosecute me to the fullest extent of the law.' That in turn, then, shows just how much the judge is protecting that system that is perpetrating that act."

"Did Martin Luther King do that as well—always plead guilty?" asked Sheila. "I've always been interested in the Gandhi/King approach, but I feel it may be more important to be all of the same mind on this, to be together."

Difference. Unity. In tandem. In tension.

This Littler Light

> As iron sharpens iron,
> so one person sharpens another.
>
> —Proverbs 27:17

Ever since then, I'd been idealizing this ideal, intentional community, without realizing I had already been living something akin to it. The New Monastics' hospitality was so inspirational, I'd thought I had to do more, to expose myself to greater challenges of love. And then when Lily left, I'd concluded that I just wasn't up to the task. Clearly, a single intimate relationship was more than I could handle, even without trying to save the world. I guess because it was my family, my flesh and blood, I'd thought the DeConto Estate didn't count, even though we were sharing a kitchen, the site of so much iron sharpening iron in any household. The truth was, I hadn't needed Lily or the tenant-biologist or anyone besides Mom, Dad, my siblings, or my daughters in order to slam headlong into difference.

While Mom's standard of neatness was lower than Lily's (she let me wear shoes in the house, for example), it was still higher than mine. I would leave breakfast dishes in the sink or empty oatmeal packets on the counter, only to find everything washed and put away when I got home. I was never sure whether to feel guilty or thankful for this. I decided on gratitude—along with prompter efforts to clean up after myself.

One morning I was rushing out the door for work, trying to grab some breakfast to go. Mom had found my crate of Clementine tangerines on the counter, some of them starting to mold, so she'd put them in a basket in the back of the refrigerator. Thoughtful. Meanwhile, in a further attempt to help, she'd stacked my single-serve yogurts, two high, at the front of the same shelf. So when I reached back for a Clementine, I knocked over the yogurt, which in turn toppled an uncovered drinking cup one of the girls hadn't finished, milk dripping from one shelf, to the next, to the next, and into the crisper at the bottom of the fridge.

"AAAAARGGH!" I grunted, full of purpose, loud enough for Mom to hear out past the door to the addition. "MMMRRRGGGHH!"

"I'm sure glad someone stacked these fucking yogurts for me," I muttered, pulling a bag of milky lettuce out of the drawer and grabbing for a rag hanging on the handle of the oven door.

"Jesse, what is it?" asked Mom, concerned, entering the kitchen.

Intentional Community

"Oh, nothing," I said, my voice dripping with sarcasm. "Someone just set a booby-trap for me in the fridge. Why the hell do we keep these half-empty cups of milk?"

"Why don't you just let me . . ." Mom started.

"No, I've got it," I barked, eager to prove a point.

Somewhere out there, the New Monastics were on their doorstep with a clipboard, just waiting to sign me up.

> Young women will dance and be glad,
> young men and old as well. I will turn their
> mourning into gladness; I will give them
> comfort and joy instead of sorrow.
>
> —Jeremiah 31:13

I first saw Julie at The Pour House, a bar and music venue in Raleigh. I'd gone there with my friend Adam from Emmaus Way. He and Julie knew each other. In fact, she and I had so many mutual friends, it was odd we'd never met. She seemed excited to run into Adam, so I immediately excused myself to the bathroom. I noticed her beautiful blue eyes.

I was there chasing another girl, someone I'd met at my band's concert a week earlier at a bar in Chapel Hill. A musician friend of mine, Brett Harris, had opened that show. He was a former music minister and his back-up band was full of guys from another local church. This Other Girl was one of their friends, and we'd talked before my set. She'd told me where she worked as a teacher, so I found her e-mail address, apologized for stalking her online and then arranged to meet her and her friends at The Pour House.

But by the time I came out of the bathroom, a group of my friends had coalesced—Julie, Adam, Trigger, and others. I joined them. The headliner that night, Thad Cockrell, had managed to build a bar-band career singing explicit gospel lyrics, and you could count on finding twenty-and-thirty-something churchgoers at his shows, faces you at least recognized if they weren't already your friends.

"So you're Julie," I said, stopping her as the opening band tuned up and she started to leave the circle to move nearer the stage. I'd overheard her name while having a separate conversation.

"Yeah," she said, smiling.

"I'm Jesse."

"Hey. How's it going?"

"Good," I said, speaking right into her ear over the stage noise. "So you work for some kind of disabilities ministry?" More fodder from my eavesdropping.

"Yeah, I work for Reality Ministries," she said, talking into my ear. "We have programs for kids and adults with disabilities and after school for at-risk youth."

"Oh, that's great," I said, trying to think of my next question.

"Hey, I'm gonna move up and listen to the music," she said.

"Oh, OK," I said. "Well, it was nice to meet you."

"Nice to meet you too."

She disappeared into the crowd, and I spied another friend from church, Jenny, atop the second-tier of wooden benches along the wall closer to the stage. I joined her there, standing about five feet above the floor. From this perch, I spotted the girl from my show in Chapel Hill, up front, just off center stage. After a few minutes, I excused myself and made my way over to her.

The Other Girl was nice enough, but she was obviously distracted by something (or someone) else, and there was yet another guy hovering nearby, someone she knew better and who apparently wanted her attention like I did. He was trying to get her to go dancing after the show. She was also talking with a girlfriend, and for an hour, we'd trade a sentence or two here and there between songs, but I wasn't getting any traction. At the end of Thad's set, I said it was nice to see her again, and she inexplicably invited me to go dancing with her and her friends. Somehow the same invitation had circulated to Julie and other friends, and so we all ended up in a dance club down the street.

At the club, guys and girls were packed tight, shoulder to shoulder, hip to hip, arm in arm—whatever body parts two consenting adults could negotiate. This was new territory for me. My childhood preachers had sermonized against dancing, and when I tried grooving to Boyz II Men at fourteen years old, Mom's friend had called me "stiff," and I'd never recovered. My friends had formed a wide circle out on the dance floor, moving and staring at one another like some kind of wallflower support group, or maybe a boozer Bible study or an AA meeting gone horribly wrong. I didn't know where the Other Girl was hiding. I went to the bar for cocktails. That ought to kill some time! After fighting my way through the crowd to deliver drinks to my friends, I swayed back and forth a few times. Then I spotted Trigger sitting alone, wallflower-like, at the edge of the floor. Clearly, he needed me.

Intentional Community

Moshing, Trigger knew. He loved Fugazi, and the indie punk of his native Arizona. But dancing, with girls in short skirts, strobe lights flashing, bass thumping, guys in tight graphic T-shirts—this was not for him, and he needed a ride home.

"Hey, you're cute," said a girl who might have been of legal drinking age, but I doubt it, stumbling toward us, another cocktail in hand.

"Oh, thanks," said Trigger.

"Are you just going to sit there?" she asked him.

"Yeah," he said. "I'm not much of a d . . ."

"Hey, you're cute too," she said, noticing me for the first time. Everybody's cute.

"Are you guys interested in a threesome?"

"Uh . . ."

"Uh . . ."

"Oh, gross," she said. "I'm just kidding, you perverts."

She looked back and forth from Trigger to me a few times, sharply exhaled her annoyance, rolled her eyes and stumbled away.

"OK, well, you sure you don't want to come join the dance circle?" I asked him.

"No, you go ahead."

On my way back toward Adam, Julie, and Jenny, I passed the Other Girl.

"Oh," she said. "Sorry we didn't get to hang out. I'm leaving."

"Oh! OK," I said. "See you later."

Back at the support group, I tried to talk to Julie again, mostly about what had just happened with Trigger. Once again, the loud music intervened, so we just danced. Jenny turned her palms up and danced with her forearms extended out in front of her, like she was carrying one of those gigantic Bibles that lie open on a table at the front of a church. I started mimicking her.

"The Bible dance," I said, yelling in Julie's ear.

She giggled.

I milked that one for a good twenty minutes. She laughed every time.

That was a Friday night. The following Monday at work, I got an email from Adam, forwarded to me at Julie's request, inviting me to Reality Ministries' annual fundraiser later that week. One theory might have been that she thought I had money to donate for a good cause. But that was not the theory I chose to operate on. My theory was that she thought I was pretty damn funny. It goes without saying that I stalked the blog-link at the bottom of her email signature.

This Littler Light

"I am a Christ follower," she captioned her blog photo, a big grin on her face beneath a red umbrella. "I was raised as a Southern Belle, I've got spunk and a bit of hippie mixed in."

Yeah, that sounded about right. At The Pour House, she'd worn a short plaid dress over black leggings and slouchy gray suede boots. Hippie? Hipster? Who can keep them straight?

In her most recent post, she had written about her job managing the office at the Reality Center—no, not her job exactly, but her volunteering after-hours at Tuesday Night Live, a weekly gathering of food and music for people with disabilities. She served as a "buddy" for James, a teenage boy with a cognitive disability.

"James is such a happy young man, he loves to play the drums, loves to sing 'Who stole the cookie from the cookie jar' and 'Go Tell It On the Mountain,' he loves to joke around, and loves to listen to (pop station) G105," she wrote. "He tells me he loves me all the time, he holds my hand, and gives hugs generously. He is radiant and full of pure joy! Hanging out with him is truly a blessing; I can clearly see the face of Jesus in his smile. He has taught me lessons on the power of presence, patience, uninhibited love, participation in what God is doing, and resting on the One that is able."

Presence, not solutions. Patience, not efficiency. Doing with God, not for God. Resting, not working. Weakness, not power. I was more comfortable with handshakes, the greetings of powerful men, than hugs and their vulnerability. This woman had much to teach me.

Her prior blog entry quoted a long passage from Martin Luther King Jr.'s *Letter from a Birmingham Jail*:

> Was not Jesus an extremist for love? "Love your enemies, bless them that curse you, pray for them that despitefully use you." Was not Amos an extremist for justice? "Let justice roll down like waters and righteousness like a mighty stream." Was not Paul an extremist for the gospel of Jesus Christ? "I bear in my body the marks of the Lord Jesus." Was not Martin Luther an extremist? "Here I stand; I can do none other so help me God." Was not John Bunyan an extremist? "I will stay in jail to the end of my days before I make a butchery of my conscience." Was not Abraham Lincoln an extremist? "This nation cannot survive half slave and half free." Was not Thomas Jefferson an extremist? "We hold these truths to be self-evident, that all men are created equal." So the question is not whether we will be extremist but what kind of extremist will we be. Will we be extremists for hate

or will we be extremists for love? Will we be extremists for the preservation of injustice—or will we be extremists for the cause of justice? In that dramatic scene on Calvary's hill, three men were crucified. We must not forget that all three were crucified for the same crime—the crime of extremism. Two were extremists for immorality, and thusly fell below their environment. The other, Jesus Christ, was an extremist for love, truth, and goodness, and thereby rose above his environment.

"[MLK's] words are powerful and challenging and call me to live out extreme reconciliation and extreme love," Julie wrote. "I am far from figuring out how exactly to do that but it is a journey worth exploring."

In the blog post before that, she listed random quotes that inspired her.

—Franciscan brother Richard Rohr: "We cannot attain the presence of God. We're already totally in the presence of God. What's absent is awareness."

—Her boss, Reality founder Jeff McSwain: "To know who we are, we first must know WHOSE we are."

—St. Augustine: "Novem te, novem me." (May I know You, may I know myself.)

Julie was even un-self-conscious enough to quote herself, apologizing that she couldn't remember whom she'd plagiarized:

—"I love the poor, the sick, and the weak because I see the face of God in them, not because I am called, but because I am desperately loved by God."

—"Grace is what makes Christianity different from all other ways to God. It allows us to be embraced."

—"I want to be in a community where you are giving and receiving so much to each other that eventually you forget who is giving and who is receiving."

I wanted her.

A few months before that, she had quoted one of her favorite authors, Henri Nouwen, whose spiritual writing had been offering healing to me, too:

> Every time we make the decision to love someone, we open ourselves to great suffering, because those we most love cause us not only great joy but also great pain. The greatest pain comes from leaving . . . the pain of the leaving can tear us apart. Still, if we want to avoid the suffering of leaving, we will never experience the joy of loving. And love is stronger than fear, life stronger

> than death, hope stronger than despair. We have to trust that the risk of loving is always worth taking.

We both had much to fear: I because love had already crushed me; she, for the same reason—my pain would be treacherous for her.

"Oh Henri, good word," she'd blogged, never having contemplated a relationship with a divorced father of two. "It is a good risk."

Among her list of New Year's Resolutions: "Dance more."

Let's dance.

And, yeah, about that fundraiser:

Julie,
I'll try to make it!
Jesse

Translation: "The Taliban could not keep me away!"

> Jesus said, "Let the children alone, and do not hinder them from coming to Me; for the kingdom of heaven belongs to such as these."
>
> —Matthew 19:14

Julie was healing from some wounds of her own. Just a year before we'd met, she'd been fired by Young Life, the nationwide evangelical youth ministry. Right out of East Carolina University, she'd turned down jobs with major hotel chains, moving to Colorado to work at Young Life youth and family camps in the Rockies. For four years she was there, taking reservations, setting up activities, running a ropes course.

She even fastened a big, athletic guy into his harness one summer. Finding an unusual crowd at the bottom of the ropes stand, she asked,

"What's going on? Who was that guy?"

"Uh, it's John Elway!"

In 2006, Julie came back to North Carolina to work as an office assistant and to mentor Duke and Carolina girls who volunteered with Young Life. Her boss, Jeff McSwain, the Chapel Hill-Durham area director, was Young Life royalty. His dad had known founder Jim Rayburn since the fifties, and Mal McSwain spent fifty years working for the parachurch organization.

Intentional Community

Jeff himself had been on staff for more than a decade, but over the years, he began to notice a rift between Young Life's theology and its practice. In its ministry, Young Life offered grace to every kid, going right into their schools or sports teams, extending hands of friendship, not expecting teens to come find God at church. But in its doctrine, Young Life taught that sinners had to acknowledge their sin and believe in Jesus before they could live into a sense of Christian belonging. In other words, Young Life offered practical belonging, but not theological belonging. Jeff was trying to reattach redemption to creation, teaching that every person had already been created in communion with God and they just had to recognize it and embrace Jesus's invitation into his resurrection. They already belonged, whether they knew it or not.

Since 2001, Jeff had been visiting Young Life summer camps as a speaker, preaching a gospel of belonging first, repentance second. He'd become a marked man. If kids thought God accepted them unconditionally, went the Young Life thinking, they would not conjure the contrition necessary to receive God's forgiveness. Preaching sin first, cross second had certainly brought millions of people into faith. But was it a faith situated so as to pay-forward God's grace into the world? Is God's love conditional? If you wanted to include people in Christian community, did you have to change them first?

Complicating matters was Jeff's conviction that not just suburban kids, Young Life's typical targets, were the ones who needed Jesus, but under-resourced, poorly-educated, prisoner-parented, inner city minority youth, and alienated, ignored, marginalized kids with developmental disabilities needed him too. Kids like these didn't need someone like Jeff to tell them about sin; they were well aware of just how broken they are, how far from heaven the world is. "I AM FOR YOU!" was the divine message Jeff thought they needed to hear. "We habitually embrace kids at their worst because that is the way God is!" he would say.

Jeff's conflict with his employers came to a head in the fall of 2007. Jeff said he could assent to the tenets of a new document, "Non-Negotiables of Young Life Proclamation," but his bosses weren't convinced. In a meeting, a Young Life executive pointed to one particular statement, which included: "People must respond to and embrace the Gospel in order to be saved." Jeff, though, heavily influenced by Barth, believed salvation was by grace, accomplished for all through Jesus's death and resurrection. For Jeff, the central message of gospel proclamation was: You are forgiven, therefore repent and believe! People mistook his message for universalism, but Jeff did not go that far.

"What about this on page six?" Jeff's boss asked.

"Well, I don't agree with that, but you're not going to ask every staff person to sign off on every detail of the paper, are you?"

The executive said he'd get back to him. The next day Jeff got a phone call: "You and all Young Life staff will have to sign off on every point of this paper. This is like wedding vows; you don't just agree with some of them. We know you are a man of integrity and that you will not be able to sign off on the document without retracting the things you have written and said."

Jeff refused, and Young Life fired him. With Jeff gone, Young Life leadership confronted Julie and several co-workers with a choice: Endorse the statement, or share Jeff's fate.

Julie didn't know what to think. She wasn't facile in the language of Arminian volitionism, or Calvinistic determinism, or Barthian election like Jeff was. She just saw her boss leading her in the way of loving kids—and getting slammed for it. She and the rest of the staff refused to sign and also lost their jobs.

But their ministry to at-risk and disabled kids was not over. They had been developing a special needs program under Young Life's Capernaum, named for the site of many of Jesus's healing miracles. The local Young Life board believed in their mission. An army of supporters—funders, volunteers, and prayer partners—followed them in founding Reality. Jeff had a five-year plan to open a community center, but within the first year he spotted an old church building across the street from Durham School of the Arts, downtown's only high school, which also houses a middle school. Supporters put up half a million dollars to buy the building and open the Reality Center.

Hundreds of kids would cross that street one afternoon a month when Durham schools let out early for teacher prep time, eating burgers and playing games at "Grill & Chill." Scores of others would come every day after school for tutoring, ping pong, video games, basketball, billiards, prayer, mentoring, and Bible study. Upstairs, about a dozen kids who'd dropped out or been expelled from the public high schools would try to finish their education at New Horizons, an alternative school funded through Reality. College and high school volunteers, some from Young Life, would come a couple of nights a week for eating, singing, and praying alongside teens and adults with disabilities. If you go to the annual King and Queen's dance, you might see the prom queen from a local suburban high school slow dancing with a guy who has Down Syndrome.

Difference and intimate unity. The image of the Trinity.

Intentional Community

> Again, truly I tell you that if two of you on earth agree about anything they ask for, it will be done for them by my Father in heaven. For where two or three gather in my name, there am I with them.
>
> —Matthew 18:19–20

Julie had me dreaming of an integrated life, living, working, loving, worshiping in central Durham. Emmaus Way had relocated from its downtown storefront and started renting space on Sundays at the Reality Center, in the old Durham Christian and Missionary Alliance Gospel Tabernacle, its pews removed and wood floor refinished for an afterschool basketball gym. Aurora was good with ink and paper, and Rowan was a little Gwen Stefani with or without a microphone, dancing and singing and bantering in a stage voice, even if I was her only audience. Maybe they could one day go to the arts magnet middle and high school across the street and walk over to Julie's office after school if I couldn't pick them up on time. Maybe I could put a new band together from the Carrboro musicians who were moving to Durham, chasing cheaper rents and newly-opened venues.

I'd finally graduated from UNC after writing my thesis on the Industrial Areas Foundation's "10 Percent Is Enough" campaign to cap credit card interest rates. Barack Obama had served as an IAF community-organizer back in the 1980s, and Emmaus Way's pastors, Tim and Dan, had gotten involved in the campaign through Durham Congregations, Associations and Neighborhood (Durham CAN), where Emmaus Way could learn how to be the "beloved community" alongside the mainly black churches that had fought for physical freedom back in the civil rights movement and were now fighting for economic freedom in this anti-greed revolution. That's how I had come to be singing "This Little Light of Mine" in the lobby of the Bank of America headquarters, with the Charlotte-Mecklenburg police eyeing me suspiciously. Maybe I could do more of this writer-activism in partnership with CAN and my neighbors at Rutba House.

And, yeah, maybe I could go to Duke. The Religion Newswriters Association had been nice enough to pay my tuition to take two Divinity School classes, "Christianity and Contemporary Literature" and "Journalism as Christian Practice." The RNA wanted all reporters, even City Hall reporters, to cover religious topics more accurately. As for me, though, I was still trying to figure out how to write good literature and practice good journalism as a faithful Christian, if such a thing was possible.

I'd struggled for months to find a house in Walltown. One deal fell through during negotiations. I broke off another contract when an inspection found major termite damage. These homes were listed around $130,000. I'd passed on one that would have been perfect, except the owner wanted $180,000, more than I thought I could afford. The house had a new kitchen and baths, a fenced backyard for the kids, and unique walnut flooring in the front dining room and central hallway, its finish distressed to look like a barroom floor. The owner had lived there with his wife and renovated it to their taste several years earlier before renting it out. Unlike most of the others I'd looked at, it needed no work. It had a master-bedroom suite with an attached office and bathroom, two more bedrooms and 1,800 square feet. It would meet our needs if our family grew by one or two more. But, still, even borrowing $30,000 from Durham's Neighborhood Improvement Program at two-percent interest, I would have to cut back on things like eating out or traveling just to make the mortgage payments.

"I don't know what to do," I told Julie. "I'm so tired of looking at houses. I just want to be done with it."

"I don't understand why you don't just buy the Clarendon Street house," she said.

"I'm scared," I said. "We've had layoffs at work every quarter for the past two years. What if I lose my job?"

She sighed and went quiet.

"What?" I asked. "What is it?"

"It's like you think you're alone in this," she said. We'd talked off and on about marriage, but I wasn't ready. "If we get married, I can help you pay those bills."

I'd been doing it alone for so long, married and unmarried, having help was not a scenario that had even crossed my mind.

> Do not let what you know is good be spoken of as evil... Make every effort to do what leads to peace and to mutual edification ...Whatever you believe about these things keep between yourself and God.
>
> —Romans 14:16–22

Intentional Community

Earlier that year, Julie and I had been dating for two months when we saw an opportunity for her to meet my girls. We'd wanted to wait until we could seriously contemplate marriage, and that time had come sooner than we'd expected. We felt she had to enter fully into my family life if we were going to be able to discern whether we could make a lifelong commitment.

Reality was hosting another fundraiser, this one at the local Fuddrucker's burger joint, which would donate twenty percent of the cost of anything purchased on this particular night.

"Fuddrucker's has amazing milkshakes! So get excited!" Julie wrote in an email inviting friends. "In the words of Kelis, 'my milkshake brings all the boys to the yard.' I don't really know what that means, but I think of that song every time I think of milkshakes!"

I forwarded the invitation to eight Emmaus Way friends, and then replied to Julie with a link to the Urban Dictionary definition:

Milkshake: A girl's body and the way she carries it.

"I like your milkshake," I wrote to her.

Except the first time I wrote it, I didn't reply to her but replied-all to my eight church friends.

"That was quite awesome, my friend!" Trigger wrote. "Well played!"

"For some reason I have a feeling this will come up and be used against you at some point in your life when you are not expecting it," Julie wrote. "But I am happy you like my milkshake!"

Now don't tell me you've never done anything like that before. Email, in the wrong hands, is an atomic bomb.

I also forwarded the invitation to my family and a few friends, including Prudence. "I'm bringing Aurora & Rowan for a low-key way to meet Julie," I wrote. "It'd be great if a few other people were there." Prudence replied:

> Jesse,
>
> Because your relationship with Julie has become more serious, I wanted to fill you in on my position regarding any romantic relationship post marriage. I don't support remarriage after divorce. I feel that it is unscriptural. I think that scripture is very clear on divorce and remarriage (see Malachi 2:13-16, Matt. 19:3-9, Mark 10:2-12, Luke 16:18). I personally have taken this stand, despite how frequently I wish it weren't so. I know that you and I interpret scripture differently. I can only tell you how I do interpret it, and allow that to explain why I do not support some of your actions. I want you to know that I think Julie is an

amazing woman. And, I think that you're a pretty amazing man. This isn't about my opinion regarding you, or her, it's regarding what I feel scripture says about divorce and remarriage. I know that my interpretation of scripture is not popular, or pleasant. I know that there is so much I don't understand about your divorce, and what you and Lily went through together. I respect you and Julie both a lot.

Lots of love,

Prudence

Where was John Lennon when I needed him? Dear Prudence, can't I see a smile? Here's what I wrote back:

Prudence,

I'm not sure why you are telling me this. God doesn't need you to impose your interpretation of Scripture on me or anyone else. God calls you to love. Period.

But since you brought up the subject, let me to respond to your proof texts, which are just grains of sand in the vast story of God's redeeming the world but which can nonetheless help us understand the grace that Jesus offers to people who suffer divorce and other effects of a broken world.

Malachi 2:13-16 says nothing about remarriage. It says God hates divorce. And so do I. I hope and pray that you NEVER, EVER come to hate it as much as I do because that will mean you have suffered from it in the way that I have. Until then, you cannot understand the depths of God's hatred of divorce. You can only understand it as some sort of moral, judgmental stance, which it is not. It is the stance of our loving God alongside those who suffer in this world, the poor, weak woman who could not support herself in first century Palestine, or the young father whose wife suffers from mental illness and cannot make wise choices.

In Matthew 19:3-9 Jesus said if you divorce your FAITHFUL wife and remarry, you are liable for adultery. Here, Jesus specifically, unequivocally, clearly "makes an exception" when your spouse is unfaithful—precisely my situation. [To the reader: I realize this might make you think Lily physically cheated on me, which she didn't, as far as I know; at this point, I had come to see her financial betrayals and her leaving as forms of infidelity.]

Mark 10:2-12 concerns ONLY the situation where a person divorces his/her spouse IN ORDER TO marry someone else.

Intentional Community

That has nothing to do with me and Julie. I was legally divorced before I ever met her and physically, emotionally, and spiritually divorced long before that.

Luke 16:18 talks about exploiting the letter of the law to avoid the spirit of the law. That has nothing to do with my situation.

I worship a God of second, third, fourth, fifth, sixth and seventh chances. Your proof texts, especially the Matthew passage, have only confirmed the position of my faith community that God celebrates remarriage as part of the redemption of sinful, fallen, suffering people into the life of community and mutuality that God wants for us.

I am sorry that you feel compelled to believe what you believe. I don't think it has any basis in Scripture and, like so many beliefs rooted in fear, it causes conflict between us and will continue to cause conflict between you and anyone who interprets Scripture outside of the very tiny minority community that you have chosen to side with. There is a great big world of Christians out there who could teach you a lot if you did not cling to fundamentalist dogma.

I also love you and will continue to love you, even if you continue to sit in judgment over me. I will offer you grace as someone who hasn't matured enough to realize that grace is the only thing worth offering each other. But you create conflict, not shalom, when you try to impose your own extra-biblical moral positions on other Christians. There's not much I can do about it but to stoically let it bounce off of me. That's too bad.

Jesse

Hey Jess,

I'm pretty hurt from your response to my email mostly because I feel really misunderstood. I know my stance is pretty unpopular and I understand how you would be offended by it, but I'm not sure that I'm in a minority. Still, I know that even at my church it's not the popular stance.

It's a conviction that I feel from the Holy Spirit, and I have no choice but to submit to it and be open to His changing my heart on the matter. It is something I have begged God to reveal in greater clarity to me, hoping that I would see how others come to such different conclusions. I don't like having a conviction that does not support "tolerance," convictions like that seldom seem to fly.

This Littler Light

The references I sent were merely there to back my conviction, not to change yours. I'm aware of your clearly stated interpretation of these verses, mainly because I have found myself dialoguing with countless believers about this very issue, in order to explore the basis of my own conviction. My stance of remarriage is a result of my belief that God has revealed it to me as truth. I understand that not all believers share the same conviction, and that's okay. There are many differing beliefs in Christianity that have valid arguments for both sides, take predestination for example. The Lord has put an extreme passion and sensitivity in me to mourn over broken marriages in a way that I believe exceeds my experience. I must agree that grace is worth giving, but I think you have to agree that there's absolute value in living a life based on godly conviction. Because I feel a certain way, doesn't mean you have to, but it does mean that I will try to line up my actions with my convictions. That's all I wanted you to know. The reason for my actions (i.e. not coming for the girl's first encounter, or encouraging a relationship which clearly seems to be headed towards remarriage). As I said before, my conviction has nothing to do with how valuable and amazing I think both you and Julie are. I'm sorry that wasn't clearly conveyed before, and I hope that you can receive that now.

love

Prudence

I rattled off another e-mail:

Prudence,

I guess the only way forward is to agree to disagree. I don't believe the Holy Spirit convicts individuals against the witness of the community of saints, therefore I cannot believe that God has revealed it to you as truth. I believe there are multiple valid interpretations of a lot of Scripture passages; I just don't believe yours is among them on these passages. You have to do interpretive somersaults to reach your conclusion. I'm not sure I agree that "there's absolute value in living a life based on godly conviction," because "conviction" so often means "I'm right and you're wrong." I believe there's absolute value in living a life based on love. That's the only absolute value I see handed down from God. As I understand the Gospel, grace is worth giving, and there is no "but."

Intentional Community

> Prudence, I'm going to be brutally honest because I love you and want you to know the divine grace that I have received through some brutal experiences. I have felt judged by you for about as long as I have known you. I'm afraid that deep down you are uncertain of God's love for you, feel ashamed in his presence, and need to prove your worth to him through moral perfectionism. The truth is that God loves you because he made you beautiful, intelligent, and strong, in God's own image. God has nothing to prove, and neither do you. He loves you enough to die for you. He does not need you to skip a meal with your friends in order to prove how much you love him. If it wasn't about changing my mind, you could have just said you couldn't make it. It's not hard to find an excuse to skip dinner: I'm tired, I'm busy, etc. In fact, you didn't have to respond at all. But for some reason you needed to express your disapproval of the make-the-best-of-the-shit life I am trying to build. Who gains from that? Not me. Not God. Not you. Nobody. The only result is a disintegration of relationships. That is not the work of the Holy Spirit, no matter what you might think. If you really believe that, I guess we'll have to agree to disagree. But I can't see how we can have a meaningful relationship if you continue to sit in a posture of judgment over me. That is not love.

But I didn't send that e-mail to Prudence. Instead, I sent it to friends for vetting.

One wrote back:

> hey jes,
>
>> reading this was strange because i wrote an email to Prudence with some very similar content in it just a few days ago. i agree with everything that you've said—i think that it's tough, and that it might change things forever, but, as i had to accept when i sent my email, things are already changed, and honesty is the only chance for improvement. i hope that Prudence sees all of this clearly and knows that we're not trying to gang up on her, but only trying to enter into something more real.
>>
>> the only other thing that i have to say is that you should make sure that everything in here is purposed for enlightenment and not vindication. i think that it is, but as the author, you have the best perspective.
>>
>> i find this whole thing heartbreaking and hope that, by the grace of God, we'll all be stronger on the other side of it.

This Littler Light

My Dad wrote:

> I think it's pretty right on. The main problem with people, myself included, is that they hang on to these ideas once they are ingrained, like it is something that cannot be wrong or they invalidate their very existence.
>
> I do think that unconditional love is the key and I also believe that this is only possible for God, not us, but should be the object of our striving. This is the kind of thing that rips people apart. We came close to that with you and Lily. I pray that grace and love along with understanding will rule the day and everyone can come through this with healing.

This is what I eventually sent to Prudence:

Prudence,

I'm not sure what to say, but I want to say something because I love you. Your posture of judgmentalism has caused me pain and caused conflict and tension for as long as I have known you. These are circumstances which we tolerate because we love you. I just wish I could soak you in the depths of God's love. A person sure of God's love does not need to live with conviction. Conviction is a cheap substitute for love, an attempt to codify obedience within a set of rules rather than tremblingly responding to the loving touch of the Savior. Conviction is how we seek to earn God's love, rather than basking in God's grace. I don't recognize the Gospel in your priority of living by conviction. That sounds like every other religion in the world, but not the story of God offering His own Son to redeem the world. I want something better for you. God wants something better for you. I don't need your approval of my choices. You can believe whatever you want, and I will still love you, even if you hurt me. But our relationship is compromised when you make choices that express self-righteous judgment rather than humility and grace. I cannot trust you and offer you my whole self when you cling to moral perfectionism. God, my Father, has welcomed me back from the pigsty, throwing me a party in the form of a wonderful, godly woman named Julie. I wish you would come to that party, instead of grumbling about the integrity of your convictions.

I wanted to sing, "Dear Prudence, can't we just go out and play?"

The girls did meet Julie, surrounded by family and friends, but not Prudence. More than a year later, Prudence and I finally tried to put a cap on that discussion, agreeing to disagree and never talking about it again.

Intentional Community

Our relationship has never been the same. I wish I had never responded to Prudence. I wish I had followed my own advice to just live and let live. I did the very thing I had accused Prudence of: I tried to impose my sense of morality on her. I tried to teach her love, instead of just showing it. I used grace as a weapon, trying to force Prudence toward what I thought was a truer vision of God, instead of leaving that work to God alone.

I was speaking out of my own pain, trying to throw off the shackles of my fundamentalist past, just as she was speaking out of deep concern for her own troubled marriage. Neither of us could see that clearly in the moment. We each talked as though it was our spiritual values at stake, but, in truth, it was the shape of our very lives. If my marriage could fail, permanently, so could hers, and that might have been her worst fear. On the other hand, her judgment was a threat to my future, the redemptive life I was dreaming of. In her act of disapproval, I heard condemnation to a life of loneliness. For two years I'd been going to Lily every few months, asking her to reconcile, asking her to go back to counseling with me. She'd never responded. I'd done all I could, but Lily didn't want to be my wife. I couldn't understand why Prudence didn't see that. I couldn't hear that Prudence was trying to be true to herself more than she was judging me. She couldn't see that I was gasping for the air of freedom. In those moments, there was too much at stake for us just to let each other be, and we hurt each other badly in the volley. She, at least, was true to her beliefs. I was so busy defending mine that I forgot to live them.

> Solomon overlaid the inside of the house with pure gold. And he drew chains of gold across the front of the inner sanctuary, and he overlaid it with gold. He overlaid the whole house with gold, until all the house was finished.
>
> —1 Kings 6:21–22

Two years later, Julie's parents came up from Goldsboro in eastern North Carolina to help us paint. Yes, to paint. We freshened up the dining and living room on Clarendon Street—one big open space the previous owners had created when they tore out walls and turned this duplex into a single family. The drab cream color became "silver sage"—a very light shade of green Julie picked out to go with the sylvan tones of my living room furniture. She didn't really like my couch or cushy chair but didn't feel good about replacing them for their good condition. Her frugality rivals mine and sometimes outpaces it.

We painted not only the walls but the ceiling. The project started because a rat had gotten into the house, and I'd gone up into the attic to screen the gable vents with heavy mesh. My stepstool had tipped, and my legs had fallen through the ceiling on either side of a joist, just feet from where Julie's friend Manda was sitting below. So as a bonus for her painting project, Julie had gotten the dated popcorn-texture removed from about 600 square feet of ceiling because matching it after repairing the damage would have been impossible. She and the rat were in cahoots. It turned out to be a low-dwelling Norway rat, not a climbing roof rat. I finally discovered and blocked off its entry point—some holes around the wiring behind the dishwasher—but by then it was too late. Julie would have her smooth ceiling and her new paint.

We'd been married about nine months at that point. We'd bought a long, ten-seat banquet table made of aged, unfinished wood rescued from a demolished house, wood that I stained dark to go with the floor. I'd found ten used black Ikea chairs being sold by an out-of-business pole dancing studio, B'risqué Fitness. Julie was sure to wipe them down with disinfectant. The wide-open front area of our house was made for entertaining of a different kind. We'd been hosting an Emmaus Way small group for almost a year prior to the wedding, while dinners and parties brought together Reality volunteers, Duke Divinity students, local musicians—a community of friends I could never have imagined just a few years earlier.

"I want to remind everybody that you are their wedding party today—you are their community of love and support," Pastor Tim had told the 150 gathered at the Reality Center for our ceremony.

We'd had too many important people to choose just a few for bridesmaids and groomsmen. We'd arranged the chairs in a circle, just like in worship at Emmaus Way. My friends from the farmhouse were there, along with the women from Julie's college girl Bible study at ECU. They'd been getting together at least once a year and sharing intimate friendship through weddings, births, sicknesses, layoffs, infertility, and family traumas. These were communities that had sustained us over many years, blending with our families and our new community to hold our relationship in their strength. We exchanged our vows at the center of the circle, and the crowd stood to lay their hands on us in prayer.

Intentional Community

    A hundred of us paraded from the Reality Center to a restaurant retrofitted into an old tobacco warehouse, with an outdoor courtyard that would first serve as part of the dining room and then as our dance floor. The music had started back at the Reality Center, where Dad and my brothers and sisters had led the throng in the Beatles' "All You Need Is Love," reprising their performance from the start of the ceremony, when Aurora and Rowan had marched in, my youngest throwing Hershey's Kisses into the crowd because she didn't see the point of throwing flower petals on the floor. The people marched and sang, or hummed through kazoos and beat tambourines, stretching out over two city blocks, stopping traffic as we crossed over two busy streets, like John, Paul, George, and Ringo on the cover of *Abbey Road*.

    My buddy Brett Harris put a band together to play sixties and seventies cover songs. Mom and I danced to Crosby, Stills, Nash, and Young's "Teach Your Children," with Aurora, Rowan, Julie, and her dad joining us to form a goofy, ring-around-the-rosie circle halfway through the song. Julie's parents had struggled with my divorce and my fatherhood, but they'd eventually come around and threw us the funnest, most scrumptious party of my life. Mom, Dad, my brothers, and sisters had choreographed a dance to Michael Jackson's "Smooth Criminal," with fedoras coming on and off their heads in rhythm. Brett had given way to Dad, the band backing him up on Tom Petty's "Breakdown," one of his favorites. I also danced with Nanny, for a minute or two. Then she had to rest. We'd thought she might die of breast cancer back in 1986, and my sister was named Katie because Nanny demanded the family name. She survived, and then in 2008 she'd been diagnosed with lung cancer. The radiation therapy made her bones brittle, and she spent most of her time in bed or on the couch.

    "My favorite part is that I'm here," Nanny kept saying.

    With Rowan occupied as "Candy Girl," flower girl duties had gone to Julie's maid of honor, Kim.

    "You often say that it's an honor to be here," Kim said during her toast. "That's how you start speeches. But to say that today is almost an understatement because being friends with Julie is one of the greatest privileges I've had in my life."

    "Awww!" said the crowd.

    "Oh, OK," said Kim. "But I'm not just saying that for 'awws,' I really mean it. She's the greatest friend that one can imagine. I appreciate that today was a celebration of community, because our community here in Durham is just greater than I could have ever imagined, and Julie and

Jesse are really the ones that hold it together. Them coming together today means so much to so many people. Who doesn't like a wedding that has raining candy?"

It was greater, too, than I could have ever imagined. In my first marriage, I'd wanted to represent the Trinity on earth. In this one, I knew imperfect love was the best I would ever manage, and I knew I would need this community to help me reach even that.

Epilogue

The Silence of the Lamb

Several months after Lily had left, I'd gone to New York for a reunion of the Phillips Foundation, that conservative grantor that had funded my writing on immigrant Christmas-tree workers. There at Forbes Headquarters on Fifth Avenue near Union Square, I met Father Richard John Neuhaus, the hoary founder of *First Things,* a Roman Catholic magazine in the Big City. If you wanted to write for a respectable religious publication, *First Things* had to be near the top of the list. It leaned to the right, and over the years my freelancing had landed in evangelical-left magazines like *Sojourners* or *Prism.* But, still, Father Neuhaus knew a thing or two about how to write on faith for the public square, so I was eager to stop him out in the lobby and pick his brain. How could I transition from newspaper reporting to longer-form, more thoughtful, provocative writing on practicing faith in the twenty-first century?

"So you want to be a public intellectual," he'd said.

Now, hold on. That sounded pretty highfalutin. I just thought Christians should know about the oppression of immigrants who farm their Christmas trees, or the elderly, diabetic, wheelchair-bound mother who waited up for the state to stick a poison needle in her son's vein, or the Jesus-loving activists trying to keep people in their homes and food on the table, instead of dough in the bankers' pockets. I just wanted to help people see the kingdom of God, where it was, and where it could be.

"Yeah," I'd told Father Neuhaus. A *public intellectual.* "I hadn't thought of it in those terms, but, yeah, I guess that's what I'm saying."

"Well," he'd said, "you've just got to do it."

Within weeks would come the apex of my *News & Observer* career. I broke the news that UNC-Chapel Hill student body president Eve Carson had been robbed, kidnapped for her ATM pin number, murdered, and left lying in the street, in a quiet residential neighborhood near campus. This was Chapel Hill's worst nightmare: a smart, kind-hearted, blond-haired princess shot to death by two black "thugs" from Durham. How could this happen? People wanted answers. I'd taken over the Chapel Hill crime beat months earlier, so I was the local guy with exclusive news via the police chief's cell phone while the national media staked him out from their satellite trucks in the parking lot at the police department.

I got voicemails from TV producers wanting me to go on shows like *On the Record with Greta Van Susteren*. I didn't have time to return most of them, but I finally ended up taping an interview for *America's Newsroom*. My friends would make fun of my stiff, matter-of-fact delivery while the Fox News anchor tried to stoke my outrage toward the "monsters." The story seemed sensational and tragic enough without inserting my emotions into it.

Two years later, I would end up on national TV again, having covered the Durham murder trial of Shannon Crawley, a mistress convicted of killing her rival Denita Smith, the fiancée of her lover, Greensboro cop Jermeir Stroud. That was right around the time Julie became my fiancée, despite her fears about dealing with Lily. Sure, I had to argue with Lily about things like weekend custody and pediatrician's bills, but Julie didn't know she had it so good! The Oxygen Network, founded by Oprah Winfrey, interviewed me for an episode of *Snapped*, a show about women who kill. My fifteen minutes of fame.

Because of all the layoffs, *The N&O* had added Durham crime and courts to my responsibilities. I was covering alone what had been three separate beats. It could get pretty frantic sometimes, bouncing from courtroom to courtroom, from crime scenes to curbside interviews of grieving family members, trying to beat the local TV stations with online breaking news and still provide the detailed analysis I wanted to give and that *The N&O* had always given. For the second half of 2010, my job became almost all Crystal Mangum, all the time.

In February, the Duke lacrosse accuser had been charged with arson, child abuse, and a host of lesser crimes after setting fire to a pile of her live-in boyfriend's clothing in a bathtub, with two Durham cops and Mangum's three children still inside their apartment. Though Mangum had lunged past one of the officers and threatened to stab her lover, no one got seriously hurt. It was the type of routine domestic disturbance we ignored every day because there were many, many bigger crimes to cover.

Sometimes even homicides spurred nothing more than a few paragraphs on one of the inside pages.

But *The N&O* higher-ups were still embarrassed because they had fallen for Mangum's rape claim and helped to shake up the lacrosse players' lives five years earlier. My directive was to show we didn't play favorites: Mangum wouldn't get an all-out blitz of reporters at her home and the DA's office like in the Duke case, but I would need to cover this one closely, to make sure we hadn't let her sully those boys' reputations and then let her get away with attempted murder. That was the dubious charge that at first accompanied the arson count, with a $1 million bond, leading some observers to speculate the Durham police and prosecutor were trying to punish Mangum for leaving egg on their faces in the lacrosse case. So my bosses had reason to think these power-brokers needed scrutiny as well.

After one of her bi-monthly court hearings where Mangum got scolded for having custody of her children in violation of her pre-trial release order, I struck up a conversation with another reporter, a fellow Christian with our local competition.

"I can't believe I'm here again," I said.

"Why? You don't think we should be covering this story?" he asked, raising his eyebrows.

"Not really," I said. "People fight with their boyfriends and girlfriends everyday."

"Yeah, but this is Crystal Mangum."

"I know," I said. "That's the problem. It just feels icky, like we're exploiting her. She's obviously got some mental health issues, and I can't see how all this publicity is helping her or her kids."

"Yeah," he said. "But that's why I think the story is important. You've got a single mother, in poverty, trying to take care of her kids ..."

"Yeah, but you could find a million stories like that," I said. "This one won't ever be anything more than a circus. If you want to write about the broken system, this can only be a distraction."

In a year's time, I wrote more than forty stories about Mangum: bond reductions; dropped charges; new charges; her rotating cast of public defenders; pre-trial release violations; a spat with Durham County Social Services who ratted her out to a judge after she applied for a daycare subsidy when she wasn't supposed to have custody of her children; a mysterious letter signed by Mangum's boyfriend—saying he set his own clothes on fire!—and delivered to the DA's office by a coalition of conspiracy theorists, the Friends of Crystal Mangum; an astonishing five days of jury selection to find twelve peers who would give her a fair shake. They finally convicted her on some misdemeanor charges, and the judge sentenced her to time already served—about three months in the county jail awaiting her trial.

The Friends of Crystal Mangum were being investigated for witness intimidation—and that after one supporter in the gallery had already spent five days in jail for contempt of court for calling the jury's slow deliberation "ridiculous." She said it loudly enough for the judge and jurors to hear. "The latest chapter in Crystal Mangum's public saga is nearly over," I wrote on January 26, 2011, after the prosecutor decided not to renew the felony arson charge, which had yielded a hung jury a week before Christmas.

But, no. Two months later, on Sunday, April 3, police charged Mangum with stabbing her boyfriend—a different boyfriend. Ten days later, the man died. The Duke lacrosse accuser was facing a murder charge. Lord, no.

Two months later, I quit. I'd been been watching my colleagues get laid off, fiscal quarter after fiscal quarter, for almost three years straight. Through hours of mental health counseling and long conversations with the people who knew me best, I'd been forced to try to imagine what I would do if I was no longer a newspaper reporter. And that wasn't hard, because I hadn't really wanted to be a newspaper reporter to begin with. I was a writer, and I needed the money, but I'd always dreamed of other things: making music, writing magazine articles, books, maybe teaching. *Just Do It*, Father Neuhaus had said, as though Nike made pens and notepads and gigabytes to store my musings.

Six months after the wedding, Julie and I had been able to pool our savings together for a down payment on the duplex next door to our house. I'd wanted to invest in it earlier, but it had needed too much work, so Dad and his business partner had bought it, fixed it up, and sold it to us for rental income, replacing about a quarter of my salary at *The N&O*. Soon after that, Reality Ministries agreed to cover me and the girls through Julie's health insurance benefits, so I didn't have to hang onto my job just for that.

Over my years of freelancing on nights and weekends, my network of magazine editors had grown. Jason Byassee, a former editor with *The Christian Century*—the mainline progressive answer to *Christianity Today*—had been the professor in one of my Duke classes. Since then, he'd become a mentor, serving on my thesis committee when I'd finally finished my master's at UNC, writing about the anti-usury campaign. Jason helped me get one of my thesis chapters published as a cover story for the *Century*,

The Silence of the Lamb

and an editor there started asking me for more. My band was in the middle of recording our first album, and I hoped it would eventually sell enough copies to pay for itself, or maybe a little more. Between these new and potential revenues, the rental income, Julie's insurance, and my existing web of magazine opportunities, I felt like I could give the entrepreneurial-artistic life a try.

"It feels like a worthy risk," Julie had said. Just like when I'd been having doubts about our potential engagement. Just like Henri Nouwen had said in her blog before we ever met.

I don't think everybody should quit their jobs and try to do something they love. For my first decade of adulthood, that wasn't an option for me, as a sole breadwinner and then as a single father. Some amazing things have fallen into place for me to make this possible, and I'm still not sure it's going to work. We've had to say no to trips to visit dear friends. Julie my hipster fashionista has had to be happy with the clothes she's got.

But it's not just the money. It's the power. With *The N&O*, my stories reached 200,000 people, across demographics: black, white, Asian, Latino; Christian, Muslim, Buddhist, atheist; rich, middle class, poor. Quitting the paper has given me time to write this book and to think about writing others, and that's a kind of power, a freedom I can't take for granted, but who knows if people will read it? I've had time to record my music, but that costs money, rather than earning it right away. My band is working to build an audience, one fan at a time. Right now, we're happy to have seventy or eighty people come to a show. Who knows if more people will listen? I know that I can't continue to give it time, if it does not give back money. It's not fair to my family. I also get to focus my time writing on things I care about: faith, social justice, the arts. But I have to *sell* every story, instead of just turning them over to an editor and knowing they'll be published. And selling, as you know, is not my strength. I am immersed in my own weakness. We are the downwardly mobile.

I am exceedingly grateful to *The Christian Century*, which pays me a fair wage to explore "what it means to believe and live out the Christian faith in our time." That's what I've been trying to do for the past thirteen years as a fraction of my professional life, and now I'm able to do it more or less full-time. But, for me, *The Christian Century* is a magazine title full of irony. The *Century* took its name at the turn of the 1900s, before the Nazis and Jim Crow and clergy sex abuse undermined the church's claim to the moral high ground. In 1900, the Social Gospel progressive movement may have had the power to influence American and even global politics. Today, though, it is clear we are no longer living in the Christian century, if ever there was such a thing.

One of my first assignments from the *Century* as a full-time freelancer was to cover the first annual Wild Goose festival in rural Chatham County, North Carolina, not far from Durham. Modeled on England's Greenbelt Festival, Wild Goose brought together Emergent and progressive Christians from all over the U.S., including some of my heroes like Over the Rhine and Derek Webb. As part of my reporting, I had to interview the Reverend Nadia Bolz-Weber, the church planter at House for All Sinners and Saints, an Emergent Lutheran community in Denver. At the end of the interview, Nadia invited Julie and me to assist with the "bluegrass liturgy" her church would be leading that night under a big white tent.

Our job was to stand near the stage at the end of the service. People lined up in front of us. We would ask their names, apply holy water from little bowls onto their foreheads, and read a baptismal blessing: "Loving God, sustain [Name] with the gift of your Holy Spirit: the spirit of wisdom and understanding, the spirit of counsel and might, the spirit of knowledge and the fear of the Lord, the spirit of joy in your presence, both now and forever." It was simple but profound, to look into another person's eyes, to have him or her look back at me, to pronounce words of blessing, to seal it with a touch of water on their skin.

It was a step backward in time, back behind my transition in college from Marjory to Heloise, when I began to theorize my faith, to try to get my beliefs just right, to try to establish myself as a possessor of truth. For a time, this sort of intellectualism shone in my songwriting, too, as I thought more about *telling the truth*, like a prophet, and shied away from the pastoral task of inviting people into mystery.

Seeking truth serves us just fine when the task is journalism; but it's not all there is. I had been striving for freedom from the strictures of modern newswriting so that I might be able to bear witness to the mystical experiences that drive a spiritual life and empower activism. Yet, at the same time, I was living amidst my own mysteries as a musician—the unique connection between souls when we create together, the interplay of melody and metaphor that somehow make truth truer, the combination of sounds that invoke divine presence even when not a word of theological truth is spoken. Having this profound liturgical experience at Wild Goose, and singing along with Nadia's bluegrass band, or shouting old favorites in the festival's Beer & Hymns tent, I saw the possibility that worship music could be mystical without being manipulative, that people could sing together without anyone demanding that we share the same emotional response to the music. I began to wonder whether the communion I have with God and others when we play music together might expand to include an entire congregation in worship. Back at Cedarville, I had set careful theological thinking over against emotive, mystical worship experiences. Now I found myself wondering whether I could be a worship musician—a different sort of worship musician, but a worship musician all the same.

As you know, I struggled with my sense of calling throughout my twenties and into my thirties.

"Anyone can be a pastor," my friend Vince, the pacifist-Catholic, once told me, with perhaps *just a bit* of exaggeration. "To work in the newsroom—the belly of the beast—that's something worth holding onto."

"I don't feel like I'm making much of a difference," I said.

"But just the possibility of being there when the gospel ethic might come into play . . ."

For me, those times did not come often enough. I spent nearly all my time writing the stories I needed to write in order to hold on to my power and influence, so that every six or twelve months I could write about some anti-usury activists or the oppression of immigrants. I finally gave up that power for a set of powers I think might be even better: giving people permission to feel the intense joy or intense sorrow that sometimes only art can give, even if it's Saturday night at the tavern; creating space for collective experiences of praise and lament, even if some people think worship is the world's biggest waste of time; bearing witness, over and over again, to the beloved community in stories of faith in action, even when it doesn't seem to make a damn difference; singing for the meek, even though it means I become one of them.

These powers look an awful lot like weakness. I don't always know where my next paycheck is coming from. I can't be sure my stories or songs will find an audience. I am a dead-beat husband chasing his rock 'n' roll artist's dream, a welfare king living off the largesse of my nonprofit-salaried sugar mama.

Ok, I overstate. I'm a landlord and a well-paid journalist when I chase down the work. I recently finished a one-year degree at Duke Divinity School and then took a part-time job to help start a new roots music service at a rural Methodist church. Anybody with two graduate degrees is pretty darn privileged. We're not dumpster diving, and we don't have to split our mortgage payment with a few roommates like at Rutba House. We are far more ordinary than radical.

This Littler Light

I'm just trying to live in the radicals' neighborhood, to be there when they befriend a kid with disabilities or march on Bank of America or sit in the prison driveway, when they confront power with weakness and ask power to empty itself. I'm just adding my little voice to the chorus, my little flame to the candlemas. So what if my "influence" is small? So what if only other Christians read what I write? I've seen some things they should see, things that might brighten their own little candles. I used to think it was my job to shine a light on great acts of Christian faithfulness, so that the world might see and believe. Now, though, I think the church's trying to hide its hypocrisy is a greater obstacle to Christian invitation than is the world's ignorance of our moments of holiness. If my work illuminates radical discipleship, it's more to remind the church of its own calling than to change the world. I think telling the truth about our own sin is a better evangelistic tool than trying to convince people of what a difference Jesus has made in our lives, because often he hasn't made much difference at all. We love and we fall short of love just like everyone else.

One of our small group members said he and his wife kept coming to Emmaus Way specifically because of my honesty about failure and suffering and how I believed God was still present in it all. This was the same gift Mark and Wade had offered me. My weakness, and the weakness of those I write and sing about, is all I have to offer. My heroes at Nazareth House couldn't hold their community together. Langley and Sheila moved back to New York, while Scott and Roberta got divorced, yet they all still work on behalf of the condemned and hurting. They're giving faithfulness their best shot, missing often, but still trying, and their failures may reveal as much about the world's need for salvation as does their radical service. As Barth wrote,

> When pilgrims on the road of God meet one another, they have something to say. A man may be of value to another man, not because he wishes to be important, not because he possesses some inner wealth of soul, not because of something he is, but because of what he is—not. His importance may consist in his poverty, in his hopes and fears, in his waiting and hurrying, in the direction of his whole being towards what lies beyond his horizon and beyond his power. . . . For this reason he is something to others: he is able to share grace with them, to focus their attention, and to establish them in waiting and in adoration. The Spirit gives grace through him. Possessing nothing, he has nothing to offer, and so, the more he imparts, the more he receives; and the more he receives, the more he

imparts. There is therefore no question of Christians saying to one another—"Did you receive from me?" or "Did I receive from you?" Since neither is, or possesses anything, nothing passes from the one to the other. It is sufficient that what is, is—above us and behind us and beyond us. Faith it is—the gospel of faith, the content of faith, the faithfulness of God—that, in all the human frailty and tribulation with which we are surrounded, provides comfort alike to the beginner and to him that hath the pre-eminence. Though fellowship is assuredly in itself an empty and a trivial thing, we cry out for it, because we long to join hands in knocking at the doors of the Kingdom of God and to be moved together by His Spirit.

When I look at my life—my dear friends; my parents and siblings who have followed me down the Eastern seaboard; my peaceful, loving home with Julie, Aurora, and Rowan—I am tempted to call it "Redemption." I had my Passion and my Good Friday with Lily, and now I have my Easter. But no.

Throughout the turmoil of my life, one thing has remained: The moment of each day, when I am most aware of the presence of God, when I tuck the girls into bed, praying over them, thanking God for them and their special gifts, asking for protection through the night and for blessings in the day that dawns. Every now and then, one of the girls will remind me to pray for the people who don't have anything to eat or anywhere to sleep that night. This is good: We humans were put on earth to walk and talk with God. It was good when Aurora was a toddler, when these prayers were the things that got her to stop squirming, to curl up on her little pillow, to close her little eyes, and to curl her little mouth into the most subtle, satisfied smile I have ever seen. And it is good now, when negotiating an ex-spouse, co-parenting, living an inconsistently-paid creative life, and just plain old dealing with adulthood combine to make prayer just about the last thing in the world I want to do.

My life is not good because it was bad and now it's better. The kids at Reality Ministries don't need to know what sinners they are so they can understand God's love. Resurrection is good, whether you live a long, beautiful life, surrounded by people who love you, with a successful career, real teeth and a head of hair, or you get beaten and whipped and fed vinegar and have your hands and feet nailed to a wooden cross. To be sure, there are wrongs to be righted, and that's why God came to earth in the flesh. The Incarnation might be the most important expression of God's enduring presence, but the Cosmic Christ of self-giving love endures—before

This Littler Light

Jesus of Nazareth, within Jesus of Nazareth, and after Jesus of Nazareth. God is love. "I am what I am," God told Moses from the burning bush.

The point is, God is there on our crosses, and God is there in our empty tombs. It's too cheap to say that God took the bad of Lily's and my marriage and gave us the good of our girls. No, our marriage was good. Let me say that again: Our marriage was good. Aurora and Rowan were born because Lily and I loved each other. All the deaths we died along the way should not obscure that fundamental truth. God created those girls out of a young couple in love. Even Lily would come to admit that she did love me once, but there was too much pain to recover it. Ultimately, we were not up to the challenge of loving each other. We tried and we failed. That just means my daughters were born from an imperfect union of love—perhaps more imperfect than with parents who manage to stay together, but love nonetheless. In that sense, they're not any different from any other human who has ever lived. We're all born into broken love.

I don't know why Rowan and Aurora's lives emerged within this particular environment of pain. I don't know why God made humans who would deny our creaturehood, hurt one another, and reject God's Godhood. I don't know why there are hurricanes, tsunamis, and wild animals who kill people. I don't know why some people hoard while others starve. If you want satisfying answers to these questions, you need a wiser book than this. All I know is, there is good, there is bad, there is resurrection and death, there is marriage, there is divorce, and somewhere in the midst of it all, there is love, and it is good. I wouldn't give up the good of being Rowan and Aurora's dad for all the perfection in the world.

As I wrote this book, Nanny was dying. The feisty little woman had fought for months to stay at her condo in Florida, but Mom, my aunts, and my Uncle David finally forced her to move here to Durham, where Mom could take care of her and Poppy. They'd be surrounded by us five of her grandkids, Julie, Aurora, Rowan, Marco's wife, and their baby, a third great granddaughter. We hope Nanny felt loved in her last days.

One day, I found another letter she'd written me at college, when her dear cousin was dying of cancer.

"He sure keeps fighting. I wish he would let go. It's probably not even up to him," Nanny wrote. "I really think the day you're born, the day you'll die is written right next to it. What happens in between is up to us.

"Have to say, I'll never understand why anyone has to suffer. Death should be more peaceful. There is no purpose served when the dying makes the living want to go with them. It's really weird, Jesse.

"When you're alive and well, you tell the dying person to let go, and yet you're alive. It's so easy for us. There's so much we don't understand about the end of life as we know it. Someday we'll all find out. I just hope it's not in pain."

Nanny's imminent death had Mom thinking about the Great Sadness of her family, another death, when my twenty-year-old Uncle Steven just went to bed one night and never woke up. I was still a baby. Mom had just left the Catholic church and "gotten saved," and she was worried about her family's eternal destiny. Just before Steven died, she'd asked him if he knew he'd go to heaven one day.

"It's OK," he said. "I'm still Catholic, and I believe in Jesus, just like you."

"You do?" she'd said. "Oh, I'm so happy to hear you say that."

"That meant everything to me after he died," Mom had told me, with Nanny on her deathbed, "to know that he'd be in heaven. But now, with my mother, I don't think that way anymore. I just leave it in God's hands."

Tell Mom how I feel, Nanny had written on the outside of the envelope, with that first letter she'd sent me at Cedarville eighteen years ago, the one about young and old, idealists and realists, heaven and hell, Father and Son.

"Remember that letter I sent you, Nan, trying to convert you?" I said to her a few months before her death.

"Everyone was always trying to convert me," she said. "You were so intense about religion. I worried about you."

No one was trying to convert her anymore. We'd seen good and bad, divinity and sin, love and bitterness in her, just like in everyone else. We hope her salvation doesn't depend on anything she did or didn't do, believed or didn't believe, but on what God has done in Christ. Maybe this is what it means to follow the Slain Lamb, the Suffering Servant: We give up the power to try to change even our eighty-pound grandmothers, and we simply love. We leave the saving to Jesus, and we love. That alone is a calling beyond our capability. The best we can do is to reflect what grace we've been given, little moons for the Sun.

This little light of mine, I'm gonna let it shine.

www.ingramcontent.com/pod-product-compliance
Lightning Source LLC
Chambersburg PA
CBHW031355230426
43670CB00006B/548